Christmas on Television

Christmas on Television

DIANE WERTS

The Praeger Television Collection
David Bianculli, Series Editor

Westport, Connecticut
London

Library of Congress Cataloging-in-Publication Data

Werts, Diane.
Christmas on television / by Diane Werts.
    p. cm. — (Praeger television collection, ISSN 1549-2257)
  Includes bibliographical references and index.
  ISBN 0-275-98331-5 (alk. paper)
  1. Christmas television programs—United States. I. Title. II. Series.
PN1992.8.C5W47 2006
791.45'634—dc22   2005020499

British Library Cataloguing in Publication Data is available.

Library of Congress Catalog Card Number: 2005020499
ISBN: 0-275-98331-5
ISSN: 1549-2257

First published in 2006

Praeger Publishers, 88 Post Road West, Westport, CT 06881
An imprint of Greenwood Publishing Group, Inc.
www.praeger.com

Printed in the United States of America

The paper used in this book complies with the
Permanent Paper Standard issued by the National
Information Standards Organization (Z39.48-1984).

10 9 8 7 6 5 4 3 2 1

Christmas is, well, it's about the best time of the whole year. You walk down the street, even for weeks before Christmas time, there's lights hanging up, green ones and red ones. Sometimes there's snow. And everybody's hustling someplace. But they don't hustle around Christmastime like they usually do. They're a little more friendly. They bump into you, they laugh and they say "Pardon me. Merry Christmas." Especially when it gets real close to Christmas night. Everybody's walking home, you can hardly hear a sound. Bells are ringing, kids are singing, the snow is coming down. And boy, what a pleasure it is to think, that you got some place to go to, and the place that you're going to, there's somebody in it that you really love—someone you're nuts about.

—Jackie Gleason, *The Honeymooners*, 1955

Really, I guess, Christmas has a way of calling up the best in people. It's a time to review your blessings, and to renew your faith; to share the warmth of the season with the new and the old friends, with family. It's a time of joy, and closeness; a time to look backward in gratitude, at being able to come this far, and a time to look ahead, with hope and optimism, to a future day, when there'll be peace on earth and good will towards all men.

—Bing Crosby, "Bing Crosby's Merrie Olde Christmas," 1977

What's my point? Well, it's that Christmas reveals itself to us each in a personal way, be it secular or sacred. Whatever Christmas is—and it's many things to many people—we all own a piece of it. It's kind of like Santa's bag. Inside, there's a gift for everybody.

—John Corbett, *Northern Exposure*, 1991

Contents

Photo essay follows page 114

Introduction:
Welcome to a TV Christmas

I've always loved Christmas—and Christmas TV. My childhood family celebrated the season like many, with a garishly decorated tree and elaborately wrapped presents, brightly colored lights along the roofline, badly warbled Christmas carols, and the pageantry of Midnight Mass. As a tube-tied tyke of the 1960s, I'd extend the festivity in front of our enormous "portable" black-and-white General Electric TV set. Anything about Christmas, I watched. The first airing of "Rudolph the Red-Nosed Reindeer." The premiere of "A Charlie Brown Christmas." Holiday episodes of *Mister Ed* and *Green Acres, Gunsmoke* and *Bonanza*. The yuletide music specials featuring the Bing Crosby and Andy Williams families, their kids all cute and cuddly in their holiday finery. Even the commercials. I liked the sledding Norelco electric shaver, and *loved* those Budweiser Clydesdales hoofing through the snow.

When VCRs emerged in the 1980s, Christmas episodes were among the first shows I taped for a home library that would grow to thousands of programs, archived for both professional use and personal immersion. Soon, hundreds of those shows were Christmas-related. My interest mushroomed into an obsession. During December, I might have three VCRs running at once, eventually joined by DVD recorders, to capture every holiday episode I could find. Delight turned to despair if I missed one—even though I had 500 on tape already. Why? Because Christmas always seems to hold out the promise of perfection—of peace, brotherhood, warmth, and generosity, of good things to come, and bad things kept at bay, at least for the holiday season. I know from my earliest memories, I loved Christmas. And I loved Christmas on TV.

Was it because things always seemed so ideal there? In the 1960s, happy endings were almost always guaranteed. Characters didn't stay mad at each other. They ultimately accepted others for who and what they were. They were kind, supportive, understanding. And they were magical. Especially in that whimsical decade, when beautiful witches cast good spells (*Bewitched*), pigs went to school (*Green Acres*), wacky monsters lived next door (*The Munsters*), mothers were reincarnated as automobiles (*My Mother the Car*), and families like mine rocketed to the stars (*Lost in Space*).

As TV grew and matured, so did I, and I came to appreciate the complexities of *All in the Family*, *Hill Street Blues*, *China Beach*, *The Simpsons*, and *The Sopranos*. I started writing about the medium and eagerly exploring the back roads of its cable landscape, trying to keep up with dozens and then hundreds of channels, offering everything from first-rate drama to third-rate infomercials. As broadcasters like CNN and MTV increasingly had an impact on the world they covered, television ever more genuinely became our window on the world and a mirror of our culture—a truly enormous force in shaping and reflecting our lives, worthy of intense scrutiny and debate.

And the more intellectually significant the medium continued to become, the more I found myself drawn to the nakedly visceral emotions stirred by all those Christmas shows for which I'd long held a soft spot. This psychologically charged holiday—its impact recognized even by those unimpressed by its religious meaning—seemed to hold the wondrous power to strip away much of the pretense and posturing we nurtured the rest of the year. It often mined deep into private corners of the soul kept so well hidden, we don't realize even ourselves how defining they are, how elemental, how psychologically raw.

Is that giving too much credit to TV shows that can simply be silly about Santa, dizzy about decorations, or goofy with gifts? I don't think so. Many Christmas episodes are simply handy situations for punch line possibilities, yes. But even the most frivolous series seem to reach deeper at Christmastime, simply because the holiday does. It touches us in a very tender place.

Television has become an integral part of our national yuletide observance. It just isn't Christmas anymore without Charlie Brown's cartoon winter wonderland, without misfit Rudolph the Red-Nosed Reindeer finally winning acceptance from all those North Pole cool kids, without the extreme house decorations of *Home Improvement*, without the deep-rooted family wranglings of *Everybody Loves Raymond*. We scour the TV listings seeking the new Christmas episode of *The Simpsons* or *South Park*, or a holiday repeat from the series that touched our hearts at key moments of our childhood or adolescence. Maybe it's a cold Christmas in Korea for the mobile war surgeons of *M*A*S*H*. Could be the Scrooge-y kid whose heart gets melted by the energetic affections of *The Monkees*. Christmas miracles seem to occur. An angel brings light to an abused gay teen on *My So-Called Life*.

There's a magic to this season, when hope shines so brightly, handed down from the faith-based origin of the holiday as a commemoration of Jesus' birth as a savior to humankind. Even many nonbelievers take the Christmas season to heart for its associated spirit of peace, generosity, acceptance, and reconciliation. Despite the annual shopping frenzy, the world seems to promise us a moment of tranquility and togetherness, of shared traditions and experiences, of a spiritual plane where people put aside their differences, where all is right with the world.

That doesn't mean Christmas is all sweetness and warmth, and certainly not on TV. When the brutal prison drama *Oz* portrays the holiday, it's with inmate murders, race riots, and rat bites. Even in comedy, Santa splatters after jumping from a helicopter on *Married ... with Children*. The mad minds behind *South Park* turn an animated piece of excrement into a holiday icon, while pitting Santa against Jesus in a nightclub duel of self-centered seasonal songs.

But even TV's satires and subversions of Christmas recognize (and indeed, even elevate) the holiday's unique place in our culture—its complicated heightening of our emotions and expectations. Crass consumerism may rise for this occasion, but so do compassion and sacrifice. Situations simply seem that much more urgent, imperative, even life-changing.

The tube isn't the first to recognize this intensity, of course. Charles Dickens had something to say about it in his literary classic *A Christmas Carol* nearly two centuries ago. Movies, recorded music, radio, and other modern media have done their part in boosting the seasonal spirit. Yet none has had the pervasive reach and impact, plus the intimacy, of television. Once considered a mere electronic fad taking up temporary residence in the living room, this metal, glass, and plastic box has grown over the past 60 years into a virtual member of the family for most Americans. We leave it on for hours and hours a day, whether we're actually watching something being transmitted from afar or simply leading our lives bathed in its emitted light. We expect it to entertain us, explain us, enrich us, keep us informed, and keep us company. We measure ourselves by what we see on its screen.

And the people we see on its screen—especially the characters on long-running series, the comedy and drama families we invite into our homes on a weekly or even daily basis, people we come to know better than most actual humans in our lives. We share our lives with them, so we share our holidays, too—with all their attendant hopes, joys, disappointments, and hard-earned lessons.

We might rather, in fact, share those fictional feelings than real-life ones, if TV's mushrooming Christmas programming is any indication. The various permutations of TV's Family Channel (Fox Family, ABC Family) have all retained the "25 Days of Christmas" stunt that runs holiday episodes, cartoons, movies, and specials daily till Santa comes. Nick at Nite's annual grouping of yuletide episodes into one evening or overnight has grown and grown into corporate sibling TV Land's "Merry-thon," up to 48 straight hours of holiday comedy and drama gems. Cartoon Network schedules continuous yule toons. Even public TV stations run marathons of "Britcom" Christmases or black-and-white holidays from TV's early years. In an era of 200 channels, the yule provides an easy episode hook and a handy promotional platform. But that's only because we care about Christmas so much already.

1
Christmastime Is Almost Here

CHAPTER 1

TV Waits in the Wings:
Christmas in Other Media

Christmas cultists don't revere Charles Dickens just for writing *A Christmas Carol*. Dickens did much more than pen a single yuletide tale. The nine-teenth-century author actually helped vault Christmas from religious and family holiday status to annual multimedia extravaganza.

A Christmas Carol, published in 1843, was his first seasonal salute—"the one great Christmas myth of modern literature," pronounces *Encyclopedia Britannica* —but it was such an instant sensation that Dickens would keep up the output with a new short holiday work nearly every year through 1867. If none matched his original inspiration, they laid the groundwork among both the public and the literary world for an entirely new genre of artistic expression—one seizing upon the familiar season and spirit of the year-ending celebration to deliver wider-ranging allegories of human morality wrapped in the seductive openheartedness of the yuletide season.

Dickens himself loved Christmas beyond its literary purpose; he saw it as an embodiment of what he called "Carol philosophy," or the spirit of generosity, compassion, and forgiveness, all throughout the year. Up until nearly the moment of his death, Dickens would traverse England and even the United States offering histrionic readings of his most famous tale, further cementing its appeal throughout the year. These Christmas stories played a huge part in building for Dickens an astonishing celebrity during his own lifetime—and sustaining his legend in the popular culture in the decades after he passed away in 1870.

During Dickens's life in the mid-nineteenth century, many other secular Christmas rituals were gaining a grip on Western imaginations. (Indeed, the holiday had begun as the Christian church's attempt to co-opt pagan rituals of the season into religious symbolism.) The advent of mass production was making more elaborate celebrations more widely possible. Thanks to the postal delivery improvements enabled by better roads and increasingly efficient rail travel, greeting cards were more widely sent to mark the holiday season. Trees of evergreen could more easily be brought indoors and decorated. Many seasonal carols were introduced in the popular music realm, including such standbys as "Away in a Manger" and "The First Noel." Clement Moore's 1822 poem "A Visit from St. Nicholas" popularized seasonal images apparently drawn from several European traditions, such as the Dutch legend of St. Nicholas and the Norse use of reindeer and sleigh. In 1860, *Harpers Weekly* artist Thomas Nast published his famous drawing of Santa Claus—the jolly old roly-poly man with the long white beard and "Santa suit"—by which the mythical character would forever be measured.

In other words, Christmas as we know it crystallized.

A Christmas Carol was also taking to the stage at this point, expanded beyond Dickens's readings to full dramatic theatrical stagings as a December perennial. It's no surprise that as motion pictures grew into their own art form at the dawn of the twentieth century, its rudimentary technology (and embryonic storytelling skills) began to churn out short, silent, black-and-white versions of Dickens's enduring tale. Shorts from 1908, 1910, and 1915 are known to exist. In the often raucous nickelodeons of the day, *A Christmas Carol* had the advantage of being brief, widely familiar to audiences already, simple in its structure, and clear in its archetypes of greed, grace, and the redemptive quality of Christmas.

But it was hardly the only seasonal story on the big screen. The celebration traditions that had grown throughout the nineteenth century were documented in turn-of-the-century shorts from motion picture companies like Thomas Edison's, quick slices of life that cost little to produce but were guaranteed to amuse viewers. More creative filmmakers used seasonal rituals as a jumping-off point: Fantasy master Georges Méliès's 1900 short "Le Reve de Noel" ("A Christmas Dream") incorporated scenes of Santa, children's stockings, presents, church bells, and the holiday dinner.

Pioneer silent directors used the season as a backdrop for their short presentations. Edwin S. Porter of "The Great Train Robbery" fame filmed Clement Moore's poem "The Night before Christmas" in 1905 using miniatures, and *Birth of a Nation* innovator D.W. Griffith earlier made "The Christmas Burglars" (1908) and "A Trap for Santa Claus" (1909). The yule offered handy plot devices for westerns (1911's "Bronco Billy's Christmas Dinner," among a half-dozen Christmas shorts made by Bronco Billy Anderson) and comic strip characters ("Snookums' Merry Christmas," 1926). The centuries-old traditions of reenacting the birth of Christ with nativity scenes based on Bible descriptions in the book of Luke were making their way into modern media, too. But most often, the spiritual approach took more the form of a morality fable. The 1911 title "The Goodfellow's Christmas Eve" featured popular Francis X. Bushman as a bachelor whose heart is opened when he helps an abandoned boy.

Meanwhile, the burgeoning advertising industry was nurturing the modern notion of Christmas as an occasion for lavish gift-giving. It wasted no time employing Santa Claus as a spokesperson (which wouldn't, after all, have been possible with Jesus Christ). Magazines were becoming much more widely read in a nation rapidly shifting from a rural to an urban society. And then radio materialized in the 1920s as a powerfully persuasive, and pervasive, national medium, thriving on a kind of immediacy the public couldn't get enough of. Supported in the United States by commercial sponsors, radio networks CBS and NBC were more than happy to stoke Christmas sentiment.

As the voices of its emerging series stars became familiar guests right inside the American home, why wouldn't they celebrate the holidays almost as part of the family? Comedians such as Jack Benny, Bob Hope, George Burns and Gracie Allen, and Edgar Bergen with his ventriloquist's dummy Charlie McCarthy did episodes in which listeners tagged along through their holiday shopping, parties, and other festivities. Scripted programs got seasonal, too, as they thrived throughout the 1930s and 1940s. Christmas provided December storylines on top comedies including *Fibber McGee and Molly* and the 30-year run of *Amos 'n' Andy*. Dramas found ways to incorporate the holidays, even thrillers like *The Shadow* and action shows like *The Lone Ranger*. Lionel Barrymore's reading of Dickens's *A Christmas Carol* became a holiday tradition lasting nearly two decades. (His 1939 broadcast featured as its narrator the up-and-coming performer/producer Orson Welles.)

Silent movies had learned to talk, too, with the surprise sensation of Warner Bros. Studios' 1927 Al Jolson vehicle *The Jazz Singer*, with its synch-sound musical numbers. "Talkies" had replaced silent films entirely by the early 1930s, in another of the lightning shifts that twentieth-century technology seemed to foster. Both movies and radio also proved a powerful engine for driving fame and sales in the music business. It had evolved from a publishing business at the turn of the century, dealing mostly in sheet music, into an industry of recording and distributing shellac platters to be played on home Victrola machines.

These new media's voracious appetite for fresh entertainment could be fed late each year with Christmas tunes. Both filmed short subjects, with which movie theaters filled out their evening-long presentations, and radio play promoted recording stars' releases of classic carols and a flurry of new compositions, including "Santa Claus Is Coming to Town" (1932), "Winter Wonderland" (1934), and "Carol of the Bells" (1936). A holiday that had been devoted to religious celebration became increasingly secularized—some might say commercialized—by the flood of festivity rituals popularized through all these robust new pop culture delivery systems.

Even the motion pictures themselves latched onto Christmas in a new way as the holiday seemed to reach critical mass in the 1940s, during and after the global cataclysm of World War II. Bing Crosby's 1942 feature *Holiday Inn* introduced Irving Berlin's immortal "White Christmas." Judy Garland debuted "Have Yourself a Merry Little Christmas" in 1944's *Meet Me in St. Louis.* Postwar theaters would see *Christmas in Connecticut* and *Miracle on 34th Street.* The flood of new carols continued with "The Christmas Song" (1946) and "Rudolph the Red Nosed Reindeer" (1949). The Allies' 1945 victory allowed American industry to turn its focus back to civilian innovation, bringing to the fore such new technologies as long-play record albums. Hot off its impressive war news coverage, the pervasive sound of radio was at its zenith. NBC, CBS, and the Mutual Broadcasting System presented hundreds of national comedy, drama, and musical series, including the network arrival of such postwar sensations as folksy host Arthur Godfrey; the mystery drama *Yours Truly, Johnny Dollar;* the Lucille Ball comedy *My Favorite Husband;* Allan Funt's *Candid Microphone;* and Groucho Marx's quiz show *You Bet Your Life.*

But radio's greatest years were among its last. A new living-room medium was shaping up to take its place. The long-promised wonder of television—first encountered by many Americans in prototype at the 1939 World's Fair—would finally come to fruition. This new communication tool would add video to audio, amplifying the immediacy of radio to create a worldwide cultural force like none the world had ever seen.

CHAPTER 2

The First (TV) Noel:
Christmas in Early Television

Even before the medium officially existed, TV was in the Christmas spirit. Sketchy historical records tell of an experimental broadcast of "A Christmas Carol" in New York City by the pioneering Dumont network in 1943. That would place it during World War II, when the commercial development of television had officially been put on hold in deference to the war effort. When peace came in 1945, those who'd previously been dabbling in the nascent technology went back to work on turning "radio with pictures" into a widespread reality. Dumont returned to the familiar (and royalty-free) territory of "A Christmas Carol" with stars John Carradine and Eva Marie Saint in 1947, when NBC was also trying to demonstrate television's potential to rival the then-dominant radio networks. A year later, CBS and ABC had joined the fray, all three sending out signals from New York to link their few outlying stations in "far-flung" locales like Schenectady and Philadelphia.

Networks as we know them today were in place by the fall of 1948, and so were some familiar programs—NBC's Milton Berle's *Texaco Star Theater* variety hour, CBS's *Arthur Godfrey's Talent Scouts*, and, in evening prime time then, NBC's news interview show *Meet the Press*. Because commercial sponsors weren't yet fully committed to this new invention, and because video equipment was bulky and technically demanding, most shows tended to feature singers, dancers, games, and interviews that could be staged relatively easily and cheaply in New York studios.

But the public had become accustomed to more elaborately scripted stagings on radio—dramatic stories detailing police investigations or western action, comedies about familiar family situations, melodramatic soap operas of domestic crises. In 1949, these began flooding onto the video waves by simply transferring known formats from radio, often with some of the same microphone-trained actors, who were suddenly seen behaving rather stiffly before cameras they'd never had to please before. CBS's *The Goldbergs* and NBC's *The Life of Riley* and *The Aldrich Family* made the move that year, with radio favorites like NBC's *Dragnet* and CBS's *Our Miss Brooks* and *Gunsmoke* to follow. Some of radio's biggest stars would soon make the leap, often bringing along a tried-and-true format. On CBS, George Burns would continue to be confounded by wife Gracie Allen's mental meanderings. Jack Benny kept playing himself, moaning about money to friends and family. Over on ABC, Ozzie and Harriet Nelson brought sons David and Ricky into the video age for more household adventures.

And sometimes they brought their scripts right along with them, which was never so evident as in their Christmas episodes. CBS's *Amos 'n' Andy* continued its annual tradition of Amos reading The Lord's Prayer. TV's 1957 holiday half-hour of *The Jack Benny Program* featured the same jokes delivered on radio by the same actors a decade earlier. And they recycled it again in 1960. *Father Knows Best* adapted its 1953 radio story of the family stranded in a snowstorm for its 1954 CBS TV episode. *Dragnet* kept retelling the tale of a baby Jesus statue stolen from a barrio church; it was used on radio in 1953, on TV that same year, and yet again during the series' second TV incarnation in the late 1960s.

Other programs were new to television—even if their stories weren't. Constrained by budgets consistent with the limited audience using TV in these early years, encumbered by awkward equipment and cramped studios, confined by live TV to whatever could be staged within the show's real-time length, the first Christmas episodes were homespun simplicity personified. As the father in ABC's family heart-warmer *The Ruggles,* film veteran Charlie Ruggles helps his kids visit the home of a schoolmate whose father has died. He admires her nativity scene, leads the singing of Christmas carols, and delivers a hammer-it-home homily. "Happiness is within one's self," he said in this 1950 live broadcast, offering "a lesson for all of us."

Some shows did get outside the stagy box of the studio living room, especially those dramas beginning to be shot on film by movie studios rather than aired live like radio. *Racket Squad,* 1951's "real-life story" of "the confidence game," had its police narrator announce "I had to arrest Santa Claus" before laying out his woeful saga of an old man recruited by swindlers at holiday time. In the overt style of the era, the detective decried "a parasite that fed on one of the finest charities we know: the street-corner Santa Claus."

Faring better was the one-to-one approach of the many variety programs of the era, speaking directly to us as if inviting us into their homes to share their celebration—a conceit that would flourish into the 1960s. Glittery mama's boy Liberace would indeed bring Mama onto 1953's syndicated *Liberace* holiday show, along with his siblings, nieces, and nephews—and his dog. They all "dropped by" the popular pianist's Hollywood studio, where Lee lamented they had to "create that Christmas spirit" out of fake snow that made him "a little lonesome for the Christmases back home in Milwaukee, Wisconsin." While playing such secular carols as "White Christmas" and "Santa Claus Is Coming to Town," Liberace also warned, "We forget the true holy meaning behind this wonderful holiday." A reading of the Nativity was quick to follow. This was the formula for Bing Crosby, Perry Como, Judy Garland, and other variety stars of the 1950s and 1960s, annually ushering their real-life family members into the studio—meant to be seen as "home"—and including viewers in the "casual" festivities.

Television also brought these characters into our homes, positioning them as our "friends" even more than radio had, now that we could see their reactions and emotions. It built a bond that kept viewers returning to spend time with lovable characters in subsequent weeks, months, and, for the lucky, even years. That relationship also mattered more to advertisers at the time, who usually sponsored an entire program, rather than buying the spot ads that would become the norm by the 1970s. The sponsor's name might even be in the title, as with *Texaco Star Theater,* and some sponsors were aligned with the same celebrity for decades (as Texaco was with Bob Hope). Echoing radio, TV stars often delivered commercial messages them-selves, sometimes in character. The more disposed viewers were to spend-ing time with these characters, the more likely they were to think favorably of the products those characters pitched.

Soon, no continuing series was complete without a Christmas install-ment. Getting in on the act, too, were the era's anthology series, those dramatic-play showcases in which sponsors presented a different story weekly. ABC's *DuPont Theater* offered an unusual ethnic take on the holi-day in 1956's "Three Young Kings," taking place in a Latin American vil-lage (staged in Hollywood). Its story sprung from the January 6 tradition of re-creating the arrival of those Biblical kings in Bethlehem, with three boys of the town riding horses to distribute parents' gifts for their children. ABC's *Telephone Time* was topical in 1957, setting "A Picture of the Magi" in

Budapest during the anticommunist uprising as an activist family seeks to escape the Soviets' clutches by crossing the border.

Even feature-film fright-meister Alfred Hitchcock went seasonal. In his first year of supervising the CBS anthology suspense show *Alfred Hitchcock Presents,* he introduced the 1955 episode "Santa Claus and the 10th Avenue Kid." While bricking over the fireplace end of a chimney, the imposing Hitch intoned that "Santa Claus is always bringing surprises to others. I thought it would be interesting if someone else surprised him for a change." Master of irony Rod Serling did a holiday *Twilight Zone* for CBS in 1960, "Night of the Meek"; that episode would become a perennial classic featuring Art Carney and be remade quite effectively with Richard Mulligan during the network's 1985 series revival.

Americans weren't the only ones making Christmas episodes, either. British shows and international productions were widely imported in the 1950s into syndication for local stations trying to fill the many broadcast hours in which the networks did not feed programming. (And they never programmed late-night then. Local stations signed off the air anytime from 11 p.m. to 1 a.m., and began the next broadcast day between 6 a.m. and 9 a.m.) Because that unfilled airtime often fell during the afternoon or on weekends, many of the imports were aimed at children and families.

Shot on location in Morocco, 1955's *Captain Gallant of the Foreign Legion* featured Flash Gordon himself, Buster Crabbe, as a legionnaire parenting a young boy. When the child runs off into the desert in search of a Christmas tree, Crabbe and his men give up their holiday to go find him. On 1955's *Long John Silver,* the title pirate's crew helps a group of orphans catch a break (and some presents) from a stern and stingy housemother who believes "children should not expect things for nothing." Even *Sherlock Holmes* in 1954 discovered Christmas pudding could be used to disguise contraband that enabled a jailbreak.

These early holiday episodes are rarely seen today, though some 1950s celebrations turn up occasionally in the wee hours on small cable channels or public television stations. The price is right for those uses. Major TV programmers avoid these pioneering efforts because the quality is often lacking—poor film prints, primitive production values, slow-moving stories, and that particular bugaboo of the modern viewer: They're almost all in black-and-white. (*Long John Silver* is a rare color exception.)

But "modern" television was then starting to take shape. CBS's 1954 staging of *A Christmas Carol* with Fredric March and Basil Rathbone, to songs by acclaimed soundtrack composer Bernard Herrmann, was apparently one of the earliest programs broadcast in color. The implementation of videotape was just around the corner. The simplistic look and ragged feel of live programs was evolving into a prerecorded polish familiar in the shows of the 1960s. That decade would establish the style of drama and comedy to reign in network prime time over the next 40 years. And it would launch all sorts of other ways to celebrate America's favorite holiday.

Amahl and the Night Visitors

One of early television's great triumphs was a Christmas premiere. And it was an opera. *Amahl and the Night Visitors* was composed by music giant Gian Carlo Menotti to debut on NBC Christmas Eve 1951 as the first-ever presentation of the soon-to-be-legendary *Hallmark Hall of Fame* showcase.

It was an enormous sensation for a medium barely half a decade into its existence and still frequently derided as a classless, passing fad. The live hour-long telecast was lauded for both its cultural and emotional impact, telling of a lame boy who follows the three magi to the manger of Christ and offers up his crutch as tribute. That such an artistic work could be seen by millions of Americans in one night—and present such a high level of creativity—marked a turning point in perceptions about television.

Because *Amahl* was aired live, however, in the era before videotape, this landmark production has existed largely in memory and repute. Hallmark restaged the entire performance the following Easter and each of the next three Christmas seasons, a practice often followed in live radio and early TV. Menotti made a 1952 original-cast audio recording that has become beloved in its own right, and NBC presented a new color videotaped version in 1964. This one-act gem would go on to such a long life in regional and religious presentations that it is often cited as the most performed opera of all time.

CHAPTER 3

White Christmas:
Vintage Movies Come to TV

The new medium of television helped push the popularity of Christmas with help from an old source of content—movies. Holiday-themed motion pictures had been made since the medium's beginnings at the turn of the twentieth century. With Hollywood movies then a prime source of entertainment, Americans would see these productions in theaters upon their making, but the shelf life thereafter was limited. Film prints would be lost or damaged. The content itself would begin to look dated to "modern" audiences. Many if not most Christmas-themed titles of the early twentieth century have been lost to time, neglect, and the archival apathy of an industry forever looking forward rather than back.

But TV changed that. Upon its post–World War II advance, the home screen developed a need for cheaply obtained programming to meet its audience's voracious appetite for new shows to fill all those hours on all those channels. Movies were a quick answer, but a tricky one. Hollywood movie studios saw the small screen as a competitor to their big one and resisted selling prints and rights to TV in those early years. British moviemakers, however, had a different outlook. Their films found hard sledding in penetrating the American theater market, dominated by Hollywood monopolists, and so to them, television was hardly a competitive concern.

As TV programmers cast about for novel offerings and seasonally timely ones, the twain met in English-accented Christmas films. Yuletide sentiment could lure 1950s viewers to showings of the 1935 foreign feature *Scrooge*, starring Sir Seymour Hicks as Dickens's classic *Christmas Carol* character, as well as Alastair Sim's newer-made 1951 tale of the same name.

The Sim film—less often promoted on-air with its original British title *Scrooge* than with its source material's more familiar name *A Christmas Carol*—became a particular tube favorite. Its more recent vintage and more lively mood, together with Sim's memorably effective performance, were such instant crowd-pleasers that TV programmers began relying on the film's appeal. Never mind an annual appearance—Sim's Scrooge could be seen on a practically daily basis during holiday seasons of the 1950s and 1960s, airing in the era's popular "Million Dollar Movie" format, in which the same title might unreel nightly for a week, sometimes even repeatedly each day.

Some Hollywood product did make its way to TV more expeditiously. The short subjects that rounded out movie nights in the 1930s and 1940s found their way into filling time on the tube, too. Behind-the scenes peeks with holiday themes could be found, like MGM's "Jackie Cooper's Christmas Party" with the 1930s child star. Cartoons were another big-screen import to the small. Kids grew up watching animation along the lines of Fleischer Studios' 1936 "Christmas Comes But Once a Year," in which an inventor cooks up homemade toys to delight an orphanage, and MGM's 1941 Tom and Jerry romp "The Night before Christmas," in which cat Tom takes holiday pity on mouse Jerry.

As the 1950s progressed, Hollywood's movie studio heads began to realize that TV could be regarded as not a threat to their existence, but as a potential revenue pipeline. Then its holiday features flooded onto the small screen, too. The generation of children raised with TV would also be raised on holiday movies. MGM's 1938 version of *A Christmas Carol* starring Reginald Owen began airing. Barbara Stanwyck could be seen yearly as a hard-driving journalist pretending to be homey—a prototypical Martha Stewart—in the 1945 romantic comedy *Christmas in Connecticut*. Bing Crosby and Fred Astaire teamed up in *Holiday Inn*, the 1942 resort musical that introduced Irving Berlin's song "White Christmas." The 1947 drama *Miracle on 34th Street* delighted families with its depiction of child actress Natalie Wood meeting the "real" Santa in Macy's kindly kid greeter Edmund Gwenn. TV turned to other stories not about Christmas per se but set during the season—Cary Grant as an angel in 1947's *The Bishop's Wife*, or Stanwyck as a reporter again, first betraying and then saving Gary Cooper's everyman/corporate pawn from suicide in director Frank Capra's 1941 drama *Meet John Doe*.

Capra's sentimental brand of "Capra-corn" would influence the holiday season yet more profoundly with another Christmas-set saga. His 1946 feature *It's a Wonderful Life* had been such a flop upon its original release that its rights passed from original short-lived studio Liberty Films into corporate hands that somehow neglected to file 1974's copyright renewal. TV stations came to believe they could air the film without rights payment, a situation that had already made a holiday constant of 1935's public-domain feature *Scrooge*. Suddenly, a crazy quilt of local network stations, PBS affiliates, and anybody else with a video signal was throwing the James Stewart feature onto its schedule, seemingly for days and nights on end throughout the Christmas season. Many Americans got to the point they could practically recite Stewart's dialogue as despondent small-town businessman George Bailey, convinced his provincial life has amounted to nothing until his guardian angel Clarence shows him how much worse off the people of Bedford Falls would have been without him.

It's a Wonderful Life and Alastair Sim's *A Christmas Carol* would be the holiday mainstays of the 1970s and 1980s, with other more recent films occupying a second tier of Christmas popularity: Crosby's splashy 1954 color feature *White Christmas*, the campy 1964 kid flick *Santa Claus Conquers the Martians* (later to double viewers' pleasure as a mock-object on Comedy Central's *Mystery Science Theater 3000*), the 1970 Leslie Bricusse musical *Scrooge* with Albert Finney, and the 1988 satire *Scrooged* with Bill Murray. But it turned out to be a 1983 theatrical disappointment that would join *Life* and *Carol* as the sort of cherished holiday perennial viewers anticipate seeing again and again.

A Christmas Story was based on the childhood memory tales of Jean Shepherd, who had long been enthralling New York radio audiences with late-night stories of his Indiana steel-town youth. His personal mythos of colorful characters and legendary calamities had been collected in books (*In God We Trust—All Others Pay Cash*) and adapted to TV in PBS's 1976 TV movie *The Phantom of the Open Hearth*, narrated by his fictionalized childhood alter ego, Ralph Parker. Young Ralph would be the center of Shepherd's 1983 holiday movie, cowritten and narrated in Shepherd's inimitable voice, and directed by, of all people, Bob Clark, who'd made his name with the gross-out antics of the frat-boy comedy smash *Porky's*.

But Clark's next film captured all the innocence of childhood, with its classroom antics, bullies, double-dog-dares, and desperate expectancy of Christmas—rendered as memory by an adult narrator putting the proceedings in ironic perspective. That attitudinal choice, plus the use of daydream sequences and a slightly loopy tone, made *A Christmas Story* a distinctive offering. So distinctive, in fact, that in the film's November 1983 release, audiences unsure what to make of this little mutt stayed away in droves.

It wasn't until cable TV started playing this family-suitable film endlessly a decade later that viewers realized what they'd missed. Suddenly, TNT or TBS was airing *A Christmas Story* for 24 hours every Christmas, starting a new screening every two hours. Then everyone came to root for Depression-era 10-year-old Ralph Parker and his wide-eyed quest for a Red Ryder Carbine-Action Two-Hundred-Shot Range Model Air Rifle. Shepherd's anecdotal storytelling made it a perfect watch-again experience, to see Ralph's hapless friend Flick stick his tongue to the frozen flagpole, and Ralph flee the school bully, say "fudge" during the Christmas tree run, get Santa's boot in the face, and be repeatedly warned, "You'll shoot your eye out."

Over time, TV had marched into many more American homes— 10 million in 1950, 47 million in 1960, 80 million in 1980 and 100 million by 2000. The most familiar Christmas showings became perennials; re-viewing them each year developed into a holiday tradition of its own. Adults who'd grown up with movies and radio were raising kids for whom TV was the primary source of entertainment, and, increasingly, a cultural touchstone shared with their peers. They marked the coming of the holiday not by the calendar but by the arrival of commercials hawking holiday gift suggestions and programs celebrating the season with familiar characters. When kids across the nation saw Macy's Thanksgiving Day Parade beamed live from New York on the networks, they knew Christmas was not far behind.

Television soon learned to hold that holiday attention for many days, in many ways. Just as the movies had eyed Christmas from various angles, the home screen was warming up a wide range of festivity. There would be homespun holiday comedy, seasonal drama, and variety revues with old-fashioned carols and modern songs. From silliness about Santa to reverent religious faith, television's growing ranks of original series would tap Christmas sentiment to more effectively connect with viewers. They would even put a fresh spin on *A Christmas Carol* or *It's a Wonderful Life* using the continuing characters Americans were welcoming into their homes weekly. These surrogate families would come to share our yuletide traditions from season to season. They would gather together, decorate the tree, exchange gifts, visit Santa, work Christmas jobs, and even confront social issues in the holiday spirit. Before long, viewers could choose among at least 12 kinds of TV Christmas. It's a wonderful holiday.

II
The Twelve Kinds of Christmas (A Baker's Dozen)

CHAPTER 4

I'll Be Home for Christmas:
Family and the Holidays

'Round the middle of December, if you're alone you start to feel like an outsider. You know it's the nature of a family holiday to make a single man feel disenfranchised. You're made to feel like a hungry vagrant with your nose pressed up against a window, staring at somebody else's dinner.

—Barry Corbin, *Northern Exposure*, 1991

Togetherness has always been one of the primary qualities of the Christmas season, and it's the one that television tended to spotlight in its early years of scripted series. Family shows especially dominated the half-hour comedy format in the 1950s, so reunions—or the obstacles thereto—became a familiar holiday plot device.

Danny Thomas provided an archetypal example of this standby story in the first season of his long-running sitcom *Make Room for Daddy*, showcasing the nightclub entertainer as—what else?—a nightclub entertainer. (Hey, it had worked for bandleader Desi Arnaz on *I Love Lucy*, produced by the same Desilu studio.) With a cab double-parked to get him to a flight to New York for the 1953 holiday, Danny is informed by Detroit's "plain Scrooge" club owner that he's being held over through Christmastime thanks to the illness of the following act. ("If you can't find it in your heart, you can find it in your contract.") Danny lets him have it as "the meanest man in the whole world." But of course, the owner is secretly arranging to have wife Jean Hagen and the kids flown in to surprise the temperamental entertainer, who then turns to sentimental mush and tops this ABC episode with a Christmas song.

The Patty Duke Show also has a happy ending in its more jet-set 1960s approach to a doubtful reunion. Teen Oscar-winner Patty Duke (*The Miracle Worker*) starred on ABC as both groovy Brooklyn teen Patty and her more refined "identical cousin" Cathy, who'd moved in with Patty's family bearing a vague European accent from her time abroad with her foreign correspondent dad. He's the crux of the 1963 holiday plot, expected home after a year but unable to make it when he's imprisoned for espionage while covering a revolution in Kurdistan. "He'll get here," coos a confident Cathy. "He always spends Christmas with me." And so he does, after "identical brother" William Schallert heads out on Christmas Eve to find a fake mustache to impersonate him lest Cathy be let down. So is that her uncle who rings the doorbell to thrill the girl? Or is it the real dad, after all? Anyone who's ever watched a sitcom knows the answer to that one. (It's both, of course, engendering classic sitcom confusion.)

The question of dad resurfaces in that 1950s-set hit of the 1970s, *Happy Days*. By the time of the ABC sitcom's sixth-season Christmas episode in 1978, the nostalgic show had long been ranked in Nielsen's top five, and Henry Winkler's leather-clad Fonzie character was an established national sensation. His hip-and-casual loner status faces a challenge when a Singapore acquaintance of his long-lost dad drops off a holiday gift from the old man Fonzie hasn't seen since he was three years old. But it's clear before long that the briefly visiting bar buddy was in reality the father Fonzie longed to know. "I didn't even get a chance to see his face real good," the resentful son moans as he vacillates between anger and ache. Reading a letter left by his dad makes Fonzie comprehend that his seaman father just didn't know how to settle down. "I thought I did something wrong and made him leave," the softie tough guy confesses to Tom Bosley's resident father figure. "I don't feel so much hate anymore....He couldn't help himself." Fonzie proudly wears his gift—a Chinese robe from Singapore ("That's in the Orient")—as he spends an especially happy Christmas with his surrogate Milwaukee family, the Cunninghams.

These "traditional" sitcoms tend to be perennial favorites in repeats precisely because of their predictability. The viewer goes in with the expectation that all will be made right by episode's end—and that the "rocky" road to that conclusion won't really be any more challenging than a fleeting pebble or two, easily brushed aside on the path to holiday happiness. However, 1980s television would begin shaking the security of that wistful cliché, even—or perhaps especially—in family comedies, which began to reflect a less rosy and more real portrait of holiday stress and its accompanying discoveries, revelations, and conflicts.

FATHER DOESN'T KNOW BEST

Many critics in the 1990s considered *Home Improvement* as emblematic of the old-time familycom, yet the Christmas episodes of this ABC hit weren't all about leading man Tim Allen's mania for power tools or holiday décor rivalry with the neighbors. Allen and TV wife Patricia Richardson spend Christmas 1994 trying to patch a rift between her visiting parents. By the 1997 yule installment, dad has died and daughter is now upset by mom (Polly Holliday) bringing along a new date. That's after 1993's announcement by oldest son Brad that he wants to spend the holiday skiing with friends, which prompts dad Tim to reprimand, "Christmas is not about being with people you like, it's about being with your family!"

But it's middle son Randy ('tween idol Jonathan Taylor Thomas) who first leaves the family, to study ecology in Costa Rica. (Thomas wanted to make feature films.) When Randy makes a return appearance in the 1998 holiday half-hour, "I just feel like I don't fit anymore," he tells his parents. "You guys are just getting on with your lives, and I'm having trouble keeping in step." That is, until klutz dad Tim falls off the roof arranging his latest Christmas display. "Then again," notes Randy, "some things never change."

ABC's *Roseanne* was already well known for taking a frank and often contentious approach to family dynamics in its working-class household. Certainly the holidays are a time when relatives let their guard down, perhaps too much, and often with the aid of excessive alcohol. Sara Gilbert's teen Darlene gets a 1992 dose of Christmas reality when she visits pal David's house, where his uncaring mother (Sally Kirkland) fails to hide her abusive side. *Roseanne* also was famous for stretching cultural boundaries, which proved both elastic and prescient in the show's 1995 Christmas outing. Roseanne's extended family and friends had long included the gay couple played by Martin Mull and Fred Willard, who finally decide on a holiday wedding. (And isn't that early TV cross-dresser Milton Berle catching the "bride's" bouquet, in drag?)

The long-running series' final yule outing took place in that ill-advised last season when the struggling Conners won the lottery and began living it up. But it deals with a touchy issue in its own roilingly insightful way. John Goodman's husband character Dan had been absent early that season, supposedly taking care of his ailing mother and even himself after a heart attack. (The actor, now busy making movies, wanted to appear in fewer episodes.) He comes home in the 1996 Christmas episode for a poignant reunion that, true to this show's unflinching form, is a difficult reconciliation involving infidelity and other deep-seated marital issues.

But family get-togethers were never as turbulent as on *Grace Under Fire*, ABC's 1990s vehicle for tough-talking comedian Brett Butler as a Houston single mom trying to make ends meet. In its five seasons, this hard-edged show did five Christmas episodes rotating among troubled family members: Grace's sister, having an affair with a married man; her depressed ex-mother-in-law ("Just because I fell asleep with my head in the oven doesn't mean I'm down"); her ex-father-in-law, whose death brings the revelation of his male significant other; her pot-smoking oldest son; and Grace's mom, asserting ideas about raising Grace's tomboy daughter in a more "ladylike" manner. The atmosphere on the *Grace under Fire* set was no less tense. Star Butler's substance abuse and conflicting notions about the show drove such a wedge between her and the producers that ABC let the show expire halfway through its fifth season. It was probably for the best—Grace was running out of distressed relatives.

SITCOMS GET SOPHISTICATED

On NBC's *Frasier*, however, distressed relatives were never in short supply. The spinoff's first Christmas episode in 1993 focuses on the anguish of Kelsey Grammer's cultured radio psychiatrist upon learning his pre-school son Frederick won't be visiting from his ex-*Cheers* home of Boston. Mom Lilith has instead arranged for the boy to live out his favorite movie, *The Sound of Music*, by spending Christmas in Austria with Julie Andrews. Frederick does show up in 1995, when Frasier is made to understand he can't mold his son into his own intellectual image by buying him "brainy" toys. By 2003, Frederick has grown into a black-clothed Goth teen, who'd rather spend time with his friends than his uptight dad. He comes around by episode's end. But by then, Frasier's even more uptight brother Niles (David Hyde Pierce) has tried to rectify his youthful lack of rebellion by "wildly" planning to eat a dope-laced brownie—which gets accidentally consumed by the brothers' elderly ex-cop dad (John Mahoney). In 2002's Christmas episode, the brothers had battled over whose home would host the annual holiday celebration, sending dad fleeing instead to his security guard job.

A lack of togetherness can also create problems, as it does in CBS's acclaimed single-camera comedy of high school cliques, *Square Pegs*. In

1982, divorced dad Tony Dow (earlier a TV teen himself on *Leave It to Beaver*) makes a rare visit to take daughter Sarah Jessica Parker ice-fishing ("He wants me by his side silently baiting hooks with frozen eel chunks"). She'd rather spend the holiday with her friends. Not that she isn't hungering for her father's attention. As he keeps perkily pestering her for gift ideas, she finally has to state the obvious for such a distant dad: "I wish he and his only daughter would get to know each other better." Well enough, anyway, to realize when he's intruding on her social life.

At least these TV characters know who their father is. On NBC's *Friends,* Lisa Kudrow's gullible Phoebe never has, believing her mother's tale that he was a "famous Burma tree surgeon guy" (represented by the man whose photo comes with newly purchased picture frames). Finally learning that he's actually an upstate small-town pharmacist, Phoebe spends Christmas of 1995 driving her grandma's cab from Manhattan to meet the man. But she can't bring herself to actually knock on his door. In various attempts, she gets only as close as the mailbox before turning back and telling companions Chandler (Matthew Perry) and Joey (Matt LeBlanc), "What if he's not this great dad guy? What if he's just still the dirtbag who ran out on my mom and us?" Consoles Chandler, "Someday when you're really ready, you'll make it past the hedges."

But Phoebe's right. You never know what you'll find when reconnecting with that long-lost parent. On NBC's *Night Court,* hip magician Harry Anderson played equally cool young judge Harry T. Stone, whose father turned out to be even wackier. John Astin, already beloved from *The Addams Family,* surfaces several years into the sitcom's run as Harry's breezily loopy dad, usually on leave from the mental institution. His Christmas 1988 visit finds him decorating Harry's office with collard greens for mistletoe and presenting court staffers with shop-class blocks of wood ("Don't tell me you already have some?"). On CBS's *Due South,* the father of Paul Gross's upright visiting Mountie was dead, but that didn't stop him from appearing on the whimsical comedy/drama's 1994 holiday hour of Chicago cop heroics. Gordon Pinsent, one of Canada's most beloved actors, popped up periodically as a bemused role model, replete with his own Mountie uniform, seen only by his son as he'd spout advice. Along on a Christmas case, he tries to give his a son a weapon—"I appreciate the offer," replies Gross, "but it's imaginary"—and finally keeps him company in a down-and-out diner. "This is the first real Christmas dinner we've had together in 20 years," says Pinsent, "and I'm not really here." The episode neatly dovetails portrayals of cop partner David Marciano's dad and its central suspect, a father assisting in bank robberies to support his son.

THE (NOT ALWAYS) HAPPY ENDING

> Brad Sullivan's Father Leo: I don't care much for Christmas myself. Expectations—they're too high. My mother always wanted us to be so joyful. And Father would drink himself into a rage. Now it doesn't even feel like Christmas until the first punch is thrown.
>
> Kevin Anderson's Father Ray: Well, that's a great Christmas tradition, right? You got the Christmas tree. The Christmas turkey. The Christmas fight.
>
> —*Nothing Sacred*, 1997

Spending holiday time with TV's adults and their parents isn't always happy-ending time. The anticipated warmth and togetherness of the season too easily degenerate into emotional button-pushing. As in life, old behavior patterns kick in to heat up simmering rivalries and long-held grudges. CBS's hit sitcom *Everybody Loves Raymond* was designed to depict that situation every week, but other shows use the holidays to heighten family tension by bringing in the in-laws and grandparents, often played by celebrity guest stars.

Mothers prove troublesome to their grown kids on CBS's *Still Standing*, when Sally Struthers insists on having 2003's holiday dinner for son Mark Addy's family at her too-small apartment, and on ABC's *According to Jim*, in which Kathleen Noone inadvertently fuels her daughters' rivalry in 2001 by giving one a family heirloom. Even CBS's short-run 1995 blue-collar city sitcom *Bless This House* found time to bring in Broadway legend Elaine Stritch as the know-better parent of young mother Cathy Moriarty, forcing husband Andrew Dice Clay to referee.

Two parents can conjure twice the tension. Or even four times. CBS's *Yes, Dear* has two visiting couples vying for their grandkids' affections in 2001. "Everybody wants to be the 'A' grandparents," slob son-in-law Mike O'Malley informs more successful in-law Anthony Clark, prompting Clark to warn his less-effusive folks Tim Conway and Vicki Lawrence, "You guys are falling behind!" Their attempts to relate to the youngsters get increasingly awkward, while rivals Dan Hedaya and Alley Mills throw candy in the air for the kids and present their adult offspring with the perfect gift: family burial plots.

Sometimes it's a widowed or divorced parent's new "significant other" who sparks tension, as on *Home Improvement* or Fox's realistically animated family comedy *King of the Hill*. At Christmas 1997 in the latter, Texas propane dealer Hank Hill goes temporarily blind after inadvertently glimpsing mom and friend making whoopee on the kitchen table. (But dad causes his own *King of the Hill* consternation in 2001, when Hank and his cranky ex-military father go at each other so spitefully during a Habitat for Humanity house-raising that ex-president envoy Jimmy Carter has to mediate.)

On ABC's 1998 *Drew Carey Show*, it's the visiting parents who get the surprise. Son Drew finds it difficult explaining to mom and dad that sixty-something Shirley Jones isn't his housekeeper, as they assumed, but actually his girlfriend. Equally dismayed is her adult son (played by loud-mouthed Danny Bonaduce, Jones's *Partridge Family* son from the 1970s), leading to a very unmerry holiday dinner. The adult children in CBS's *The King of Queens* aren't sure what to say, either, when working man Kevin James's parents make an inconvenient visit in 2001 during the "fertile time" of wife and would-be mother Leah Remini.

Other relatives can cause their own Christmas crises by reopening lingering familial wounds. Danny DeVito's volatile *Taxi* dispatcher Louie loses it (again) when his poker-playing brother Nicky pays a visit in 1978 during the ABC sitcom's first season. The Vegas visitor would rather sit in on the garage card game than drop in on the mother he rarely sees. "Every Christmas Eve for the last six years," moans the loathsome Louie, "Ma stayed up all night crying. It was really hard on me. I hated having to put her out in the hall." But holidays are the perfect time for softening harsh characters. Louie does take care of his mother, after all. He wants her to be happy, as well as out of his rapidly receding hair. So he does a bad thing—bankrolling Judd Hirsch's driver Alex against Nicky with the company receipts—to do a good thing. When Nicky runs out of money, all he has left to bet is taking their live-in ma with him if he loses. Thanks to Alex's acumen, Louie gets to savor some seasonal joy.

The sibling reunion is again lukewarm on Ellen DeGeneres's one-season CBS sitcom *The Ellen Show* in 2001. Because Ellen's small-town mother hasn't seen her "big-shot reporter" sister in ages, Ellen has her flown in—which makes for a second reunion, when Mary Tyler Moore guest stars alongside 1970s *Mary Tyler Moore Show* cast mate Cloris Leachman. Old rivalries resurface when the well-heeled Moore spends lavishly on gifts, despite Leachman's $15 limit. It takes Ellen to tell mom that Moore, without a family of her own, "wasn't trying to be better than you with those presents. She was trying to be necessary." (Episode's end brings another nostalgic reunion, when *MTM* co-star Ed Asner is unmasked as the local mall Santa.)

Cousins and uncles also get into the mix. On ABC's *Dharma & Greg*, straitlaced Thomas Gibson sees free-spirit wife Jenna Elfman take his teenage cousin under her wing for the 1997 holidays, when the resentful girl visits while her serial-marrying mother goes on "a honeymoon in Bali with a rich old guy who's been clinically dead twice." The girls share "cheesy movies and dairy-free pizza," make prank phone calls to Greg's mom, and head to the mall pretending to be German tourists. But that's downright everyday compared to the fancifully sweet 1990 Family Channel cable series *Maniac Mansion,* adapted from a computer game for the Lucasfilm studio by former *SCTV* parodists. Its science-dabbling family includes a brother in the form of a tiny fly and a four-year-old the size of a linebacker. There's also wacky Uncle Lenny, who spends the Christmas episode trying to reach the homestead in a snowstorm, first by dogsled, then dangling from the landing gear of an airplane and, finally, hitching a ride with Santa. Lenny makes his arrival head-first down the chimney.

More serious reunions were a specialty of TV's early years. The 1950s staple *Father Knows Best* had the middle-aged sister of star Robert Young come to visit the NBC series in 1956, when her discomfort around kids makes youngest child Lauren Chapin uneasy. Grumps her character Kathy, "It never seems like Christmas with her around!" She only adjusts to her persnickety aunt when an immigrant plumber fixing a broken water pipe on Christmas Eve tells her an old Scandinavian holiday folk tale. The family enacts the snowy story as Kathy imagines it—a village girl wanting to buy a sweater for an angel she meets, but then giving it to the town's nasty old woman, who miraculously becomes beautiful upon receiving "the greatest gift of all"—love. No sooner does Kathy tell starchy Aunt Neva she loves her than church bells chime and Christmas snow starts falling outside the Andersons' window. "That's part of the miracle," cries Kathy.

Mismatched temperaments prove less warm than wacky in ABC's 1990s sitcom *Coach,* when batty defensive coordinator Jerry Van Dyke's Luther Van Dam orders a family heritage book that informs him "there are over seven thousand Van Dams living in this country right now!" Craig T. Nelson's head coach Hayden encourages him to attend their local holiday reunion in 1993, but Luther frets, "What if we don't have anything in common? What if they don't like me? What if I don't like them? What if it turns out just to be awful?" (Which of course it does, when awkward Luther scares the kids, feeds cake to a diabetic and knocks over the Christmas tree.) "Well," Hayden responds, "then you'll know you're really a family."

But family members don't always have to be related by blood. Prime time also loves the seasonal run-in with the former spouse, as in 1990s NBC episodes of *Veronica's Closet* for Kirstie Alley and NBC's *Jesse* for Christina Applegate. *Taxi* played it well just after moving from ABC to NBC in 1982, when droning Louise Lasser *(Mary Hartman, Mary Hartman)* appeared as Alex's self-pitying ex, certain to make life miserable for anyone with whom she comes into contact. And that's everybody, after she shows up on Alex's doorstep: "My other ex-husband recently won a court order that forbids me to get within 400 yards of him." Alex feels forced to bring her to the holiday party being thrown by oddly indeterminate foreigner Andy Kaufman and equally accented wife Carol Kane. "The holidays are time for family, friends, and joy," says Lasser, "and since I have none of those, I'm happy to be here."

IF ONLY IN MY DREAMS

Occasionally, it isn't the presence of loved ones that incites Christmas clashes; it can also be their absence. The continually surprising *King of the Hill* employs animation's detachment from reality to reveal average suburban lives in ways that live-action shows can't. And never more so than at Christmas 1998, when Hank Hill's neighbor Bill gets suicidally obsessed with his (seven years past) marital breakup. He takes to toting around a pet iguana named after ex-wife Lenore and repeatedly tries (ineptly) to kill himself. "I don't think he's gonna snap out of it," drawls pal Dale. "All we can do is sit back and watch the bloodbath." It's only an emotional disaster, though, when Bill dons Lenore's clothes and "becomes" her, to the embarrassment of everyone at the Hills' Christmas party. Wanting to help Bill, Hank puts on his own dress, enacting Lenore himself to decisively tell Bill that she's gone for good. This is an episode that's outrageously funny: A hairy man in a dress has worked ever since Milton Berle. Yet the story never loses sight of the dire human pathos it's portraying. *King of the Hill* manages that rare TV feat of revealing the often-concealed emotions of real men in the guise of cartoon ones.

Another absent relative looks to be oddly present in Fox's Emmy-winning 2003 docu-soap spoof *Arrested Development*. In this ultra-dry single-camera show about the richly dysfunctional Bluth family, Christmastime finds shady CEO patriarch Jeffrey Tambor cooling his heels in jail, awaiting trial for corporate frauds too numerous to list. Just as the show's title has multiple meanings, so does this episode's: "In God We Trust." Tambor may win temporary release to play his traditional role of the Lord in their Southern California community's annual pageant reenacting famous paintings (based on Laguna Beach's summer outdoor Pageant of the Masters). His "adult" children are bickering over who plays which other role, and self-involved wife Jessica Walter starts driving a wedge between her estranged twins Jason Bateman and Portia DeRossi at the very moment they're actually starting to get along. Lunacy runs rampant, highlighting each charac-

ter's particular fear or phobia, climaxed by Tambor hoofing it away from
the pageant in God costume to evade authorities. After he's stunned into
submission with a Taser, the clan gathers at the prison for Christmas Eve.
Even equally neurotic attorney Henry Winkler shows up. "It's like any other
day," he shrugs, "except I bill double."

Comedy and drama haven't been the only genres concerning themselves
with family intimacy or estrangement at holiday time. Variety hours during
their heyday in the 1950s and 1960s were known for having popular entertainers gather their real-life wives, kids, and parents for seasonal celebration. It was even required when the marriage was falling apart, as Sonny
Bono and Cher learned when they forced holiday happiness on their soon-
to-implode 1970s CBS show. In a late series revival, they strained through
a joint celebration despite their divorce (and Cher's new baby with Gregg
Allman). Daytime's soap operas have always cooked up ways to incorporate
the season's home-based traditions as part of their year-round depiction of
ongoing family sagas.

And it's true of whatever genre into which all-star hours like *The Love
Boat* fall. In one of the stories of its 1980 holiday cruise, father and son
singers Allan Jones and Jack Jones (the latter sang the series' theme song)
haven't spoken in the 10 years since Jack's character left their joint act, but
mom Dorothy Lamour and daughter-in-law Laraine Stephens scheme to get
their men together aboard ship. Subtlety was never the strong suit of this
hour from "eye candy" producer Aaron Spelling (*Charlie's Angels*). "What's
he unhappy about?" Allan grouses of Jack. "He's rich, he's famous. He's a
big star!" "I know," moans Stephens, "but it doesn't mean a thing to him
without your love!" The men huff and puff. But they eventually reunite on
stage for a big hug and a duet on Allan's signature hit "Donkey Serenade"
after mom slips Jack a scrapbook of review clippings. "Dad? You mean he
did all this?" marvels Jack. "Your father loves you," coos Lamour. "It's just
that he didn't know how to tell you." The script does, naturally, with its
trademark schmaltz.

FAMILY DRAMAS

More serious hour-long series have also found the yuletide a handy time
to tackle sensitive family issues, introduce far-flung relatives, explore surprising aspects of the regular characters' personalities or depict self-revela-
tions coming through close-knit interaction. NBC's long-running *Bonanza*,
top-ranked among the late 1950s–early 1960s profusion of westerns, used
Christmas to show how tender its all-male family of Nevada ranchers could

get when they took in a little orphan girl. CBS's homespun 1970s hit *The Waltons* actually debuted with a holiday theme: Its 1971 pilot movie "The Homecoming" centered on whether the mountain brood's hard-working Depression-era father would make it home in time for Christmas, providing a chance to view the relationships of all its characters through the eyes of the eldest son and would-be writer played by Richard Thomas.

Northern Exposure normally focused on a makeshift family of residents in a small Alaska town. But the quirky CBS hour's 1991 Christmas outing found Barry Corbin's crusty old Maurice discovering some blood relations of his own. The Emmy-winning script of "Seoul Mates" features the persistent presence of a visiting Korean woman and the adult son she claims Maurice had fathered during military service there 40 years earlier. The cantankerous Alaskan insists, "I don't like the way he looks, I don't like the way he talks. I don't like what he eats." But father and son finally bond after a broken-English karaoke rendering of "Fly Me to the Moon," some arm wrestling, and a barroom chat where they identify their similarities.

Relatives of different ethnicities also find common ground on Fox's school drama *Boston Public*. Fyvush Finkel's elderly Jewish teacher has discovered he has a son from a long-ago liaison with a black woman, and he's in a dither because they've asked him over for 2002 Christmas dinner. "I don't care if they're Christians or Jews or Buddhists," counsels black principal Chi McBride. "They're a gift, and if you break bread with them or have some eggnog, or even watch a Christmas movie or two, you will not be lured into the darkness." Finkel finally arrives for dinner bringing a Christmas ornament, only to discover his son displaying a menorah: "I recently realized that I'm half Jewish." "Lesson number 1," says Finkel. "Hanukkah ended three weeks ago."

The family culture clash is a bit different in 2002 for *Sue Thomas, F.B.Eye* on the wholesome seventh broadcast network, PAX. In this inspirational drama, deaf actress Deanne Bray plays the title federal agent, newly striking out on her own after being raised by protective parents with normal hearing. Sue has to take on an assertive new role when officious mother Kate Trotter insists on doing things her way during a D.C. visit, from buying and decorating the tree to running her daughter's holiday party. "This isn't your life, it's mine," Sue finally insists, while mom admits "I was afraid if I didn't push you, you wouldn't make it" in a hearing world. "I've been your mother for so many years, I didn't know how to be much of anything else." The rapprochement is inevitable, of course. But it's movingly reinforced in a unique rendition of "Silent Night," mom playing the piano as her deaf daughter sign-sings the carol with her hands.

It's politics that come between Martin Sheen's President Jed Bartlet and his ambitious son-in-law on *The West Wing*, the NBC White House drama normally more concerned with national affairs than domestic ones. In 2003, Sheen is determined to bring his wife and three adult daughters together for a holiday dinner. First Lady Stockard Channing is only newly back from an estrangement sojourn to New Hampshire. And now, while Sheen tries to dissuade his son-in-law from running an unwinnable congressional race, he faces down the daughter married to this man, who still feels neglected from her own childhood. "We didn't beat them," Channing wryly consoles Sheen, whose sarcastic comeback is "There's still time." While this scenario hardly reflects the idealized Christmas perfection still sought by so many Americans, the tension and rancor of relatives in close quarters with cross purposes is indeed a holiday befitting this First Family, and many others. As Channing puts it, "We were never Currier and Ives."

Neither are the various clans represented by the hospital staff of NBC's hit *ER*, where Christmas chaos has been sparked over the show's decade-plus run by an assortment of relatives, from nurse Carol's (Julianna Margulies) folksy Ukrainian mother to Dr. Carter's (Noah Wyle) junkie cousin and his divorcing father. Eriq LaSalle's prickly Dr. Benton usually had the most happening, whether he was taking in a street kid, romancing girlfriend Carla or, later, angling to see their son. When tests after Carla's death revealed in 2001 that her deaf preschooler was fathered by someone else, Benton nevertheless sought custody of the kid he'd helped raise. The single-minded surgeon finally chose family over career when the decision came to a head in that year's Christmas episode. Benton relinquished the adrenaline of the ER for a cushy suburban practice in order to make more time for raising the child, and that Christmas hour was LaSalle's last in the cast—a rare holiday exit. (*ER* would stage another in 2004, when Ming-Na's Dr. Chen left after enabling her ailing elderly father's death.)

At least a move like that was definitive. Would the Christmas episode of UPN's 1995 thriller *Nowhere Man* offer a long-awaited family reunion and finally the end of the nightmare for Bruce Greenwood's photographer? Or just another of the incredibly elaborate ruses that bedeviled him during the sleek intrigue drama's one-season run? His entire life had turned upside down after he'd taken a mysterious photo of an execution involving Latin revolutionaries and what seemed to be U.S. military troops. One night in the middle of dinner, his wife claimed not to know him, his credit cards no longer worked, and his existence seemed wiped out utterly. He could only go on the run with the photo's negative, trying to unravel it all while being pursued by sinister forces capable of creating fake realities to acquire that incriminating piece of evidence. For the holidays, "federal agents" reunite him with his wife and estranged mother at a "safe house" complete with decorated tree—asking only that he testify at a "Senate hearing" and turn over the negative. He does the former (or so he thinks) and refuses the latter—only to awaken alone in a torn-apart house, fleeing yet another masquerade.

The characters knew who everyone was, but were agonizingly unsure of themselves, in the 1999 Christmas installment of ABC's *Once and Again*. The moody study of divorced mom Sela Ward and divorced dad Billy Campbell falling in love also found them coping with two sets of kids. And exes. Should they make joint appearances with former spouses to celebrate with their respective kids? Or try a holiday getaway together? The pressure forces them to reassess their escalating relationship—and to make the sort of hard choices (and painful confessions) that made the series such an authentic depiction of the heartache involved in wondering where you stand in both romance and family. The episode doesn't flinch. It ends with Ward and Campbell split up, a rift that must wait for the new year to be repaired.

Other alienated spouses take their issues to court over the holidays. In NBC's *Highway to Heaven* in 1987, angel Michael Landon has to play referee for a little boy caught between battling lawyer parents. For them to see the error of their ways, it takes one of the show's overtly maudlin speeches, from a Santa Claus involved in a case that pits the two attorneys against each other: "The boy loves you both and he's living proof that once you loved each other . . . . Neither of you has to win and neither of you has to lose. All you've got to do is love your son and work together even if you're apart to raise him." The situation arises again in a 2001 episode of CBS's *Family Law*, but it's resolved without intervention from either heaven or Santa—at least the "real" one. Mediator Tom Bosley arrives in Santa gear to face down warring parents after he's called away from playing the role at the local Y. But this series' quirky mix of legal cases and lawyer shenanigans viewed modern life much less earnestly.

Another playful mix was *Gilmore Girls*, The WB's hour-long drama about a 16-year-old girl's tight friendship with the single mother who'd given birth to her at about that same age. Stars Lauren Graham and Alexis Bledel converse a mile a minute about life, love, literature, and pop culture in one of those rare shows that talks up to its audience. The family fracture created when Graham's character kept her baby and stayed single, to the horror of her aristocratic parents, is only beginning to be repaired at 2000's first-season holiday. When Graham's inn job delays her arrival at her parents' fancy dinner, decorous mother Kelly Bishop huffs that she may as well not come, "since it's obviously an enormous burden for you." But then father Edward Herrmann collapses, and Graham's character rushes to the hospital for a caring, if temporary, reconciliation.

Family was an extremely earnest matter in Fox's 1994–2000 drama *Party of Five*, with its focus on five orphaned siblings, ages infant to independent young adult, who are forced to forge a tighter bond after their parents have been killed by a drunk driver. As the series progresses, they grow up and grow further apart again, until a joint celebration in the 1998 holiday hour seems all but impossible. Matthew Fox as eldest son Charlie is delighted when girlfriend Daphne's mom shows up to see their new baby: "This is the way it should be, the holidays, really—grandparents, grandkids, a house full of family." But the visit reopens old wounds

There are plenty of new ones, too. Scott Wolf's Bailey discovers that kindergarten brother Owen feels pushed out by the baby and starts acting out, stealing the Jesus doll from the school nativity play. Neve Campbell's Julia gets preoccupied by a college boyfriend, while Lacey Chabert's Claudia is in the doghouse for ditching boarding school. Claudia's attempt to orchestrate a "proper Christmas Eve" finds everyone exiting the house for various reasons, so when Julia finally arrives home, no one is there. "I love them all, and it's nobody's fault," she says, "but I don't want to go back to all that stuff."

She isn't the only one. Benjamin McKenzie's alienated teen in the hip Fox soap *The O.C.* learns how to celebrate a new way in 2003 when he's introduced to the merged holiday Chrismukkah, created by his new Orange County foster family. It's better than the festivities of his birth family: "My holiday memories pretty much consist of my mom drunk and me getting my ass kicked."

Christmas often strips away pretensions and lays bare cold, hard relationship realities that TV characters normally shy away from. In 1993's first season of ABC's police hour *NYPD Blue*, we learn a bit more about star David Caruso's enigmatic detective when he makes a holiday visit to his mother's rest home, where the confused woman takes him for his late father and suggests he spend more time with his son. Even personality-oriented hours can focus on friendships and romance to the exclusion of relatives. On NBC's lighthearted *Ed*, a portrait of a bowling alley–owning lawyer, Tom Cavanagh's title character is fleshed out a bit when his wheeler-dealer brother (guest Timothy Busfield) blows back into their small hometown at Christmas 2002 with a new scheme to sell "man makeup." His brother's arrest amplifies their long-simmering rift, until they have it out over old resentments. "You like that I'm the screwup brother," declares Busfield. "It makes it easy on you." Cavanagh finally opens up about his own life's mistakes: "You've said 'I'm sorry' to me a thousand times," he tells Busfield," and no matter how angry I am at you, I've always accepted your apology, 'cause you're my brother. And now I'm asking the same."

THE MAKESHIFT FAMILY

> We try to cram all this love, peace and understanding into one day, and our
> little miniscule human brains can't even hold it all, so we explode.

—Brett Butler, *Grace Under Fire*, 1994

Shows like *Ed*, in which dealing with relatives is less than central on a weekly basis, often create their own kind of family unit from coworkers and best buddies. Think NBC's *Hill Street Blues* police squad, or CBS's Vietnam vet pals on *Magnum, P.I.* Dramas learned that trick from the spate of workplace comedies that poured out of Hollywood after the 1970s success of adult-oriented ensembles led by CBS's *Mary Tyler Moore Show* and *M*A*S*H*, and ABC's *Barney Miller* and *Taxi*. The following two decades were filled with nonrelated sitcom "families" who'd share in life-changing events and spend holidays together—the mixed-gender roommates of ABC's *Three's Company*, the barflies of NBC's *Cheers*, the diner patrons of CBS's *Becker*, the urban compatriots of NBC's *Friends*, *Seinfeld*, and *Will & Grace*. Never mind the fellow workers of CBS's *Alice* and *Murphy Brown*, NBC's *Night Court* and *Wings*, and ABC's *Coach* and *Spin City*.

The epitome of the workplace family was the radio station staff of *WKRP in Cincinnati*, whose actual relatives were rarely seen in the 1978–82 CBS cult hit. Though most of the DJs and office staff have their own separate plans for Christmas 1979, they rally together when it seems Loni Anderson's romantically busy receptionist Jennifer might actually be spending the holiday alone. One by one (or two), they flock to her apartment, each delivering a Christmas tree ("In the spirit of Christmas," quips Howard Hesseman's Johnny Fever, "we killed a tree for you"), which can barely fit amid the lavish gifts arriving from her "admirers." But Jennifer has a confession to make about her high-powered holiday companionship: "The admiral is flying me to Bethlehem in his private jet." "Now that," says Fever, "is a down-home Christmas."

But not as warm as one spent with a character's TV-certified family. Who needs real relatives when you've got real friends? Not the students of NBC's *Facts of Life* boarding school or *A Different World* college; not, at the other end of the age spectrum, the retiree roommate quartet of NBC's *The Golden*

Girls; not even no-longer-related-by-marriage antagonists like the title character of *Grace Under Fire* and her ex-mother-in-law. Trying to cheer up the depressed woman at the 1994 holiday, Brett Butler expresses TV's new family credo: "I'm family even though I'm your ex-daughter-in-law. In kind of a dysfunctional '90s sort of way, that's family. Family's just who you're with and how you treat 'em." It's sweet enough to make the two battlers make up. But as usual, Butler gets the final punch line: "This doesn't mean we can't fight anymore, does it?"

Certainly not. You're family. And this is Christmas.

CHAPTER 5

(Not) Home for the Holidays: At Work and Away

I didn't say they had to work (on Christmas). I just said if they don't work, they might not get cabs with the luxuries that they've grown accustomed to. Like reverse.

—Danny DeVito as the tiny-terror boss in *Taxi*, 1982

You know, between decorating the tree with thermometers, and Radar singing those Christmas carols on the PA, and that little below-zero nip in the air, this place really manages to capture that good old-fashioned Christmas depression.

—Alan Alda amid the Korean War, *M*A*S*H*, 1978

Obstacles to yuletide togetherness keep popping up more frequently in TV storylines as the hectic pace of real life continues to accelerate and family members find themselves spread across the country. The hurdles can be as simple and temporary as Burt Reynolds's 1992 car trouble on CBS's *Evening Shade*, or a power failure that forces the title star to trudge home on foot through the 1973 snow of CBS's Chicago-set *The Bob Newhart Show*. After the tour bus for ABC's rock-singing *The Partridge Family* breaks down in a ghost town on Christmas Eve, mom Shirley Jones and her kids meet a lonely prospector for whom they stage an elaborate 1971 holiday. A dodgy dog holds celebrants at bay in 1996 in both NBC's *Something So Right*, destroying the belongings of New York apartment dwellers Jere Burns and Mel Harris, and CBS's *Pearl*, in which a canine outside a classroom door traps adult student Rhea Perlman and antagonist professor Malcolm McDowell.

But with the explosion of affordable jet travel in the 1980s—and the increase in TV news coverage of same during the slow-news/high-travel holiday season—came a new kind of can't-get-home script staple.

STRANDED AT THE AIRPORT

Full House may have set sitcoms' stuck-at-the-airport standard with its 1988 ABC episode in which widowed San Francisco dad Bob Saget, room-mates John Stamos and Dave Coulier, and Saget's three daughters get caught in a "totally incredible blizzard" Christmas Eve on their way to a family reunion in the Rockies. This awww-some Friday "TGIF"-block familycom builds layer after layer of kid cuteness and hokey sentimentality. Rock-and-roll bachelor Stamos is urged by his dad to hit on the fellow traveler and Saget colleague played by comely series-wife-to-be Lori Laughlin. ("Times of crisis always bring people together," counsels dad. "Trust me, I met your mother the day Elvis got drafted.") Middle daughter Jodie Sweetin frets, "Santa will never find us now!" at their unscheduled stop. But somehow, just as the crankiest passenger on their plane disappears, a Santa Claus arrives to conjure presents on the baggage carousel while the Scrooge-y man's laptop computer screen flashes "Merry Christmas."

Even more crucial for TV's holiday annals, Stamos gets to make the quintessential it's-Christmas-anywhere-we're-together speech, complete with French horns on the music track blatantly tugging audience heart-strings. "What's the matter with you people?" he demands of the down-hearted airport stranded, leaping to his feet. "The first Christmas was in a manger—they did okay. I mean, so what if we're stuck in this crummy dump? Christmas isn't about presents or Santa Claus or cows," referring to Laughlin's mooning over her youthful rural yules. "It's about a feeling. It's about people. It's about us forgetting about our problems and reaching out to help other people. Christmas doesn't have to happen in one certain place. It happens in our hearts."

"So if you think about it," his moment-for-the-ages climaxes, "we could have Christmas anywhere. I mean, even in a baggage claim. What do you see right here?" Stamos asks of a coat stand. "I see a big beautiful Christmas tree." Vending machines are "a Christmas dinner with all the trimmings," and the baggage conveyor belt—"Okay, yes, that's a conveyor belt, but the point I'm trying to make here is that we could give these kids the best darn

Christmas they ever had!" He leads an all-around sing-along of "Winter Wonderland." Laughlin gives him a kiss under the mistletoe. And fine festivity is enjoyed by all.

Of course, that family was at least together in being waylaid. Celebrants were separated in ABC's 1995 *Home Improvement*. Detroit TV's *Tool Time* dad Tim Allen finds himself marooned Christmas Eve at a small Michigan airport when low visibility interrupts his quick trip to serve as grand marshal of an elf parade. "No matter what it takes, I'm getting home," he swears. And he does, after the pilot announces, "A tremendous beam of light has just broken through the fog!" What else could that be but Tim's annual zillion-watt household holiday display, in his absence fired up for the annual neighborhood competition by his three boys? "I can't believe we won the lighting contest," says youngest son Taran Noah Smith. "And helped land a plane," adds eldest Zachery Ty Bryan. But the final word goes to teen idol Jonathan Taylor Thomas as middle kid Randy: "This just proves one thing, guys. Dad's been holding us back all these years."

Nothing so dramatic, or so amusing, happens on UPN's 2004 *All of Us*, in which Hollywood dad Duane Martin gets stuck in a Denver snowstorm on the way to New York for a big showbiz interview. "First things were bad, then they cleared up," the script lamely has him say upon arriving home in the sitcom's last act. "I guess it was a Christmas miracle," he tells wife Elyse Neal, who's been battling and then bonding with LisaRaye as Martin's ex-wife and mother of his son. As for things on that end, "First they were bad, and then they cleared up, so I guess we had a Christmas miracle, too," Neal says, tying up the episode's message with a big tidy bow.

Things are equally spelled out in *The Golden Girls* when the title's retired Miami roommates can't fly home to their families from Miami in the NBC sitcom's 1986 holiday episode: A "severe storm front" has all air traffic grounded. As they joyously commiserate in a diner, owner Teddy Wilson wonders, "You all are not related? Really? The way you were teasing and talking to each other, I thought you were family for sure." "Well," drawls Rue McClanahan's Blanche, "isn't it funny how sometimes it takes a total stranger to point out something that's been right there in front of your face?" "We were feeling so sorry for ourselves," says Betty White's Rose, "we forget—we *are* celebrating Christmas with family."

Beyond planes, sometimes trains and automotive transport still get their moment in the modern spotlight. A bus station is the celebration haven for the 1993 holiday of Fox's Martin Lawrence showcase, *Martin*, when girlfriend Tisha Campbell's trip from Detroit home to Philadelphia is short-circuited by snow (and some very grungy terminal denizens).

It's the subway—or, as they say in Chicago, the el—on which the chief antagonists of ABC's *Family Matters* once again make episode-concluding peace for their 1993 Christmas. When a power outage strands Jaleel White's nerdy kid Urkel and Reginald VelJohnson's put-upon cop-neighbor Carl with a carful of cranky commuters, this Friday-night "TGIF" series mainstay ladles out yet more syrup: "I know you're all tired and hungry and you wanna be at home spending Christmas Eve with your families, but does sitting here being grumpy make you feel any better? Well, I think not," cheers Urkel, urging straphangers to talk about their grandkids and their lovers. "You see, folks, Christmas isn't a place. Why, it's a feeling. It's the love and warmth of friends and family," he oozes, echoing the schmaltzy cliché-spouting of its *Full House* sibling in the sugary Miller-Boyett production stable. "It's a feeling we get in our hearts this time of year, and we take that feeling with us wherever we go. Why, Christmas can even be here, on this cold dark train!" Which is, of course, the cue for the train to start up, the passengers to trade hugs, and the episode to end with the traditional Miller-Boyett carol-singing.

A helicopter provides the troublesome transport on CBS's *Magnum, P.I.* in 1983. Snow may be unlikely in its Hawaiian islands setting, but this Tom Selleck detective drama substitutes a threat yet more novel—government bombing target practice. As Selleck travels to play Santa for orphans on the Big Island, while his pals are heading to Maui and Molokai, their "oversize eggbeater" piloted by Roger E. Mosley's T.C. makes an emergency landing on a Navy "free-fire island" (based on the real-life isle of Kaho'olawe). "Who's gonna order gunnery exercises on Christmas Eve?" scoffs Magnum. But he isn't counting on Ed Lauter's grinch-y captain nursing a grudge for past holidays spent in the Antarctic and Vietnam. Before the guys get the helicopter repaired in the nick of time (did we suspect otherwise?), they conveniently experience their own heartrending yule awakening. "Perhaps in an odd way, being stranded here has been good for us," says John Hillerman as Magnum's stuffy supervisor Higgins. "I for one had been so intent on getting everything done that needed to get done, I completely lost track of the spirit of the season."

STUCK IN THE SLAMMER

Could there be an even stranger location for would-be celebrants to be stranded? There's certainly one that's much more ubiquitous—jail. TV has persistently relied on this notion since the medium's nascent days. Maybe it's what comes first to the minds of scriptwriters asking themselves: Where's the last place you'd want to spend the holiday? One of tube comedy's earliest icons, Jackie Gleason's Ralph Kramden, cooled his heels there in one of 1953's Honeymooners holiday skits on his live CBS variety hour. After answering a want ad for a sidewalk Santa job, Ralph is sneakily set up by his employers to collect bookmaking slips—and ends up arrested because of it, fretting that he'll lose his job driving the bus and be unable to find another. "Well," suggests Art Carney's even dimmer Ed Norton (playing elf to Ralph's Santa), "you've had a little experience in bookmaking... ."

Other folks go to jail voluntarily. Like Frank Faylen's storekeeping dad of the wryly narrating title teen in CBS's playful sitcom classic The Many Loves of Dobie Gillis. Its 1959 first-season holiday finds Dwayne Hickman's bundled-up Dobie at his usual perch in the park near Rodin's The Thinker statue. Confiding as always in the audience, he asks, "So why ain't I merry?" Quick cut to his bombastic dad behind bars roaring: "It ain't easy to get arrested on a Christmas Eve!" But he maneuvers it for some solitude, because "I am mad at people! People at Christmas! ... Everybody goes nuts, and it's OK—it's Christmas!" Dobie flashes us back to his dad's slow-burn stewing over his mother's dithering about her Christmas card list, over Dobie and college brother Davey wheedling for cash ("you generous, warm-hearted, affectionate old softie"), over Bob Denver as Dobie's grubby beatnik pal Maynard setting off a self-inflating life raft on Gillis's grocery counter. Persnickety store customers keep pushing the high-strung grocer's buttons, asking him to gift-wrap salami in order to cadge free wrapping paper, refusing to take specially ordered items without free Christmas delivery, returning frozen turkeys from a June sale to get December's full-price refund.

The series has an edge unusual for its era, especially when teens angle for as much as they can get from adults, who bristlingly battle back. The post–World War II "generation gap" hadn't yet been captured in terms of such blatant gamesmanship or such prickly emotion. Of course, the enmity only lasted as long as the laughs, each episode warmly coming to accord by its conclusion. In this case, the Gillis clan brings its Christmas dinner to the clink, which softens dad's heart enough for him to willingly head home.

Family also finds its jailed way together in 1960's first-season Christmas episode of CBS's The Andy Griffith Show. Just when Griffith's folksy Southern sheriff Andy Taylor has emptied his cells for the holiday, the local liquor merchant hauls in a moonshiner who's "made a batch to kind of merry up Christmas." "You just cain't do anythin' with him," Andy shakes his head of the Scrooge-y storekeeper, so he simply "arrests" the prisoner's wife and kids to share his convict Christmas. "Prison is for punishin'," rages the cranky old complainant, "not for picnicking!" But once this lonely man eyeballs the warmth of the family's detention festivity, he successively steals a town bench, parks by a fire hydrant and tears up the ticket before the bug-eyes of Don Knotts's excitable deputy Barney Fife. "If a fella was tryin' to get hisself throwed in the jug, he couldn't do a better job," drawls Andy. When it finally dawns on him, he corrals the reformed grouch to enjoy some courthouse guitar-pickin' and girlfriend Elinor Donahue's rendition of "Away in a Manger."

The Andy Griffith Show never did another Christmas half-hour in its high-rated eight-year run. But Emmy-winning scene stealer Knotts returned to the familiar territory of his star-making role 33 years later for the 1993 holiday outing of ABC's familycom Step by Step. Playing a Wisconsin deputy named Feif ("That's 'feef'! F-E-I-F! Fife would be F-I-F-E, got it?"), he puts stars Patrick Duffy and Suzanne Somers behind bars, after catching the contractor and his wife "entering with the intent to purchase" last-minute gifts at a renovating toy store to which Duffy holds the keys. The kids of the stars' blended family are initially too greedily grabbing presents to notice their parents' Christmas-morning absence, but in true Friday night "TGIF" fashion, they come to realize "the most important thing about Christmas is being with your family," in the words of daughter Angela Watson. Soon they've taken their holiday food and festivity down to the jailhouse. Says pubescent son Christopher Castile, "We couldn't let you spend Christmas alone in the hoosegow."

It's a traffic infraction that gets the title TV talk-show host of The New Dick Van Dyke Show arrested on his CBS sitcom in 1972, while he's driving back from Las Vegas to his Arizona home (attired in a painfully trendy leisure suit). "You expect everybody to go five over" the speed limit, he pleads with the officer, "and I was only going five over the five you expect everybody to go." Left alone in the small-town slammer for the holiday, he can only imagine his kids "waiting for Santa to come down the chimney and Daddy to go up the river"—until his pals arrive, having also been pulled over while speeding down to bail him out. Luckily, they're all entertained by an itinerant folk duo named (is there any doubt?) Joe and Mary, who've been left without a place to stay because (all together now) "there's no room in the inn."

A law officer is the one jailed in NBC's 1988 Night Court. Comic Marsha Warfield's tough-talking bailiff Roz has stolen a truck of toys being held as case evidence, to give them to indigent kids. "When I was eight years old, my father lost his job right before Christmas," she confides in her Manhattan cell to Markie Post's public defender. "I thought no way was I gonna get any presents this year. And the people from Toys for Toddlers came." So she knows, "When you're a kid at Christmastime, most of all you just want something under the tree with your name on it." The kids who got her toys offer to give them back to get her sprung. But the businessmen involved in the case have a handy change of heart thanks to the sly mediation of twisted judge Harry Anderson.

WORKING CHRISTMAS

The court crew is working Christmas, like many TV characters whose jobs don't afford the luxury of holidays off. This became a more commonplace plot as office comedies grew to dominate network airwaves from the 1970s. The first holiday for CBS's *The Mary Tyler Moore Show* found the star's Minneapolis TV producer character explaining over the phone to her mother in 1970 that "Christmas Eve is just like any other day when you're doing a news show." Even the cleaning crew and the night watchman will be off, but Mary has to staff the newsroom alone, clinging to the radio voice of Charlie from the station transmitter to keep her company with tales of his family's "real old-fashioned Christmas." Could Mary feel any lower? Of course not. In burst boss Ed Asner, anchor Ted Knight, news writer Gavin MacLeod, and pal Valerie Harper, bringing the holiday party to the girl who thought she wouldn't have one. (Even production company MTM got festive, coloring its three logo letters red and green on its credits-ending tag.)

The office's new gal or guy always seems to be the one holding down the professional fort. Radio psychiatrist Kelsey Grammer willingly takes the gig at his Seattle station on NBC's first-season *Frasier* in 1993: "I couldn't see my son, I had a terrible fight with my father, I was facing a horrible Christmas, and then I thought, well, maybe trying to help other people through their troubles, it might get me through mine." Their telephoned tales of woe only bring him down, though. ("You see, Dr. Crane, I've fallen in the shower so many times, they can't fit any more pins in my hip.") Heading to a skid row diner for dinner in his scruffy holiday-work clothes, he loses his wallet, only to have the bums at the counter take pity on him as one of their own. "The rest of the year belongs to rich people with their fancy houses and expensive foreign cars"—both of which Frasier has, of course—"but Christmas, Christmas belongs to guys like us," contends guest star John Finn, flummoxing the all-knowing shrink with his naïve wisdom.

Crime never takes a holiday, which means officers of the law are often called to yule duty. Manhattan's 12th precinct detectives on ABC's *Barney Miller* were virtually a family of their own, anyway, emblematic of the workplace sitcoms of the 1970s, 1980s and 1990s that seldom followed the characters beyond their occupational bond. Producer Danny Arnold's sharp and adult half-hour relied on its setting's steady stream of perpetrators, accusers, and attorneys to expose all we needed to know about the cops' personalities. Its 1976 holiday episode finds Ron Glass's slick detective Harris gibing the hookers he's hauling in, "I don't enjoy working on Christmas any more than you do." Max Gail's dense but softhearted Wojo assembles a recalcitrant toy for a father charged with throwing the troublesome contraption through a store window. As tired veteran cop Fish, Abe Vigoda goes undercover to nab a mugger who preys on Santas. And at the episode's core, Jack Soo's yearning loner Yemana makes friends with a Japanese mugging victim who is, unbeknownst to him, also a streetwalker. Learning the truth, he decides to keep their late-night date anyway—two lonely people leaving their professional roles behind to forge the Christmas connection they crave.

The same sort of makeshift alliance again takes shape in the 1981 episode, after recurring repertory player Stanley Brock's yap-happy vigilante merchant Bruno uses a cattle prod on a homeless person found sleeping in his store. When both are taken into custody, Hal Linden's title captain of the squad unravels a topical tale of urban gentrification wiping out flophouses like the one their sleeping man had lived in. "There's all these marginal people out on the street," explains Wojo, "trying to survive, sleeping in doorways, trash bins." But not this Christmas. Redneck Bruno and his mousy wife finally welcome his victim home for the holiday. Meanwhile, a greeting card writer has been busy "decking the halls with a barrage of deviled eggs" after being fired at the company Christmas party.

That mix of the serious and the silly resurfaces in hour-long series form in NBC's 1979 *CHiPs*. Erik Estrada and his Los Angeles motorcycle patrol pals search for a stolen church bell, while a man arrested for drunk driving actually comes to the station to thank the officers for nabbing him. But most cops of that violent TV era were handling more brutal business. The detective squad led by lollipop-licking New York detective Telly Savalas on CBS's hard-nosed *Kojak* spends the 1975 holiday solving pharmacy robberies and bar shootings. One cop volunteers for a stakeout to avoid brooding over his wife's summertime murder.

That same year, the quick-strike weapons squad of ABC's *S.W.A.T.* engages in its typical surround-'em-and-shoot-'em skirmishes amid a Christmas theme. A holiday-hating heiress played by Anne Francis plans her annual hospital stay for plastic surgery, and jewel thieves plot to clean her out while she's there. It just so happens that star Steve Forrest and his heavy artillery boys are already on the scene, throwing a Christmas party for the children's ward. Between hostage-takings and bursts of gunfire, they get to show off their softer side, and Francis's Scrooge-y heart softens by episode's end. Strangely enough, lots of cops seem to end up at the hospital. So does Dennis Weaver, directing as well as starring in 1976's "'Twas the Fight before Christmas" installment of NBC's mystery movie franchise *McCloud*. His drawling New Mexico marshal turned New York City detective spends Christmas saving the life of a would-be suicide jumper played by future *Dallas* star Linda Gray. He ushers her to the hospital, where his girlfriend Diana Muldaur just happens to be throwing a party in—where else?—the children's ward. When armed junkies take the ward hostage, McCloud takes it upon himself to rappel down by rope from the roof and heroically burst through the ward window.

Luckily, the next generation of police shows was more talk than action, making them more realistic in both character study and serial structure. *NYPD Blue*'s first-season holiday hour on ABC in 1993 found Dennis Franz's hard-nosed detective Andy Sipowicz reluctantly serving as a charity Santa to "all these deprived kids. Maybe some of 'em actually didn't try to break into my car on their way to school." Explored even more fully was his partner John Kelly, as played by shooting star David Caruso in his only season on the series. Kelly's generally somber mood was gracefully illuminated by a Christmas visit to his mother at her rest home, where she speaks earnestly but confusedly to her eerily calm son as if he were his father, urging him to spend less time working and more time with "John Jr."

Things are more graphically messy on NBC's gritty *Homicide: Life on the Street* in 1994, when the Baltimore-shot show has its detectives working the graveyard shift on Christmas Eve. "Ho-ho-ho, homicide," Richard Belzer's mordant Munch answers the squad room phone, before heading out to investigate a dead body in a Santa suit. "Uh-oh," he says upon arrival, "Rudolph's gonna be pissed." Clark Johnson's equally sardonic Meldrick offers philosophical observations, in that typically aside *Homicide* manner: "You know there's more suicides at Christmas than at any other time of the year?" Joining him on a stakeout, Isabella Hofmann's Russert is no jollier: "Nice way to spend Christmas Eve, huh? Watching addicts get their yuletide fix."

HOSPITAL HOLIDAYS

The medical profession never gets a day off, either, especially from the 1980s onward. The hour format was shifting away from its stalwart family melodramas and solo-star heroism, instead exploring the professional bustle of "franchise" arenas such as cops, lawyers, and doctors. In medicine, the closed-end weekly adventures of earlier lone wolves—NBC's 1960s *Dr. Kildare* or ABC's 1970s *Marcus Welby, M.D.*—gave way to the more complex continuing-tale dynamics of large hospital staffs in NBC's 1980s trailblazer *St. Elsewhere*, CBS's topical *Chicago Hope*, and NBC's smash-hit *ER*. These shows' diverse ensemble casts made it easier to introduce new actors as the series progressed (and eliminate old ones), to rotate attention from character to character, and to break form and tone at times to keep the series feeling fresh.

St. Elsewhere's broken-down Boston hospital staff couldn't have been truer to cranky form than in its sole yule outing, aired in 1985. William Daniels's arrogant chief of surgery observes tartly, "What with all the office party car wrecks, there's more chest trauma than I can than I can keep up with." Even at home, Ed Flanders's head physician and widowed father of a withdrawn autistic son tells his college-age daughter, "The holidays are something I endure, not enjoy," with those "recollections of happier, simpler times that were never there in the first place." Most morose of all, *St. Elsewhere* offers one of TV's earliest offings of Santa Claus, as the hospital's holiday-party Santa collapses in front of the kids and eventually croaks during the intensive-care visit of one boy, who subsequently blames himself.

ABC's *Doogie Howser, M.D.* was barely more upbeat, exemplifying the late 1980s spate of "dramedy" half-hours shot single-camera without a studio audience. After Neil Patrick Harris's title teen prodigy finds himself "volunteered" to work the 1989 holiday night shift, he fakes a fever and "faints" in the cafeteria to escape to a "major blow-out" party. Guilt overtakes him there, of course, and Doogie returns to an emergency room where Santa is wheeled in with a heart attack and a seemingly disturbed patient claims to be, among other outsize personalities, Darth Vader and Ethel Merman. (He's discovered to have an insulin imbalance.) Finally, staffers dressed as elves and reindeer assist a surgeon dressed as St. Nick in saving the life a kid who professes his undying belief in the red-suited gift-giver.

The Christmas shift at a hospital always seems to add extra pressure. *ER* annually specializes in working staff woe. Blizzards frequently hit its Chicago setting, resulting in overwork from disasters like 1994's first-season expressway pileup or 2004's subzero temperatures afflicting the city's homeless. Yuletide 1995 brings what one staffer calls a "Nativity on Ice vs. Zamboni" showdown, when the driver of the ice-rink resurfacer plows "right into the manger" ("Put the Virgin Mary in three," barks the room-assigning triage chief). Split-second decisions over harvesting organs for transplants haunt Eriq LaSalle's Dr. Benton in 1994 and Noah Wyle's Dr. Carter in 1998.

But the most put-upon hospital employee of all is *ER* lead Anthony Edwards. His Dr. Mark Greene can't get away from work to shop in 1994, and then faces a wrongful death lawsuit in 1995, the same year his divorcing wife has taken their daughter for Christmas in Dayton. In 1998, he's being stalked by an obsessed female staffer. By 2000, he's been stricken with a brain tumor that requires a holiday trip to New York for possible treatment. Close behind in the continuing tragedy department might be Wyle's Dr. John Carter, at various Christmases discovering his cousin shooting heroin, his own painkiller addiction resurfacing, his father divorcing his mother, and more.

CHRISTMAS AT WAR

What could be worse at Christmas than such an urban war zone? Just the front lines of the real thing. Television has only occasionally touched on the waging of declared national conflict, most notably in two separate spates 20 years after the real-life fact. The mid-1960s brought several hours showcasing World War II heroics: ABC's *Combat!*, *Twelve O'clock High*, and *The Rat Patrol*, not to mention CBS's odd and oddly enduring prisoner-of-war sitcom, *Hogan's Heroes*. But the next generation's service in the muddier moral waters of the Vietnam struggle would inspire more conflicted portrayals in reflective dramas.

CBS's *Tour of Duty*, with *St. Elsewhere* grad Terence Knox leading its grime-covered grunts, spends its 1989 Christmas episode examining the war's confusing impact on these infantrymen, both on the ground in Cambodia and among the folks back home. ABC's field-hospital cult favorite *China Beach* constructs a more colorful tapestry in 1988—radio DJ Megan Gallagher spinning "the sound of Christmas on the South China Sea," Bob Hope's troupe heading in to entertain the troops, a Santa-suited soldier "wandering around post-op with a grenade launcher," and a nativity scene featuring a monkey in a "manger" cooler. Dana Delany's nurse gets a kiss from doctor Robert Picardo, while newbie Nancy Giles gets assigned to the graves registration unit. "We give a man back his dignity," says supervisor Michael Boatman. "It isn't much, but it's something." Giles learns a key act of respect upon noticing a death tag marked December 26 instead of the correct December 24. Decrees Boatman, "Nobody dies on Christmas Eve."

The same insistence powers a memorable episode of *M*A*S*H*, CBS's long-running adaptation of Robert Altman's seriocomic 1970 film of Korean War hijinks at a battlefront Army mobile hospital where draftee staffers struggle to cope with the carnage. In a landmark instance of TV improving on the big screen, the weekly half-hour developed in 1972 by veteran comedy writer Larry Gelbart (*Your Show of Shows*) deftly maintained the movie's laughs while hitting harder on the antiwar message, for a TV audience grown weary of nightly news images from Vietnam's "living-room war."

That era's increasingly caustic sense of humor is on early display in 1980's ninth-season episode, both written and directed by costar Mike Farrell, whose surgeon B.J. Hunnicut served as comedic partner-in-crime to Alan Alda's flippant Dr. Hawkeye Pierce. The hard-drinking cynics are clucking over a supply convoy being attacked by the North Koreans during the yuletide truce—"Don't those guys know there's a war on that's off?" quips Alda—until the incoming casualties include a gravely wounded soldier unlikely to live through the holiday. "If we can delay it long enough," bargains Hunnicut, "his kids won't have to think of Christmas as the day daddy died." These jokesters want to play the date straight, and they almost make it. When the soldier dies at 11:25 p.m., Hawkeye walks to the clock and moves the minute hand to 12:05 a.m. "Christmas," says William Christopher's chaplain Father Mulcahy, "should be thought of as a day of birth."

Pierce and Mulcahy figure more prominently in two earlier holiday-themed *M*A*S*H* favorites: 1972's "Dear Dad," written by Gelbart, and 1978's "Dear Sis," written and directed by Alda. The first makes a striking break with TV comedy form: Anecdotal flashbacks of various camp crises come to life as Hawkeye writes home to his father. "The tension in the operating room is always a foot thick, but we do our best to cut through it," Alda's character pens, less to inform his dad than to gently familiarize first-season viewers with the series' unusually irreverent tone. The sitcom laugh track that backed the off-duty antics in which staffers blew off pent-up steam would fall silent during scenes of surgery, even as its cynical surgeons remained ribald, their gallows humor left to play against the bloodshed as it may. "If jokes seem sacrilegious in an operating room," Hawkeye writes, "I promise you they're a necessary defense against what we get down here at this end of the draft board." Jamie Farr's cross-dressing malcontent Corporal Klinger (not yet such a comedic character) is shown wielding a grenade against his colleagues in exhaustion, while Hawkeye ends up choppering from the camp party to battlefield casualties dressed as Kris Kringle.

A similar structure is revisited six years later, to elaborate on MASH staffers' continuing frustration at being unable to make anything more than an ameliorative dent in the combat carnage. As Father Mulcahy writes of everyday activities to his nun sister in the week before Christmas, "It's a time of anticipation and hope. Unfortunately, it's also a time when both sides get in as much destruction as they can before the Christmas truce." The escalation of slaughter leaves the gently earnest priest lamenting, "I don't seem to make a difference here. I hang around on the edge of effectiveness." Where Hawkeye reiterates his jaundiced point of view here—"We don't sleep, we don't eat, and every day a truck comes in and lays a bunch of bodies on the ground"—Mulcahy's perspective serves to encourage faith and wonder. His positive presence is saluted in Hawkeye's episode-ending Christmas party toast: "To someone who's too modest, too utterly simple a man to realize how much strength he gives us just by the decency of his life among us."

The men and women of the 4077th salute their chaplain with a graceful singing of "Dona Nobis Pacem," as snow begins to fall. "All of a sudden, this place is pretty," says Harry Morgan as crusty Colonel Potter. But *M*A*S*H* never lets us forget that even with faith's promise of heaven, war is still hell on earth. "Sorry, folks, they broke the truce," says an arriving ambulance driver. "I got some Christmas presents for you." The unit's healers go back to work on yet one more holiday slipping away too far from home.

CHAPTER 6

Chestnuts Roasting on an Open Fire: Christmas Traditions

We've always decorated the tree together. Now all of a sudden, they're too busy. It's just that there's certain traditions, especially around holidays, I still enjoy sharing with my children. And as the years go by, those things become more and more precious to me. I just wish my kids felt the same way.

—JoMarie Payton Noble, *Family Matters*, 1995

The building would be filled with the sounds of Christmas [back home in Philadelphia]. You know, jingle bells and singing and laughing, and then at the end of the evening, the traditional police sirens. People in Bel-Air don't even know how to celebrate Christmas. There's no sledding, there's no caroling, there's no winos making snow angels on the front lawn.

—Will Smith, *Fresh Prince of Bel-Air*, 1990

Gotta get a tree. Send some cards. Put up the decorations. Cook up Christmas dinner. And if ambition strikes, compose a new holiday carol.

Christmas traditions are a huge part of TV's celebration, especially on situation comedies, which mine these ubiquitously recognized customs for gags, punch lines, and character development.

O CHRISTMAS TREE

> I am against innocent trees being cut down in their prime and their corpses
> being grotesquely dressed in tinsel and twinkly lights.
>
> —Lisa Kudrow, *Friends*, 1996

> It would just have ended up as cheap furniture at Ikea if it weren't here.
>
> —Jennifer Saunders (defending her huge tree), *Absolutely Fabulous*, 2003

In many shows it all starts with the Christmas tree—the American home's
largest and most obvious symbol of the holiday. "You know, a Christmas tree is
wonderful in and of itself," muses Rob Morrow's Jewish doctor on CBS's *Northern
Exposure* in 1991, "but it evokes so much—images of snowmen, sleigh rides."

The holiday tree brought indoors and decorated is so crucial that it's
even worth risking arrest for. Just ask the title character of *The Jeff Foxworthy
Show* in its 1996 NBC incarnation, when he's hauled in for cutting down a
great one in a state park. Or the teens of Fox's *That '70s Show*, chased in
1998 after they bring home a highway specimen so they can keep dad's tree
money. Or John Lithgow's alien-new-to-Earth on NBC's delirious *3rd Rock
from the Sun*, who in 1996 naively enters a neighbor's yard with a chain saw.
"Have you ever felt a Taser?" the Emmy-winning Lithgow reports back to his
outer-space companions. "It's not nearly as much fun as it looks."

America's favorite yellow animated family celebrates the centrality of the
Christmas tree in various ways over their many Fox seasons of *The Simpsons*.
Mischievous son Bart burns it down, along with all the presents, when he
plays too literally with his new toy fire truck in 1997. Boisterous dad Homer
seeks a spectacular example in 2003 after coming into some money, crav-
ing "a Christmas tree so large, its absence from the forest will cause mud
slides and flooding!"

When holiday-happy characters just can't let go of Christmas, the tree
is what they keep around. Let's just hope it's an artificial one. It stays up a
whole year on ABC's *Who's the Boss?* when Tony Danza's Connecticut housekeeper character can't bear to disturb his father's apartment after the old man
dies. Judith Light as his high-powered executive employer finds him down at
the old neighborhood in Brooklyn, looking at last year's present still sitting
under his father's Christmas tree. He's only able to come to terms with his
loss after opening it to find a pocket knife inscribed "to my 14-karat son."

But comedic clashes are what Christmas trees usually stir on TV, especially when celebrants dispute what constitutes a "proper" display. In ABC's
Manhattan police comedy *Barney Miller*, Jack Soo's gopher cop is proud of
his 1976 find for the squad room—a baby-blue-flocked tree. But Max Gail's

hothead detective Wojo is appalled: "It's sacrilegious!" The 1978 celebration on ABC's 1950s nostalgia sitcom *Happy Days* has daughter Erin Moran moaning to Tom Bosley's hardware store owner, "Oh, Dad, not an artificial tree." "This is not an artificial tree," he insists. "*This* is aluminum!" At Christmas 1993 among the pals working the tiny Nantucket airport of NBC's *Wings*, all of star Tim Daly's efforts to provide a great tree fizzle. He's forced to resort to a two-foot blue-flocked number that unfolds out of a briefcase: "Have a merry, portable, prefab, plastic little Christmas!"

The debate over what is and isn't a proper tree gets truly heated on CBS's *The Lucy Show*, in which star Lucille Ball and roommate costar Vivian Vance nearly come to blows. As widowed mothers planning to spend the 1962 holiday together for their first time, Viv wants a white tree and Lucy wants green, along with disagreements over family traditions for dinner (goose with oyster dressing vs. turkey with chestnut), stocking-hanging (bed footboard vs. mantle), present-opening (Christmas Eve vs. Christmas morning), and other details. "Well, I might have known anyone who'd have a white tree would be a goose-eating package peeker!" hurls Lucy, to Viv's retort, "What else would you expect from an evergreen-loving chestnut stuffer?"

Their compromise attempts and slow burns escalate to lightning warfare as the two trim separate trees at opposite sides of the room. Viv steps on Lucy's most cherished ornament, and Lucy cuts Viv's light string. Accidentally or intentionally? Does it really matter? In classic comedic tit-for-tat volleys, branches get chopped, ornaments broken, candy canes snapped in half, and the trees virtually destroyed by the time the pals come to their senses at hearing their kids caroling down the block. A rush job binds pieces of both trees together to form a Frankenstein centerpiece to a living room soon filled with a boys' chorus that softens the stars' hearts. Ball looks at Vance so warmly, she appears to have stepped out of character and conveyed her own swelling sentiment for the season.

Conflict gets a bit rougher by 2003 and *It's All Relative*, ABC's one-season sitcom about an Archie Bunker-ish bar owner's son falling in love with an upper-glass girl raised by two sophisticated gay men. While bombastic Lenny Clarke wants to "walk into a house that's smelling like ham and sounding like Bing Crosby," John Benjamin Hickey's fussy Philip prefers classical music and "a room that's clean and spare." His tree can't have any tacky ornaments, as personified by the bright yellow origami angel proudly presented by Clarke's TV wife Harriet Sansom Harris after Clarke's back goes out at the gay couple's place as he's delivering a tree on Christmas Eve. The family decides to move its festivity there, but their dancing Santa figure and giant plastic snowman are less than welcome. Not that Clarke's thrilled about it, either: "I can't spend Christmas Eve with the sugar plum fairies!" But he does, of course. Clarke's clan serves its traditional "bathtub ham" alongside the hosts' gourmet risotto.

As tradition and taste vie, those who like their Christmases old-fashioned often pine for cutting down their own fir or spruce. While daughters Betty and Kathy debate modern trees of pink or purple in 1954, Robert Young's down-to-earth dad on ABC's *Father Knows Best* waxes nostalgic how "my dad used to take me up into the hills and we'd cut down our own Christmas tree"—which, sure enough, leads to a family ride up snowy Old Pine Mountain as "a good start toward learning what Christmas really means." The same situation on NBC's *Dennis the Menace* in 1961 has growly neighbor Mr. Wilson finally sympathizing with Jay North's tow-haired young scamp when he catches sight of the kid's family's four-foot white artificial number. "You can't expect a child to get the real feeling of Christmas with a little bunch of twigs like this," Joseph Kearns' Wilson rages to Herbert Anderson's suburban dad. "That boy of yours deserves a real Christmas tree—a tall, green, pine-smelling tree, from God's own forest, a tree that the boy's helped to cut down himself. By golly, let's do it right now!" There's less "gosh-golly"-ness but an equal amount of grumbly adult and annoying kid next door on ABC's *Family Matters* in 1996, when Jaleel White's nerd-supreme Steve Urkel joins Reginald VelJohnson's curmudgeonly cop Carl in a tree-cutting expedition.

Nothing is as simple as it seems, though, or where's the humor? The Andersons of *Father Knows Best* get snowbound with a hermit in a forest cabin who shakes the kids from their consumerism toward a more loving celebration. Dennis, his dad, and Mr. Wilson break their ax, lose the car keys down a country well, and finally take their tree home on the bus. (Wilson's subsequent attempt to even out the tree's shape leads the family right back to that artificial tree, after all.) And Urkel saves the day with his "trusty survival belt" and star-gazing acumen when he and Carl get lost in the woods.

Their adventures pale, however, in comparison with the dramatic setting of the 1977 episode of CBS's family period piece *The Waltons*. Its loving Appalachian mountain clan has taken in two British children fleeing Hitler's World War II bombing of London. The kids are withdrawn, but Will Geer's inspiring Grandpa Walton has an idea: "There are lots of ways to be happy in this world, and one of the best ways is to go out looking for a Christmas tree." On Walton's Mountain, of course. Out in the country air, hearing Grandpa's tales of dragging home trees with possums still hanging from the branches, the kids are soon skipping through the woods singing "Jingle Bells." But a low-flying mail plane sends them scurrying in panic into a culvert, weeping, as if fleeing Nazi bombers. This wholesome family show takes the time to remind us that, sometimes, even Christmas isn't enough to soothe a sore heart.

DECK THE HALLS, WITH EVERYTHING

The more, the merrier. That's the credo of TV characters when it comes to Christmas decor. John Mahoney's kitsch-loving dad on NBC's *Frasier* horrifies his refined son by hanging a red-light-nosed Rudolph on the front door and dressing dog Eddie in a Santa suit. CBS's *Green Acres* gang goes modern with wax popcorn and fiberglass candy canes. The title horse of CBS's *Mister Ed* spruces up the stable. Even the entire crew of ABC's *The Love Boat* dresses like Santa and decorates.

But some shows go all out, reflecting that one house in every neighborhood, decked out with life-size this, animated that, music blaring, and enough lights to illuminate a stadium.

Home Improvement probably takes the cake, and everything else inside the house or out, when it comes to household displays. With Tim Allen's tool-loving Detroit dad having a thing for big motors and "more power"— *grunt grunt grunt* —the 1991–1999 ABC sitcom just kept topping itself with elaborate, clever, and outrageous roof decorations—huge standees, lighted figures, revolving Santas, moving mangers. Despite regular visits to the emergency room and from the paramedics ("Guess we'll probably see you next Christmas"), hapless Tim remained perpetually positive he could wrest the neighborhood contest crown from 76-year-old retired proctologist Doc Johnson. (And the writers could go wild with bodily humor and still remain family friendly.) "You always think I'm competing with Doc Johnson," Allen moans to Patricia Richardson's wife Jill in 1991's first-season outing, carting yet more decorations up from the basement. "Oh," she challenges, "it doesn't bother you that he's added those extra three giant candles on his roof?" "There's four of 'em," Tim corrects, "and his little dancing elf, but that doesn't bother me." Maybe, maybe not. But sliding down the roof with a frozen hammer stuck to his tongue sure does.

Still insisting in 1992 that "I have nothing to prove," Tim swears he's "going for like a low-key approach." Except that as he premieres his extravaganza, he issues a family warning: "When I flip the switch, it's gonna be kinda bright, so you're gonna need these sunglasses. And don't look directly at the snowman." Their whited-out faces gaze off-screen in wonderment, with youngest son Mark babbling, "I see spots." When Jill's blender use trips the circuit breaker, cheers ring through the neighborhood.

The plot thickens in 1993. When Tim wonders why he's never won the neighborhood contest, Jill says, "you've lost nine years in a row, I'd think you'd

be used to it by now." He suspects espionage on the part of Doc Johnson—
"Spying on us is a lot more fun that what he used to do"—until Jonathan Taylor
Thomas' middle son Randy confesses he's got a thing for Doc Johnson's grand-
daughter and "kinda mentioned a few things." Tim's efforts to trump his rival
seem to impress the judge, who turns out to be Earl Hindman's ever-obscured
advice-giving behind-the-fence neighbor Wilson: "Oh, Tim, that is a lovely use
of neon. It reminds me of the Christmas I spent in Las Vegas." But Tim isn't
through. Climbing to the roof to fix the bulb in Rudolph's nose, he touches a live
wire and shorts himself out into a living piece of neon (thanks to special effects).
"Well, good golly, Taylors, I think you've won the contest," opines Wilson. "I did
not realize there was a full-size electric Tim on the roof."

Or maybe Tim didn't triumph, after all. *Home Improvement*'s 1994 holiday
finds him insisting, "I think this year, finally my decorations are gonna beat
Doc Johnson," as he's hauling out a plastic six-foot camel and five-foot candy
canes. ("They were all out of the big ones.") With family in town, he recruits
his brother and father-in-law to help. "We're gonna surprise the hell out of
that Navy butt doctor!" urges retired Army father-in-law M. Emmet Walsh.
The wife and kids aren't initially impressed with Tim's efforts. But that's
because they're stealthy. "They didn't see the Allies coming at Normandy,
either," roars Walsh. "You know why? Camouflage!" Up pop character figures
from the rooftop, while a manger rises hydraulically out of nowhere.

Elaborate in a different way are the 1996 decorating contest efforts
of Amanda Bearse as the tacky Bundys' yuppie neighbor on Fox's raucous *Married...with Children*. The hard-driving bank executive brags to
Ed O'Neill's sad sack Al Bundy, "I have imported a hand-carved nativity
scene from Bavaria. Cost me five grand. My holy family's gonna kick every
yuletide ass on the block!" That's until the shiftless Bundy offspring kidnap
Mary and Joseph from her lawn to hold them for ransom. By episode's end,
the kids have beheaded the statues by driving them through a tunnel sticking out the car's sunroof.

That's the kind of stunt they'd love on ABC's blue-collar sitcom *Roseanne*,
where the Conner family is proudly "white trash" and iconoclast. It's clear
there's going to be trouble in 1993, when their Illinois town's neighborhood
association sends around a notice seeking restraint from the gaudy holiday decorations of past years, such as some specific past infractions from
guess-whose house. "They've singled us out, honey," says John Goodman's
Dan. "We're the tackiest house in the whole neighborhood." "Well," grins
Roseanne Barr's Roseanne, "this year I say we go for the national title."

They come up with two mangers ("Dueling saviors!" cries Roseanne). A
life-size Liberace standee ("Because there was no room at the Desert Inn").

"Merry Xmas" in giant rooftop letters. Santa's legs sticking out of the chimney. And thanks to out-of-business café Pancho's, a neon sign proclaiming "Feliz Navidad. Wednesday Is Ladies Night. All Drinks Half Price." Estelle Parsons as Roseanne's tsk-tsking mother is suitably appalled: "The wise men are supposed to be adoring the baby Jesus, not leering at Mrs. Claus!" She's also confused: "What is Santa Claus doing?" with a fountain-like modification. "He's just telling the whole neighborhood that Christmas is number one!" says Roseanne. As viewers think that one through, on comes the Conners' holiday "music"—dogs barking out "Jingle Bells."

Not everyone goes overboard with Christmas decorations for spite. Some do it out of greed. On ABC's *Family Matters* in 1995, Carl and Urkel are once again Christmas coconspirators. "Every Christmas," Urkel coos nasally, "I design a visual yuletide spectacular on the rooftop of my house. And this year, since I'm living with you, I want to design the Winslows' roof." Carl isn't into that at all, until he hears about a $5,000 TV contest prize. Then he becomes the spirit of the season. "Well, who put the mistletoe in your boxers?" sniffs Urkel, with Carl replying, "I just realized, well, how rewarding decorating the roof can be."

With Urkel's disdain for "that tawdry contest," Carl keeps his aims a secret while building a sleigh pulled by reindeer and holding Santa and elf figures, whose heads begin to smoke and then shoot off into the sky. After a frantic Carl gives himself away by pushing to repair the damage quickly before the contest committee comes along, their weighty wonder falls through the Winslow roof into the kitchen. The kid-centric *Family Matters* always loved slapstick and broad characterizations. And it even more loved quick-fix sappiness. "You besmudged Christmas!" Urkel rants at Carl. "You tried to deck your halls with wads of dollars!" But "far worse is that you lied to me. Why, now's the time to celebrate friendship, not take advantage of it." "You're right, Steve, and I'm sorry," Carl cringes, setting everything right just in time for the final commercial break.

At least their earthy Chicago neighborhood is amenable to gaudy displays. Not so the well-heeled Southern California citizens of NBC's *Fresh Prince of Bel-Air*, as Philadelphia kid Will Smith discovers in 1990's first Christmas with his refined rich relatives. Waxing nostalgic for sledding, caroling and "winos making snow angels on the front lawn," he decides to show 'em a real Christmas, not a professionally installed display from a designer entranced with "arrogant touches of celadon and periwinkle." Will fills the lawn with brightly lit "arrogant little elves and rambunctious reindeer and little men in red suits," and the house with huge candy canes and plastic holiday characters.

The neighbors take quick offense—"The blinking Frosty the Snowman is ril-ing your attack dogs?" And one of them, the one Will challenged on the phone to a fight, happens to be heavyweight champion Evander Holyfield. But Will insists, "The house looks dope! Who cares what they think?" As it turns out, nobody—not after ex-President and local resident Ronald Reagan stops by to compliment them (in the person of a celebrity imitator): "I just want to say that I greatly admire your wonderful Christmas decorations, and I just wanted to say that because Nancy won't let me do anything fun to our house."

Those ritzy folks never will. It's up to the blue-collar types to do it up right. On CBS's *The King of Queens*, the job falls to the father-in-law played by Jerry Stiller, who originally gained fame in the 1960s for being the Jewish husband to an Irish Catholic wife in the Stiller & Meara stand-up comedy team. While Kevin James' Doug and Leah Remini's Carrie argue over the fate of an inter-net stock they've bought in 1999 (the height of the tech boom), Stiller tries to outdo a decorating neighbor with a makeshift nativity scene featuring a wooden Indian, jockey statue, and huge baby doll. The generational dispar-ity is most acute on NBC's *Frasier*, where two upper-class psychiatrist sons annually sniff at the old-time ornamentation beloved by John Mahoney's cop dad: wrapping paper covering the doors, brick paper over the fireplace, a life-size talking Santa, even dog Eddie attired in a Santa hat and a sweater with a bell. "Dad," admonishes David Hyde Pierce as younger son Niles, "you have to get out more, you've started doing old lady things."

Perhaps it takes a fresh eye to truly appreciate the wonder that American Christmas decorating excess can be. The landlord on NBC's *3rd Rock from the Sun* covers the house in 1996 with extreme strings of lights, promising "By the time I'm through with this joint, they're gonna be able to see it from the [space] shuttle!" John Lithgow's kooky clan of space aliens couldn't be happier, soaking up the wonderment of their very first Earth Christmas as its illumination's glow travels light-years toward their home planet.

ALL THE CARDS AND LETTERS

"I'd rather open Christmas cards than anything I know of," drawls Andy Griffith, as he does just that at his sheriff's desk on CBS's *The Andy Griffith Show* in 1960. Mayberry being such a small, slow town, he's got plenty of time to do it. "Haven't seen him in a looooong time," says Andy, more exuberant in this first-season episode, savoring the thought of that card's particular sender.

Reconnecting with friends and loved ones through seasonal postal greetings has long been a herald of the holiday spirit on TV sitcoms. The title characters of ABC's *The Adventures of Ozzie & Harriet* open their 1956 Christmas show admiring all the received cards on their mantle. Ozzie's only got one gripe. "You'd think they'd write a little something on it, wouldn't you?" he asks Harriet when a card contains only a family photo. "Here's what I mean, listen to this. 'May this be your happiest Christmas, and may all that follow be even happier. Merry Christmas and Happy New Year. We hope we may always be privileged to include you among our nicest and best friends.' Isn't that nice?" "Oh, it certainly is," chimes Harriet, "who's it from?" "The Acme cleaners."

TV rarely misses a chance to zing the impersonality and commercialism of the "modern" Christmas, whether it's the twentieth or twenty-first century version. Martin Sheen on NBC's *The West Wing* decides that as President of the United States, he's going to hand-sign all the cards the White House is sending out. "I don't like the whole idea of the auto-pen," he scoffs in 2000. "Let's do 'em by hand. How many can there be?" Answers Dule Hill's aide Charlie, "One million one hundred and ten thousand," explaining a "three-tiered system" of the First Family's list, contributors and campaign workers, and everyone who's written a letter to the White House that year.

Sometimes those holiday cards can be conversely too personal. In NBC's 2001 Christmas outing of *Friends*, David Schwimmer's awkward Ross makes the mistake of telling new girlfriend Bonnie Somerville that a photo of them on the town "looks like a holiday card—you know, with the tree in the middle and the skaters and the snow." When she suggests they "send this one out together," Ross sees it as a sign of commitment and descends into a state of panicked frenzy. "Married couples send out cards. Families send out cards. People who have been dating for a couple of months do not send out cards!"

Julia Louis-Dreyfus doesn't get the chance to put the brakes on her card's revealing intimacy. Her character Elaine discovers only after sending it out in NBC's 1992 *Seinfeld* that the card photo taken of her by Michael Richards' gonzo Kramer was not quite what she had in mind. "Did you look at this picture carefully?" wonders pal Jerry Seinfeld upon opening the card she sent him. "Because I'm not sure, and correct me if I'm wrong, but I think I see a nipple." "Oh my God!" Elaine wails at more closely examining her too-open shirt. "I sent this card to hundreds of people! My parents. My boss. Nana and Papa!" She's little consoled by reassurances from Jerry and Kramer. "So what?" soothes Jerry. "It's a nipple. A little brown protuberance. What's the big deal? Everybody's got 'em. Look, I got 'em," he says, while he and Kramer lift their shirts to display something Elaine wants to see about as much as the sight on her card.

Trouble is quite a bit more predictable on ABC's *Home Improvement*, in which Tim Allen's tool-mad dad is always digging himself a new hole. At Thanksgiving 1993, he's scheming not to "take the same old boring Christmas card photo," as he tells wife Patricia Richardson. "I got this vision, to capture the real spirit of the Taylor family just like we really are." Which would, of course, involve "wearing costumes at the North Pole." On a "snow"-filled set in the backyard, the three boys are reluctantly attired in green, red, and white and fake ears as elves ("We thought you said we could all be Elvis," moans Jonathan Taylor Thomas). Dad is a Canadian Mountie and mom is Mrs. Claus in a red-velvet mini. Next thing you know, thanks to Tim, his wife is coping with "burnt pies, a broken window, and a snowblower in my family room." It's another ill-fated walk on what wise neighbor Wilson calls the "fine line between genius and madness."

At least Tim's family members are (semi-) willing posers. That's not the case for country singer Travis Tritt in 1995 on ABC's *The Jeff Foxworthy Show*. When the "redneck" comic's heating contractor works on Tritt's tour bus, he sneaks into the sleeping Tritt's bed with his entire family for that Christmas picture "our friends'll get a big kick out of" ("A strange bearded man has his arm around you, and I don't have any pants on—that screams 'Feliz Navidad' to me"). Volunteers are no more forthcoming on CBS's 2003 *The King of Queens* for obstinate old man Jerry Stiller's Christmas card picture. He sneakily offers to photograph walking companion Nicole Sullivan, who's less than thrilled when he steps into the frame with her and five pooches she walks. "Arthur, I hadn't planned on you actually being in the photo," she confesses. "I'm sending these to my clients, and I'm not sure they would understand that I walk a human being." Friends of his son-in-law flee, too, when Stiller suggests "a simple snapshot" in an all-too-decorated setting: "You offer me these chocolate chip cookies, and I react with delight thusly." The final resort here is another bed-set shot, snapped in the middle of the night via remote-controlled camera to include his sleeping daughter and son-in-law.

Bart Simpson struggles with a 1995 family photo shoot on Fox's *The Simpsons* that puts America's favorite yellow tyke in a tough spot. It's at the same Try-n-Save where he was recently caught taking a "four-finger discount" (of course; they're cartoon characters) on the much-coveted Bonestorm video game. Fulfilling his worst fears, the family's proud pose is spoiled by a security guard's arm jerking returning reprobate Bart out of frame.

That's precisely *not* the sort of thing you'd mention in your annual Christmas letter. This one-telling-fits-all insert for the Christmas card mailing is among the most divisive holiday traditions. Some folks love to inform and be informed, while others loathe such an impersonal news blast, viewing it as an ego platform for the writer to boast and, by comparison, belittle the recipient. Into the latter category falls Doris Roberts' busybody mom Marie in CBS's *Everybody Loves Raymond*, who gets worked up in 2001 and decides to fire back to her cousin Teresa's written litany of accomplishments. ("You'd think that she pulled the Pope out of quicksand or something.")

Christmas Jobs

Taking an extra job to earn extra money for the holidays is another tradition much beloved of Christmas TV. Among the characters who go to work:

- Max Baer's simplistic Jethro of CBS's *The Beverly Hillbillies* plays Santa in 1966, prompting a store manager to marvel, "I've never seen anyone with such rapport with children. It's just as though he had the mind of a seven-year-old."
- Lisa Kudrow's plucky Phoebe of NBC's *Friends* gets tough bell-ringing for the Salvation Army in 1998, when passersby use her kettle to make change, leave trash, and put out cigarettes.
- Shirley Booth's Hazel of CBS's maid sitcom *Hazel* mans a department store counter in 1961, where she keeps "helping" a customer who turns out to be a habitual robber.
- Leah Remini's Carrie of CBS's *King of Queens* gets a holiday gig at husband Kevin James's parcel delivery service in 2003, driving him nuts with 24-hour togetherness.
- Bryan Cranston's dad on Fox's *Malcolm in the Middle* sells Christmas trees with his sons in 2003: "It'll be just like a Korean grocery store!... We will have so many precious memories together, as long as you don't give into your worst instincts and do something really stupid."
- Ed O'Neill's Al Bundy of Fox's *Married... with Children* unwinds with a beer at the bar after his 1992 Santa gig: "I've been peed on, spit on, snotted on, drooled on, and thrown up on, and now it's Miller time."

As usual with this incisively hilarious sitcom, that simple action sets off an escalating chain of family fury. Marie's own bragging letter riles Patricia Heaton's daughter-in-law Debra, who resents the missive's implication that "it's you having to help poor, pathetic Debra." But after Marie explains "I just want people to read about me and think Marie's doing well, too," the two stop butting heads long enough to pen a return parry. "Shouldn't we use the word *selfless*," asks Debra, "to describe your work as a piano teacher?" Then everybody wants to add his own two words. Or three. Brad Garrett's ever-sulking eldest son Robert is keeping count. He tells Ray Romano's younger sibling that he saved Marie's last holiday letter from 10 years ago: "There were six lines in your section. I got three!" Retired father Peter Boyle chimes in that it isn't enough to list his favorite cable channels and say "His love affair with bacon continues." In the end, the letter gets ripped up, and nobody's happy. Same as they were when the whole thing started. Christmas rarely changes anything.

FESTIVE FOOD

What is it with the gingerbread house? This incredibly time-consuming and idealistically edible Christmas construct seems to obsess an inordinate number of TV characters. And not always the ones you'd suspect.

Sure, it may be obvious that when *Family Matters* teen Kellie Shanygne Williams builds one in 1997 on ABC's hit Friday TGIF familycom, her handi-work is bound to be flattened by Jaleel White's nerdy neighbor Urkel dur-ing an attempt to impress the apple of his eye—an easy slapstick device to keep the kiddies laughing. And the one being assembled on ABC's *Home Improvement* in 1998 by star Tim Allen's twin nieces is like any other do-it-yourself project in his clumsy universe. When one girl frets that her sister "put her shutters on backwards," the excuse is "I wanted to feel like Uncle Tim." His helpful observation that they've used licorice for the gutters instead of for plumbing—"I think I better get my hands on this"—inevitably gets a quick shoot-down from the tykes. "No! We want it to last till Christmas!"

And it's no surprise that the small-town folks surrounding L.A. bounce-back native Ellen DeGeneres on CBS's sitcom *The Ellen Show* are into ginger-bread baking, too. The home economics teacher at the school where Ellen now works is erecting a huge house for the local mall, starting with a gin-gerbread bidet. (The comic suggests, "You might wanna slap together a little gingerbread therapist.") It's a good thing the mansion is edible. With all the town eateries closed for the holiday, her "beautiful gingerbread home" is the only thing Ellen's family can find to consume.

But did we expect to see Sela Ward's career-minded single mom fixat-ing on a gingerbread fabrication on ABC's angst-y drama *Once and Again?* "Remember childbirth?" warns a friend. "This is harder." Ward's young-est daughter, already anxious over mom and dad's pending divorce, gets freaked out about the kitchen creation's connection to Hansel and Gretel: "They get eaten." Reassures mom, "This gingerbread house is absolutely witch-free." It is, however, a haunted notion, bound to go down for the count the way the show's relationships always seemed to. "Mom, it's totally falling apart," her more aware adolescent daughter moans later in this 1999 hour, metaphorically delivering the message of a holiday episode that's no more sanguine than any other week's.

The absolute last character you'd expect to see assembling a gingerbread dwelling is idle housewife Peg Bundy on Fox's subversive *Married…with Children.* Yet there's Katey Sagal's tacky redhead becoming obsessed in 1996 with piecing together those pastry walls. "That's not for eating," she chides her hungry fam-ily, "this is what you call decorative." "Oh, that's great," whines David Faustino's son Bud. "The first time you cook something and you won't let us eat it." That's because it's such an artistic creation, with details authentic down to the crack in the walls. "'Cause it's our house," she explains. "See that cotton candy? That's asbestos." In typical *MWC* excess, Peg becomes so engrossed "that I decided to bake the whole neighborhood." Christina Applegate's slutty daughter Kelly is impressed with her depiction of their old-man neighbor's house: "You even got the telescope he uses to watch me shower!"

Fruitcake gets kicked around even more frequently than gingerbread. Sometimes literally. When the first Christmas on *Married …with Children* in 1987 finds the Bundys doing their traditional rewrapping of previous gifts, their offering to yuppie neighbor Amanda Bearse turns out to be something they'd punted around the house the previous year—" a fruitcake," she winces. "With a footprint on it." (One also gets physically kicked to the curb in Disney Channel's 2001 all-ages cartoon *The Proud Family.*) As Orlando Jones observed in irreverent musings on 1995's first-season holiday for Fox's late-night sketch fest *MADtv*, "The tradition of Santa has been passed down from generation to generation. And so have most fruitcakes." So have some relatives. At least that's what future *Everybody Loves Raymond* mom Doris Roberts claims when she plays an abhorred aunt on ABC's Suzanne Somers blended-family sitcom *Step by Step* in 1994, asking "So how come every Christmas I get passed around like a bad fruitcake?"

The supersweet baked tradition is considered so mock-able that the 1984 Christmas episode of Robert Guillaume's ABC sitcom *Benson* uses it as a punch line. This *It's a Wonderful Life* homage depicts an alternate reality in which Guillaume's governor's mansion nemesis Inga Swenson is portrayed as so horrifically pathetic, she's reduced to selling fruitcakes door-to-door. On CBS's *Green Acres* at Christmastime 1966, the only way that Eva Gabor's loving, sophisticated, bad-cook wife can scare the inhabitants of down-home Hooterville out of her holiday party is by fabricating fruitcakes out of her famously dreadful hotcakes.

It makes an even more delicious running joke on CBS's 1988 "Pee-wee's Playhouse Christmas" special, spun by snooty-cool supernerd comic Paul Reubens out of his Saturday morning kids' romp. As snickering Pee-wee gets Christmas-y with decorations, music, and more, he's visited by such playtime pals as Reba the mail lady, Cowboy Curtis, and Miss Renee, plus drop-by celebrities including Cher, Charo, Magic Johnson, and k.d. lang—all of whom seem to arrive oddly bearing fruitcakes. (In honor of Hanukkah, the Jewish Miss Renee brings eight.) But ever-resourceful man/boy Pee-wee turns his grimaces to glee by the end of this delirious hour: He adds an entire new wing to the playhouse using their brick-hard baked goods.

Obviously, though, somebody likes fruitcakes, even to eat, or their appearance wouldn't be so perennial. Some even resolve to redeem the detested delicacy's reputation. Patricia Richardson's wife/mom does her best on the 1997 *Home Improvement*, making a "special Christmas cake" out of mangos and papayas, insisting, "This is not a fruitcake. This is a Christmas cake. With fruit."

Better they should try to sell everybody on cookies. Baking these holiday-shaped sweets is a much more beloved tube tradition. And they don't only represent Christmas. Celebrity fitness trainer Jake Steinfeld's cable comedy *Big Brother Jake* on The Family Channel had him riding herd on kids at the Brooklyn orphans' home in which he'd grown up years earlier, a Jewish kid with a Christian foster mother. "You said you'd make a Star of David every now and then," he tells her in 1991 as her new young charges cut cookie dough at the kitchen table. "All I see are Santas," notes Jake. "You're letting the Jews fall behind." "You know, Jake," discerns Jewish kid Josiah Trager, "if you bite off the top of Santa's head, and squinch up your eyes, he sorta looks like Rabbi Feldman." Cookies often represent something personal. On NBC's *Family Ties* in 1987, one of the Christmas cookies comes out shaped not like Santa but a dollar sign thanks to the efforts of Michael J. Fox's acquisitional teen.

Christmas pudding gets its moment in the televisual sun in 1954 on the British-produced series *Sherlock Holmes*, which aired in American syndication. Ronald Howard's incarnation of the classic sleuth trusts his "intuition" about the "resourcefulness" of a vengeful killer sentenced to hang. Good thing. The prisoner escapes and tries to shoot Holmes, who then deduces the ribbon around the box containing the man's Christmas pudding was actually a wire file that made "a very effective cutting tool indeed."

More often, though, this British holiday favorite is a smaller part of the larger Christmas dinner tradition. The BBC's more recent Britcom *The Vicar of Dibley* casts popular comedian Dawn French as a village pastor dragooned by her parishioners into a bloating series of 1996 holiday feasts. One serves "meat and 16 vegetables—that's always been the way in Dibley." Another presents just pasta and fish. But they turn out to be mere starter courses for a huge turkey followed by pudding after pudding. The well-fed French can only crawl on her hands and knees to the next dinner house, where she immediately breaks the chair she sits in, then takes a taxi to the subsequent home, just half a block away. Her farmland yule is all about "overeating till you spew."

The Christmas goose is another European tradition that goes back centuries—all the way back to *The Adventures of Robin Hood* in CBS's British-filmed family half-hour of the late 1950s. It's such a medieval favorite that a self-involved new lord of the manor has seized a small boy's pet goose named Matilda for his holiday repast. Saving the day is Richard Greene's title hero, who teaches the greedy man "a bit of a lesson in the Christmas spirit" while returning Matilda safe and sound.

In more contemporary terms, NBC's 1993 sitcom *Café Americain* has Valerie Bertinelli living in Paris and heading for "a traditional French family Christmas" at a friend's chateau where the geese they raise keep pecking after her. "I feel like Tippi Hedren," she jests, from Alfred Hitchcock's feathered-attack film *The Birds*. So she couldn't be happier that their hors d'oeuvres are foie gras, made from goose liver. "You mean one of them has to thwkk," she says with a choking sound, "to make this stuff? May I please have some more?" Vicki Lawrence's title character on the NBC/ syndication sitcom *Mama's Family* feels the same way. Though she can't wait to cook up her 1990 Christmas present from a back-home friend—a goose named Leland—the rest of her family treats this dinner-to-be like a pampered pet. "Don't you be taking him for walks," warns Lawrence's ornery old woman. "His legs'll get tough." But we all know what has to happen when Mama totes her brand-new Shinsu knife to the goose pen. She ends up commuting the bird's sentence, bringing him to the dinner table as a guest instead to share a "mock goose" made from stuffing and vegetables.

The dinner gift from farmland on NBC's barroom hit *Cheers* in 1992 is a Christmas ham sent to Boston in piglet form by the Hoosier mother of back-home bartender Woody Harrelson. Taking pity on the squealer, bar manager Kirstie Alley schemes to "take him to the country and give him his freedom." And amazingly, Snuffles finds a way to wiggle back to his Indiana origins. "You see, he traveled all that distance to get home where he was safe and sound," rejoices Alley. "This is a Christmas miracle!" "I'll say," adds Harrelson. "Mom said he was delicious."

YULETIDE CAROLS BEING SUNG BY A CHOIR

Trying to compose your own Christmas carol is a more common theme than you might expect. Even Homer Simpson tries to write one on a 2003 installment of Fox's *The Simpsons*. He gets inspired the way many do, while out caroling himself with the family. ("Just exquisite," enthuses boss Mr. Burns. "Makes me wish I hadn't released the hounds.") After caroling at a lawyer's home where they're "forbidden to perform that song without paying royalties to the copyright owner"—public domain substitutes like "O Tannenbaum" and "Jesu, Joy of Men's Desiring" are suggested—Homer has had it. "Those suck! They're worse than nothing! I could write way better songs!" Unfortunately, however, he can't: "Christmas in December/Wow wow wow/Gimme tons of presents/Now now now."

Peggy Hill on Fox's other animated familycom, *King of the Hill*, at least has a subject for her 2003 composition attempt. Husband Hank and son Bobby are trucking his mom's furniture from Texas to Arizona. "A trucker and his boy," she realizes. "And they promise their mom to be home by Christmas. This is one of those novelty Christmas songs that always sells a million friggin' copies!" Too bad Peggy learns "there's just no good words that rhyme with truck." Niece Luanne suggests they write about a snowman. "Of course!" says Peggy. "Who needs a snowman more than a widow in Arizona? Our song will be about Hank and Bobby delivering a snowman to a wo-man with no man!" No way, as it turns out.

Two minds are no better than one on NBC's *Just Shoot Me*, either. Especially when they belong to David Spade's smarmy magazine assistant Finch and Wendie Malick's egotistical ex-model Nina. "I think all the best songs were already written," Spade concludes after their 2001 attempt at a Christmas carol. So the two decide to become Jewish and try some Hanukkah harmony. That's also part of the equation at NBC's *Friends* in 1997, when Lisa Kudrow's off-key songstress Phoebe, already known for her "Smelly Cat" tune, tries again with a holiday theme. All she comes up with is "Happy Hanukkah, Monica/May your Christmas be snowy, Joey." Multiculturalism gets another shot in 2001 on Nickelodeon's cartoon *As Told by Ginger*. The title girl's brother Carl wears an African dashiki and brings his portable keyboard to the family party, pounding out "Jingle bells/Higsbee's smells/Dreidel's made of clay/ Frosty the frigid snowman went to his bar mitzvah day/Hey."

Another specific kind of carol is the goal on NBC's short-lived *The Tracy Morgan Show*, built around the *Saturday Night Live* regular in 2003. "Our people have been in jazz, the blues, hip-hop, R&B," pal Katt Williams scoffs at holiday music playing in Morgan's car repair shop. "How come the black man can't come up with one good Christmas song? . . . If we could write a black Christmas carol, we could take the world by storm." Easier said than done. "Christmas in the 'hood, y'all" gets rhymed with "buy me a shirt from the big and tall." The final result—"Happy Christmas, your little stocking stuffer's gonna treat you right," sung by Williams adorned like superstar Prince in purple, black and ruffles—is not exactly worth waiting for.

A more successful attempt underlies a two-hour tale from CBS's hit period drama *The Waltons* in 1977, as the Depression-era family shelters two British children fleeing Nazi bombing in the days before the United States is drawn into World War II. "I'm trying to write a Christmas carol," Jon Walmsley's piano-playing teen Jason tells his mother. "It's times like these when we really need music." And his music is inspired by the times and the children's visit, as indicated by the title of both the episode and his composition, "The Children's

Carol." The family finally sings that Jesus "is one of us, untouched by hate or fear" and "we are one with him this joyful time of year."

Simply vocalizing conventional carols is enough for others—though not everyone appreciates the itinerant singing tradition. A vigilante Manhattan merchant on ABC's *Barney Miller* cop comedy in 1981 has his cattle prod at the ready: "I mean, if this night is supposed to be so silent, what are they out there singin' for?" Julianna Margulies's aptly named nurse character Carol Hathaway has trouble rounding up voices to serenade patients in 1995 on NBC's hospital drama *ER*. Friends of Tracee Ellis Ross's yule-loving Joan stage a mutiny in UPN's 2003 *Girlfriends*, after she provides Dickensian attire for their caroling and directs the outing with an iron fist: "It's very important that you turn on the right beat. If not, you miss the musical punctuation and the visual effect, are we clear?"

Even those who are into caroling have trouble enjoying the ritual the way they're supposed to. Hattie Winston's office nurse on CBS's Ted Danson vehicle *Becker* convinces grinch-y aide Shawnee Smith to accompany her church group of carolers in 2002, only to discover the girl's voice is "screechifying." Equally awful is Kirstie Alley of NBC's *Veronica's Closet*, who joins a Carnegie Hall chorus for Christmas 1997 in order to meet men. Good thing her goal isn't actually singing, since she's assigned to simply fill space as "a mouther." On that same season's NBC sitcom *Suddenly Susan*, magazine boss Judd Nelson tries to avoid vocalizing after informing star Brooke Shields and coworkers that he has "volunteered all of you" for a hospital's holiday choir. Shields manages to persuade him to participate. But then they hear how tone-deaf he is. "Get rid of him," comic colleague Kathy Griffin implores Shields, "or I'll tamper with his brakes."

There's an edge, too, to 1997's wandering carolers in ABC's culture-slash comedy *Dharma & Greg*. The sniffy rich parents of Thomas Gibson's young lawyer are appalled by the vocals of the hippie-esque clan of daughter-in-law Jenna Elfman, serenading from outside the mansion window to the tune of the 1969 rock hit and perennial sports-crowd chant "Na Na Hey Hey (Kiss Him Goodbye)": "Fa-la-la-la, fa-la-la-la, hey hey, merry Christmas." Dharma's mom Mimi Kennedy later apologizes, "Sorry if we muddied up your house," after they've come inside. "But you did turn the sprinklers on us," adds dad Alan Rachins.

PAGEANTRY

Christmas pageants are an integral part of the yuletide spectacle, especially in school-related settings. Kids' stage celebrations run the gamut from Linus's reverent Bible reading in CBS's animated 1960s classic "A Charlie Brown Christmas" to "the Bronson Alcott multidenominational holiday pageant" on UPN's TV adaptation of the big-screen comedy *Clueless*. The latter's 1997 Beverly Hills high school extravaganza playfully includes a home-viewer sing-along with on-screen lyrics, promising "no one is excluded—Sikhs, Shakers, Christians, Muslims, and Jews."

Not even pretentious show-offs, who take center stage at the high school pageant on CBS's 1982 sitcom *Square Pegs*. On this no-laugh-track portrait of misfit teens from *Saturday Night Live* writer Anne Beatts, the holiday production is overseen by an artsy male teacher—"My muse and I have risen to this challenge and triumphed over it"—who seems a kindred spirit to Merritt Butrick's apparent (but never declared) gay student Johnny Slash. "He wanted to dance, he wanted to prance," the teacher narrates as Johnny cavorts across the stage in antlers playing the "ninth reindeer" of "Ms. Santa." ("She was sort of a Bette Davis type.") "The lonesome reindeer had talent, but his moves were just too big," coos the narrator, until "one foggy Christmas Eve [when] all the regular reindeer ate bad shrimp cocktail and got sick." The moral of the story? "Being a reindeer with an interest in theater is not bad," proclaims Johnny. "Only slightly different," concludes the teaching artiste.

Art is also too much the effect on ABC's 2003 comedy *Hope & Faith*, about mismatched sisters Faith Ford as a homey mom (named Hope, of course) and Kelly Ripa (playing Faith, for confusion) as the spoiled ex–soap star who has returned home to live with her. "Why don't you help me with Hailey's play?" suggests Ford. "You can be the acting coach." But Ripa's pretentious efforts to perfect her niece's pageant drive everyone up the wall. "This isn't about you, this is about the kids. They're supposed to be having fun!" Ford tells Ripa, who's been cracking the whip in costume with an old-time director's beret and megaphone. "You spent all that time directing those kids, and you missed the whole message of the play. Life is not about what you get. It's about what you give." But this being an ABC Friday night familycom, she hasn't missed it, after all. When niece Hailey gets stage fright, Ford gives her a pep talk backstage—actually, above-stage, dangling from the flies of the stage on wires alongside Hailey's fairy godmother character. "I remember my first audition. I was terrified. I was sweating and shivering the whole time." Of course, "I got the job. Turns out it was for a cold medicine." And Hailey learns the value of "being scared to do something and doing it anyway. That's what makes you strong."

Workplace revues are more concerned with showing off than sentiment. This device to let series regulars strut their stuff was especially popular in sitcoms during TV's first two decades, when the medium's roots in vaude-ville and stage shows meant lots of performers had cut their teeth in pre-video song-and-dance acts. NBC's New York cop comedy *Car 54, Where Are You?* has its 53rd precinct "brotherhood club Christmas party" provide its 1961 holiday episode: Comic Joe E. Ross's "ooo-ooo" uttering Officer Toody sings "You're Nobody Till Somebody Loves You," magician Carl Ballantine does a sleight-of-hand act, and Fred Gwynne's Officer Muldoon leads a bar-bershop quartet—none of which has much to do with Christmas, of course, but provides a yuletide change of pace for the series. In 1963, all four stars of CBS's *The Dick Van Dyke Show* get musical in their long-running sitcom's sole holiday half-hour: Van Dyke and TV wife Mary Tyler Moore revisit their dancing pasts in original songs, while long-ago child star Rose Marie sings the comic plea "Santa, Send a Fella" and vaudevillian Maury Amsterdam plays cello, quite well but for laughs.

When holiday talent showcases pop up in later years, they're more inte-grated into the comedic or dramatic flow of the show. Both ABC's *Laverne & Shirley* in 1976 and syndication's performance-school drama *Fame* in 1986 showcase their stars by putting on shows for hospital patients—in the case of *Laverne & Shirley,* mental patients. On ABC's 2000 Andre Braugher medical drama *Gideon's Crossing,* a hospital resident struggles to find holiday show participants. Colleague Eric Dane bristles at filling "the Jew slot" but finally agrees to salute Hanukkah if he can do his magic act: "Did you like the way I magically turned one candle into eight?" Ruben Blades's hospital chief surprises everyone by having Ruben Blades's singing voice, and a towering black male staffer arrives in a red Santa dress and blonde tresses to croon Christmas carols.

Churches served as a holiday performance setting from TV's earliest days, making their mark in such Christmas favorites as ABC's 1969 *The Brady Bunch.* That's the one where mom Florence Henderson, at that time best known as a musical comedy star, loses her voice before her church choir solo, only to regain it just in time as a prime example of TV's plot-beloved Christmas miracle.

Places of worship become more common in the 1980s and beyond—ironically making natural appearances in many characters' lives just as self-styled "moral majority" activist groups increasingly griped that prime time shows were disrespecting moral values and refusing to acknowledge religious faith. Already, for instance, Tim Allen's Taylor family on ABC's hit *Home Improvement* was attending Christmas services and appearing in the annual holiday pageant. For 1991's first-season yule, Zachery Ty Bryan's Brad gripes "I'm a shepherd again" after blowing a wise man audition by saying "they were carrying gold and Frankenstein." Brad reports brother Randy has been kicked out completely for ad-libbing his innkeeper lines: "He doubled the price of the room and asked the wise men for ID." Littlest brother Mark (Taran Noah Smith) gets into the act in 1993 when mom sews him a robe for the church's NOEL boys' quartet. He wears a giant N, which dad jokes must mean "naked under this robe and no one can tell." The following year, Mark's pageant has Patricia Richardson's mom Jill racing to finish building the sets in her garage—racing so fast that she leaves Tim's beloved hot rod outside when a blizzard hits. She was preoccupied with reminiscing to Mark about her own pageant days in the fourth grade, playing Mary and having "the audience eating out of the palm of my hand. Until I threw up all over the three wise men."

A more obvious home for religious celebration was NBC's *Amen,* the Saturday night sitcom set in a Philadelphia church. Even with *Jeffersons* strutter Sherman Hemsley starring as a domineering deacon, the 1986 first-season holiday episode is more reverent than not. The main comic plot has a TV crew coming to cover the church nativity pageant, which incites Hemsley to take over coaching the kids how to make authentic animal sounds. ("No self-respecting pig says oink.") But when a snowstorm blankets the city and not even the audience shows up, the telling gets truly back to basics. Adults who arrive to cancel the program discover the kids have already started performing the nativity with heartfelt respect, even in an empty auditorium.

Another natural was CBS's pious 1990s drama *Touched by an Angel,* with Roma Downey and Della Reese depicting heavenly agents sent to aid earthly humans in crisis. Its 1994 first-season holiday celebration "Fear Not!" couldn't have been more overtly devout, from its scriptural title to its climax at the Christmas pageant of a needy church that had originally had to cancel the event because its organ was broken. Reese arrives to repair the instrument, and Downey becomes the star of the production, which includes the entire "Hallelujah" chorus and a mentally challenged young man reading "I bring you good tidings of great joy that shall be to all men." Downey demands belief as she arrives in full winged regalia, levitating over the congregation to release a dove. The episode's sincere presentation of the miraculous as the natural handiwork of a loving God was a hallmark that kept *Angel* viewers faithful through nine seasons.

But few TV series have gotten that sacred about their Christmas pageants, even as they reflect the holiday's sacred roots. Nativity scenes depicting the Biblical tale of Christ's birth often find a way to combine wit with their worship. That's certainly true of the 1999 holiday special of the BBC sitcom *The Vicar of Dibley,* premiered Stateside by PBS. Title character Dawn

French is stunned when her dimwit friend Alice (Emma Chambers) actually has a brainstorm, to do the rural church's nativity "on an actual farm, so the audience can follow the story around the farmyard. A real stable with cows and sheep. That sort of thing." Not all the townspeople grasp this simple concept. They audition by playing wise men like disabled scientist Stephen Hawking, complete with computer-generated voices, and imitating Elvis, who is, of course, The King. When the big night comes, the farmer hosting the show takes the opportunity to announce, "I'll be slaughtering Daisy here tomorrow, so do order your Christmas beef after the show." Luckily the Vicar has encouraged improvisation. When the donkey runs away before showtime, pregnant Alice is able to make her entrance as Mary riding "a small motorized lawn mower." The spirit of Dibley may be lighthearted, but it's firmly in the right, reverent place.

Even the "frankincense"-smoking gang of *That '70s Show* ends up doing their best in that Fox sitcom's 2002 Christmas show, when Topher Grace's teen Eric gets volunteered to direct the church pageant. His pals originally have their own distinct ideas—Danny Masterson's Hyde wants to be baby Jesus so he doesn't have to do anything, Ashton Kutcher's Kelso imagines an interpretation of Joseph taking place in space—but eventually come around to Eric's more traditional Christmas spirit. That respect also manifests in ABC's outrageous *Drew Carey Show* foil Mimi, Kathy Kinney's hefty fan of fluorescent fashions, extreme eye makeup, and digs at coworker Drew. In 1998, Mimi actually takes her role of Mary in a store-window nativity quite seriously.

And Donal Logue's intentions are nothing but good as a rambunctious young dad on Fox's *Grounded for Life* who plays Joseph for the 2001 church manger scene. "Come forward, rejoice, gather round, for today our savior is born," he solemnly intones, only to see his competitive father arrive dressed as Santa Claus atop a red convertible to spoil his son's moment. "No, no!" he pleads with bystanders. "Behold Jesus, not Santa!" Soon, tomatoes are hurled, and Santa's elves beat Joseph with jumbo candy canes. "Couldn't you just ruin Christmas the old-fashioned way?" wonders wife Megyn Price. "Just get drunk and fall down in the fireplace?"

Larry David in HBO's *Curb Your Enthusiasm* can ruin Christmas, just like any other day, in ways old, new, and known only to the misanthropic comic who created *Seinfeld*. Playing his Hollywood self, he's a Jewish producer who is unsettled in 2002 when his wife brings a Christmas tree into the house ("It's bad luck. My guy may think I'm switching or something"), unnerved when her relatives gather round the piano to sing carols, and unaware that the "animal" cookies they baked (and he ate) were intended for a manger scene ("The hay, the barn, I thought that was all part of the zoo"). Larry tries to make it up to them in this largely improved story. Seeing a living nativity down the street, he offers the church troupe a donation to set up at his house. But Larry's tone-deaf people skills have him quickly offending their leader: "Mary, by the way, has quite the bod. C'mon, Joe, between you and me—you and Mary? You don't feel like it every now and then?" Goodbye, peace on earth. Hello, wrestling match in the hay.

Jews, Christians, and jingle bell lovers again try to mesh on NBC's 1998 *Frasier*. Jane Leeves's Daphne is helping coordinate a community pageant that has evolved into "a mixed bag. We open with the no-room-at-the-inn scene, then it's a rousing version of 'Jingle Bell Rock,' a brief medley from 'Jesus Christ Superstar,' and the first act ends with Santa's elves and the three wise men all linking arms and singing 'Frosty the Snowman.'" David Hyde Pierce as Frasier's fragile brother Niles ends up dragooned into the show when the actor playing Jesus drops out. And that fact crimps Frasier's attempt to impress new girlfriend Amy Brenneman's mother, who thinks he's Jewish.

In one of those distinctively farcical *Frasier* moments, beautifully directed by star Kelsey Grammer, he tries to distract visiting mom Carole Shelley from observing a Christmas tree being delivered, dog Eddie romping in a Santa suit, and Niles rushing into the apartment in Jesus costume with an allergy attack. Just when the situation seems to have been saved, mom opens the bathroom door to discover Niles dressed as Jesus using nasal spray in front of their hidden Christmas tree.

But sometimes the best holiday pageantry is the simplest of all. CBS's 1991 *Northern Exposure* finds Cynthia Geary's romantic young adult Shelley pining for the religious spectacle she remembers from childhood midnight masses at Our Lady of Refuge. Her retired tavern-owning boyfriend, played by Broadway musical veteran John Cullum, arranges to surprise her alone in a deserted church with hundreds of candles, a manger scene and his own stirring rendition of "Ave Maria." So it's not as elaborate as their Alaska town's raven pageant. It's a personal response from deep inside the heart. The most memorable presentations are.

WE NEED A LITTLE (LESS) CHRISTMAS

You know you're overdoing the holiday spirit when they start calling you "the Christmas Nazi." That name is applied to Katherine Heigl's Isabel, one of the teenage aliens struggling to live like ordinary New Mexico high schoolers in The WB's youth drama *Roswell*. As Isabel rushes around town trying to create a perfect Christmas 2000, the description sets her steaming. "Is it too much to ask, that one day a year I can be like a normal human being, with a normal life, and have a *merry Christmas*?!" she shrieks.

"We have to stop the madness," begs *Hope & Faith* preteen daughter Macey Cruthird on that ABC family sitcom in 2004. Mother Faith Ford makes her entire family wear Santa caps to shop at the mall and asks sister Kelly Ripa to descend the chimney as St. Nick so her son will keep believing. "Remember when we were kids," Ford asks Ripa, "the holidays were so magical and filled with joy?" "Okay, what house did you grow up in?" rips Ripa. "Mom was always a stress case, and somebody in the house was always crying....I mean, maybe if you learned to back off a little, the Christmas spirit would return to all of us." On UPN's *Girlfriends*, star Tracee Ellis Ross is another character with a seasonal soft spot who simply can't overdo the yule. Caught recruiting carolers with her pitch pipe at a 2003 party, she rejects a friend's suggestion that maybe she should seek romance instead. "I don't need a man, sweetie, I have something better—I have holidays!"

Laura San Giacomo on NBC's publishing sitcom *Just Shoot Me* is similarly smitten. But she can be pushed too far. Into her office's 2001 holiday party bursts holiday-sweater-clad Ray Liotta, guest starring as himself, cousin to Brian Posehn's show character with the same last name. "There's just something about this time of year, isn't there?" Liotta gushes. "People are a little nicer." San Giacomo agrees, "It's like mankind is on its best behavior." "As if," he concludes gleefully, "God Almighty had given this naughty world a time-out."

But their joint joy takes a pause when he proudly ushers her into his apartment, crammed with dozens of dancing Santa figures, life-size reindeer statues, "Thomas my fiberglass camel," and yes, even two live "elves" played by dwarves in costume busily wrapping presents. "I bought the apartment right above me," Liotta enthuses, "so I can come down my own chimney!" San Giacomo's recoil prompts Liotta to explain that Christmas is crucial because "when I was a kid, my parents fought with each other all the time. But on Christmas, it was all different. Somehow there was peace and harmony. And delicious ham." Maya is persuaded to keep warming in Liotta's childlike glow until he's given her his last present. At which point, he really loses it. "It's over," he pouts. "The whole damn holiday's over! The presents have been opened, the eggnog's been drunk, we've eaten all the ham! You think I make movies because I like making movies? I make movies to pay for Christmas! I live for this holiday! And now it's over!" Liotta's beer-chugging elves confide to Maya, "He gets worse every year."

Not that resolving to take the holiday easier is a surefire solution. That's tried by dad Ozzie Nelson, also playing himself, in the Christmas 1956 episode of *The Adventures of Ozzie & Harriet*. The laid-back bandleader also wrote and directed ABC's long-running half-hour in which he, singer-wife Harriet Hilliard, and sons David and Ricky depicted an "average" family.

"I'm not going to get involved in a lot of complications this year," he promises Harriet in an episode much replayed in recent years via public TV stations and low-priced home video releases. Naturally, this vow is no sooner out of Ozzie's mouth than he's recruited by seemingly everyone in town to go caroling, play Santa at the orphanage, star as Scrooge in the local play, pick up the costumes, and more—in addition to such household duties as buying the tree, putting up the lights, and shopping for gifts. "Here we go again," he sighs. "A fine way to spend Christmas Eve."

But in the end, of course, it is. In a whirlwind montage, Ozzie gets everything satisfyingly accomplished except obtaining the tree. He thus arrives home feeling like a failure, until Harriet and the boys surprise him with a fully decorated model. As carolers serenade from outside, Ozzie gets to pensively pronounce that favorite holiday episode farewell:

"This'll be the most wonderful Christmas we've ever had!"

Their First Christmas

When it comes to Christmas traditions, some folks don't have any. That's because they've never had Christmas. Some of TV's first-timers:

Mork & Mindy finds improvisational comic Robin Williams hit with "a plague, an epidemic" he can't comprehend in his alien's first year on ABC (and Earth) in 1978. Seeing a tree wrapped for holiday delivery, livewire Mork asks a neighborhood kid, "What's this, a tree in bondage?" He feels terrorized by carolers and each street corner's scary man in red ("He's called Santa Claws!").

3rd Rock from the Sun lets its entire cast do the yule for the first time. John Lithgow leads a "family" of outrageous alien scouts who study Christmas 1996 on NBC by throwing their human-form selves into decorating, gift-giving, and seasonal mall jobs. Gushes Lithgow, "It's as if all the Earth were throwing us a party!" Amazonian Kristen Johnston bullies customers while working as a gift wrapper: "You got your mom a Dust Miser. How nice. The gift that keeps on sucking." Stuck in a teen body, Joseph Gordon-Levitt rails about his girlfriend's gift wishes: "They know exactly what they want, but they won't tell you. Nooooo. They make you guess!"

As for the massively misconstruing Lithgow, he sweats out the secret Santa routine, pilfers a tree from a neighbor's yard, and bumps into "empty sentiment and holiday hypocrisy." But by episode's end, he has learned what Americans consider the holiday's true meaning to be. "I thought Christmas was all about stress and hostility and handcuffs and Miranda rights. It's so much more. It's about giving and sharing and just being human."

The Pretender is desperate to feel those emotions. He's an earthling, but one with no more experience in human society. NBC's late-1990s cult drama stars Michael T. Weiss as a savant raised isolated from popular culture by a conniving corporation eager to tap his chameleon ability to assume various professions. When he finally escapes in his 30s, he gets to savor his first real Christmas—in Baltimore, working for the medical examiner, trying to set things straight on the latest case to intrigue him. He's using this week's identity and occupation to solve the hit-and-run killing of a Santa-playing homeless man beloved by kids at the local children's home as Christmas George.

Along the way, Weiss's character Jarod delights in each new Christmas tradition he counters. "Geez, Jarod," says a coroner colleague when he beams about a gift-wrapped box, "don't tell me you never got a Christmas present before." Ever stranger, the present is "a cake with fruit baked right in!" as Jarod exudes. "Thank you, this has to be delicious!" But Jarod can't figure kids' faith in Santa since his brainiac mind figures the fat man would have to visit 830 homes a second, traveling 700 miles a second, making each delivery in one-thousandth of a second: "It's so fantastical, why would anybody believe it?" Smiles a nun at the kids' home, "It's Christmas, Jarod. Anything's possible." That's what enchants veteran celebrants and newcomers alike.

CHAPTER 7

Here Comes Santa Claus: Kris Kringle as "Real," Imagined, Multiple, Perverse

Dennis Franz: How come I gotta be Santa Claus?

Gordon Clapp: Well, Stilwell psychoed out, and Walker's got jaundice. No offense, but you're the fattest guy in the squad.

—*NYPD Blue,* 1993

After being giant colored eggs last year, I thought the Easter bunny was the biggest bastard we ever worked for. Santa's 10 times worse. We can't get away from this guy. He knows when we're sleeping, he knows when we're awake, he knows when we're reading porn on our break.

—Ryan Stiles as a store elf on *The Drew Carey Show,* 2000

Santa Claus is sweet. He's silly. He's magical. He's demented. He's real? He's a she?!

He's all over the place when it comes to TV. The gift-delivering character that was originally made a cultural centerpiece in the mid-nineteenth century by Clement C. Moore's poem "The Night Before Christmas"—and soon forever fixed into that jolly bearded figure by Thomas Nast's newspaper sketches—has been a familiar presence from the video medium's beginning, whether in holiday episode depictions or screenings of seasonal cinema hits like *Miracle on 34th Street.*

But the Christmas rush on TV Santa sightings really hit in the 1960s. The once-earnest medium was becoming more playful. Witches and Martians were suddenly popular sitcom characters. And television advertising was hitting its stride. Ad agencies were learning to target their sales pitches to ever more specific demographic slices of the audience. Entire-show sponsorship by mainstream brands of broad-based products like household soap or toothpaste (on advertiser-shaped shows like *The Colgate Comedy Hour)* was now being replaced by spot time purchases alongside other advertisers. Instead of pitching one product or sponsor throughout its length, a single show might now contain a wide array of commercials for a half-dozen items of interest to a more targeted audience segment—say, affluent executive types or teenage boys. Who better to make the kiddies (or adult purse-string-holders) feel happy (not to mention greedy and/or spendthrift) than the jolly man said to be responsible for dispensing that consumer bounty every Christmas morning?

THERE IS TOO A SANTA

Keeping the Santa legend alive became a widespread storyline in the 1960s as modern kids were said to be getting ever more sophisticated—or, some might say, cynical. Precocious scoffers didn't come more obnoxious than worldly-wise Billy Mumy, pre-*Lost in Space,* in the first-season yule outing of ABC's *Bewitched* in 1964, its first of four Christmas tales in an eight-season run. The young redheaded smart-mouth played an orphan kindergartener staying for the holidays with Dick York's suburban advertising executive Darrin and Elizabeth Montgomery's good-witch wife Samantha. Inevitably, Sam becomes so dedicated to restoring the boy's innocence and faith in Santa that she whisks him off to the North Pole to meet the man (elderly cherub Cecil Kellaway).

Things didn't get quite so literal in the differently warped world of ABC's *The Addams Family.* In 1965, Ken Weatherwax's somber son Pugsley and Lisa Loring's vaguely sinister daughter Wednesday so doubt the existence of the gift-giving gnome that the entire quirky clan, right down to hair-covered dwarf Cousin Itt, dons the black-and-white broadcast version of Santa's red suit to persuade the skeptical tykes.

The Addams clan was in good company, echoing the Ricardos and the Mertzes of CBS's 1950s pioneer sitcom smash *I Love Lucy.* The landmark series' sole Christmas outing, a 1956 "clip show" of flashbacks to previous episodes, finds stars Lucille Ball and Desi Arnaz decorating their tree on Christmas Eve in the company of best-friend neighbors Vivian Vance and William Frawley. As the funny foursome reminisce about Lucy telling Ricky she's pregnant and later scrambling to get to the hospital, they're about to create one more memory. Toddler Little Ricky insists on seeing the holiday's big man in person: "I'll go to bed after Santa Claus gets here!" They manage to get him to sleep, but on Christmas morning, all four adults separately dress in Santa suits to make the boy believe. Frawley grumps, "You gotta get up early if you wanna be Santa Claus around here!" Indeed. The Santas in the living room number one, two, three, four—five? Tugging down each other's beards, they discover one Santa's won't come off—and he fades from view, leaving our beloved stars to gasp to the camera, "Merry Christmas, everybody."

Keeping kids in the Santa loop is a plot that TV seems to find eternally reliable. Nearly a half-century later, ABC's George Lopez repeated the same effort, with the title dad pushing hard in 2003 to make a believer of son Luis Armand Garcia—along the way re-becoming a believer himself after Santa stops by the backyard. That same year in UPN's All of Us, dad Duane Martin somehow convinces his son that he's the real St. Nick—and that son will inherit his beard someday.

Parents try to stop siblings from spilling the beans about Santa on the first-year holiday of ABC's 1990s hit Home Improvement. That's when the two older brothers of Taran Noah Smith's kindergartener Mark make fun of his faith. "Are you gonna be a dork your whole life?" asks Zachery Ty Bryan's Brad in 1991. "You're too old to believe in Santa Claus," scoffs Jonathan Taylor Thomas's Randy. The latter tries again with "Here's the truth. There used to be a Santa Claus, but he died six years ago." "Yeah," taunts Brad, "you just missed out." Dad Tim Allen later reassures his youngest about Santa's survival: "Son, I think he's old, but he's not dead." "You wouldn't lie," confirms Mark, happily heading off as Tim admits, "We just lied to him." "He's our last baby," pleads wife Patricia Richardson. "I wanted him to have one more magical Christmas." That seems assured when Earl Hindman's oft-obscured neighbor Wilson later arrives in full regalia to substantiate Santa's existence. "Sometimes that Wilson is one fine neighbor," enthuses Allen while showing Santa out the door. "You mean, that Wilson?" wonders Richardson as an un-costumed Wilson waves from his backyard.

So who was that bearded man? Home Improvement beautifully exemplified one of television's favorite devices: making Santa Claus at least conceivably real. If his existence isn't lock, stock, and barrel proven in stories like this, it's presented as a delightful and, yes, magical possibility. Even episodes aimed at adults indulge in personifying a prospective Santa, most often as a desperately needed source of enchantment and wonder in an otherwise world-weary society.

NBC's whimsical Night Court didn't mess around, presenting its first Christmas tale in only the series' second airing (which actually came

after the holidays when the midseason show premiered in January 1984).
Michael J. Fox, who'd just become a TV sensation on NBC's *Family Ties,*
guest starred here as a different sort of teen know-it-all—a defiant runaway
brought into Manhattan arraignment court the same night as Jeff Corey, the
legendary acting teacher cast as a seemingly homeless mental patient who
insists he's St. Nick. "All Santa had in his bag," testifies John Larroquette's
sarcastic prosecutor, "was a box of Chiclets and a half empty bottle of gin."
"Firing up the old yule log, eh, Mr. Claus?" winks hippie-styled judge/magi-
cian Harry Anderson.

But Harry takes a shine to the tall tales of this old man, who eventually
offers his honor the chance to take over his reindeers' reins. Corey even
manages to knock the chip off Fox's shoulder when he seems to know
things about the boy that only Santa could know. "It's all right for you not
to believe in me," he tells Fox. "Because the important thing is that I believe
in you." As *Night Court* did so well for nine seasons, this gritty/goofy episode blends the outrageous with the sentimental, the matter-of-fact with
the miraculous. Corey turns out to have read Fox's police file, which would
explain his intimate knowledge of the boy—except the police actually delivered the file of some Japanese kid instead. As "Santa" is heard exclaiming
on his way back to the mental institution, "Ho, ho, ho"....

Fox encounters the "real" Santa again soon thereafter, in 1987 on his
own series *Family Ties.* This time, the elfin actor also gets to wear the red
suit himself, when his materialistic young yuppie Alex Keaton is pressed
into St. Nick service at the mall. "I just don't know how you can celebrate
joyously when holiday retail sales are down by 4 percent," he scoffs, but
finally agrees to a friend's request to sub as Santa, only because it pays $10
an hour. Elf-playing sister Tina Yothers feels compelled to warn a visiting
mom, "I hope your daughter's interested in the commodities market." But
the "me decade" soul of Fox's self-centered character is touched by the
girl's plea to bring her traveling-salesman daddy home for Christmas—so
touched that another Santa in the store locker room takes note.

The portly white-bearded man is down from the North Pole, he tells Fox,
who retorts, "Let's try and keep our sled in the real world here, pal." But the
guy recognizes Fox's briefcase—"That was the Christmas of '73. You asked
for that briefcase, a pocket calculator, and a pardon for Richard Nixon"—and
after Fox searches fruitlessly for *Candid Camera*'s hidden lenses, he finally
believes. "Alex," counsels Santa, "I know that up to this point our relationship has been mostly financial, but this year you've changed.... You're
doing the right thing. Don't underestimate the power of Christmas. It can
work miracles." And it must. The salesman shows up at the Keaton home,

where the girl and her mother have joined Fox's family festivity. Dad reports he was in Fargo when "this great big barrel of a man with a white beard" showed up at his motel and bought everything he had to sell, asking only that he deliver a package to Alex P. Keaton. It's a model-kit Porsche. Even the "real" Santa can't come up with the life-size sports car for which Fox secretly yearns.

Santa often does come through, however, with precisely the gift the recipient needs—and in such a miraculous way that it seems no other source could be responsible. This approach was a natural for a classic anthology in which the ironic was always happening: Rod Serling's CBS suspense drama *The Twilight Zone*. Its 1960 holiday episode, "Night of the Meek," outfits Art Carney in a red suit his downtrodden character is ill-prepared to wear. The script by the acclaimed writer of such live-TV "golden age" dramas as "Patterns" and "Requiem for a Heavyweight," starts in a bar, where Carney's department store Santa is downing so many drinks that back at the store a mouthy kid later exclaims, "Look out, Mom! Santa Claus is loaded!" Made even more despondent by the holiday, Carney implores that "just one Christmas, I'd like to see the meek inherit the earth." Later that night, a bag of tin cans on a snowy city street morphs into a magic sack from which his character then "gives everybody exactly what they want for Christmas."

Helping just one person is enough on NBC's ensemble medical drama *St. Elsewhere*. In 1985, the hospital party's Santa collapses and dies—but not before the grandson of Norman Lloyd's Dr. Auschlander has asked the man to replace something the boy broke: a glass snowball given to grandma Jane Wyatt by her grandmother. "Consider it done," Santa says in intensive care. And sure enough, a package shows up under the hospital tree, containing a ball "just like the one that grandma gave me!"

A bike is what mysteriously appears for the 2002 Christmas of The WB's *Reba*, starring country music superstar Reba McEntire as a divorced Texas mom coping with her dentist ex-husband's remarriage to the office assistant with whom he'd philandered. Add to its sitcom mix the emergency marriage of her pregnant teenage daughter to a dimwit football star, followed by the birth of a grandbaby. The suddenly single Reba has been through so much that "I am so looking forward to this Christmas Eve," she drawls. "There is just somethin' so special about havin' a baby in the house." Too bad that daughter and son-in-law want to head off for time alone. And that Reba's middle kid prefers to celebrate with her pals. And that youngest son asks to stay with dad for their annual reading of "The Night before Christmas." When Reba and her ex clash over who gets to give their son his much-desired bike this holiday, it's enough to make the throaty-voiced petite powerhouse angrily grab and strangle the Christmas tree left undecorated by her departed clan: "So I suppose you wanna go back to the forest now, huh?"

The only way Reba can perk herself up is to take her Christmas dinner fixings to the local homeless shelter. "Yeah, that's why I come down here," agrees Victor Raider-Wexler's grumpy old guest in a red hat and white beard. "To feel better about myself. I used to hang around with a disfigured guy so I wouldn't feel bad about the extra weight I put on." Making things crystal clear, he explains he's sulky because "I gotta work. It's the busiest night of the year for Santa." Reba's a doubter, of course—heck, the guy has disparaged her homemade cookies—but she listens anyway to his counsel. "If your traditions meant anything," concludes the roly-poly guest, "your family's still together in your heart. Go home. Decorate your tree. End of speech." (He even departs carrying her cookies: "By the time we get to Japan, you'd be surprised what a reindeer will eat.") Back at the homestead, Reba is greeted by the return of her middle daughter, and then the married kids, and the youngest, with dad and new wife in tow. "All your kids are home for Christmas," says ex Christopher Rich. "Looks like you got your wish." Completely. On Christmas morning, there's a bike under the tree that mom didn't buy, and dad didn't either. "To Jake, From Santa," reads the tag.

Is that enough proof of Santa's existence? St. Nick rarely finds himself taken at face value or even on faith. More often, a man in a red suit who says he's the real thing is ridiculed, fired, sued, or jailed by a world too jaded to play along. The last happens on a winning installment of CBS's *Early Edition,* the lighthearted drama in which Kyle Chandler's character receives the next day's paper each morning, and then feels compelled to head off its tragic headlines. "Bomber kills 20 at skating rink" blares the front page at Christmas 1996, just as Chandler's schemer friend Fisher Stevens is thrown in the slammer for collecting 106 parking tickets. The two problems dovetail in the person of a Santa Claus, played by M. Emmet Walsh, who's been jailed for breaking and entering. "Think you got problems?" he moans. "I'm late for work."

Stevens isn't inclined to buy it, but Santa seems to know all about the presents he requested as a child (and didn't get; as Santa chastises, "You didn't believe. There's a price you have to pay for that"). Santa hatches a scheme to pinch the guard's keys and escape, and then to Stevens's amazement steals a car. "If I am who I say I am," warns Santa, "you're walking away from the one chance in your life to do something good for the world, if that means anything to you—and I think it does." Seems Santa doesn't steer very well—"I'm not used to driving with a wheel"—but he does speed them over to the bar where Chandler has cornered the would-be bomber, rigged with explosives and threatening to blow up everyone. "Howie Phillips!" Santa exclaims. "You know, you used to be one of my favorite kids. I got you your first chemistry set." Santa wheedles the bomb away, runs out-side—and vanishes. "He really believed he was what he thought he was, and you have to admire that," marvels Stevens. He then discovers that Santa "stole my keys." Stevens is later called to the impound lot, where he's been left a nifty sleigh.

SANTA GOES TO COURT

That combination of the serious and the absurd was the stock in trade a few years later of producer David E. Kelley's *Ally McBeal*, Fox's fantastical comedy/drama about Calista Flockhart's overimaginative young attorney and her emotionally arrested Boston law firm colleagues. They were forever in court with holiday cases, as creator Kelley cooked up as many as three mischievous Christmas episodes each December of the series' five-year run. (Maybe he wanted to make room for seasonal songs: His *Ally* characters were always singing in the nightclub downstairs from their firm, allow-ing Kelley to underscore his scripts with mood music from staff songstress Vonda Shepard and stage-bred costars like Jane Krakowski.)

In a 1999 *Ally*, Santa gets into a store floor brawl that involves wacky elf-tossing. He's been told that after 17 years his services are no longer required, because he's—of all things—too fat. "I'm Santa Claus! I am the spirit of Christmas, you son of a bitch! I will make you pay!" Santa rages, soon filing a wrongful termination suit. Retail execs testify they've "decided to go with a new lean, health-conscious Santa Claus," a hot bod in red spandex who's "more commensurate with the store's demographic." They sniff that "fat and jolly belongs at Wal-Mart." Though the case is lost by Peter MacNicol's neurotic firm partner Cage—who tells the judge "I'd like to personally roast your chestnuts on an open fire"—the store asks overweight Santa back anyhow. They've ultimately realized Christmas "should be more than about demographics."

During the case, though, the whole notion of Santa's existence has come up for discussion and debate. "One could argue they'd be doing a service to children by exposing the truth," claims store counsel and ex-*Ally* colleague Courtney Thorne-Smith, pooh-poohing the fat-red-suit tradition. She's dealing with her own heartache of a dissolving marriage to firm lawyer Gil Bellows, and gets teary in court about the "adult disillusionment" awaiting those kids when they grow up. "At the end of the day, life is just this big wall of reality that we all crash into. Maybe kids should get a dose of it .... My client isn't killing Santa Claus, your honor. He doesn't exist."

So says more than one TV character. And it's worse when kids hear it from a voice of authority. On ABC's 1997 *Spin City*, it's Barry Bostwick's hapless New York City mayor who inadvertently announces Santa is a fantasy, digging himself another hole that wheeling-dealing deputy mayor Michael J. Fox has to pull his employer out of. *Ally McBeal* returns to that same territory in 2000 with the case of a Santa-scorning TV news anchor who's been canned for "excessive truth telling" on his kid-viewed morning broadcast. Station management claims "we incurred the wrath of our trusted public" with his "mean-spirited, unscripted, cynical proclamation" that Santa doesn't exist. But in another of writer Kelley's Christmas ruminations, MacNicol argues it isn't finding out Santa's fictional that hurts kids, "it's the reveal that maybe their parents lied to them." He says the effort to sustain that magic is actually more needed by the adults than their offspring. "It's nice to cling to Santa and all he represents, to relive the innocence of childhood, to recapture those feelings of joy and magic and song, feelings that have long since left us. Santa is a device for the parents, sometimes, to experience the love and the gift of a child. And we need it."

Just two weeks later in 2000, *Ally McBeal* is back in court with a man who so desperately desires Santa's magic that he believes he actually *is* Santa. He's also the father of blonde firm lawyer Portia de Rossi. "Please call me Kris," says veteran actor William Windom, playing a character actually named Henderson Porter. As a retired lawyer turned schoolteacher, he's been fired for refusing to deny his Santa status to his second-graders. "We all adore him," says his principal, "but he's delusional." MacNicol, who seems to be the series' Santa specialist, contends in court, "it might be nice for more teachers to assume the role of St. Nicholas than, say, Joan Crawford. I might think that I'm Barry White," the slight white attorney says of the hefty black soul singer, but "that doesn't render me less capable as an attorney." This schoolteacher Santa "hasn't done anything wrong. The symptoms of this progressive disorder thus far have been kindness, charity, and love.... His only crime is to bring a little extra wonder to his students, make their lives a little more magical, a little more romantic." And the firm finally wins one.

Kelley revisits the question of who makes a suitable Santa in another series, ABC's *Boston Legal*, the madcap successor to his long-running courtroom drama *The Practice*. In 2004, it's a gray-haired, middle-aged man who's been sacked after eight years as a popular Kris Kringle. Of course, he's a cross-dresser wearing a skirt and pearls. "I should not lose my job because of how I like to dress," he argues, engendering an intrafirm bet between proudly peculiar counsel James Spader and straighter colleague Mark Valley, which the latter maneuvers to win by getting a reactionary judge assigned to the case. "That's where we're at now?" rages judge H. Richard Greene. "Santa Claus is being played by homosexuals? A homosexual transvestite?" The judge makes the mistake of asking the loose-cannon Spader, "Would you sit in his lap?" Which Spader does: "And he hasn't gone all 'homo erectus' on me, if that was your fear." The cunning lawyer finally calls in real-life preacher/activist Al Sharpton to bring down the house with a fervent call to "let the bells of tolerance ring out this Christmas!"

Santa finds himself in court more often than you might think. In 1987 on NBC's *Highway to Heaven*, Bill Erwin's jolly old soul sues a store for firing him, enlisting the help of angel Michael Landon on a week he's working for an attorney. Erwin is, however, the "real" St. Nick. "They want Santa to push machine guns?" he fumes at being told to steer visiting kids toward specific store toys. "I don't need the job, I've got the job, I've had it for hundreds of years," he informs Landon. "They can't take diddly-squat away from me. But what they can do is take Christmas, the spirit of Christmas away from the children." After violating a store restraining order, Santa lands in jail, which allows him to make friends with a jailer whose son desperately wants a train set his father can't afford. That problem is magically solved by Christmas, of course, as is a courtroom showdown between the lawyers on either side of Santa's case, a divorced couple battling over which gets the holiday with their son. "The boy loves you both, and he's living proof that once you loved each other," Santa lectures from the stand. "Neither of you has to win and neither of you has to lose. All you gotta do is love your son and work together, even if you're apart, to raise him."

SANTA: THE REAL DEAL

If the court never rules on what's factual or fantastical there, Santa Claus is indeed presented as the real deal on other vintage yule favorites. After Elizabeth Montgomery's Samantha on *Bewitched* makes young Billy Mumy believe, two other episodes of the ABC sitcom go on to conjure the bona fide Santa in their own ways. Why not, on a show where witches exist? In 1969, it's Samantha's mistake-prone Aunt Esmeralda (Alice Ghostley) summoning the jolly man, who promptly appears from the North Pole and can't get back, thanks to Esmeralda's unreliable spells. "I don't usually go on trips during my busy season," worries Ronald Long's Santa, remaining marooned long enough that pesky neighbors like Sandra Gould's Gladys Kravitz keep showing up and spotting him. It's enough to make mortal husband Darrin (now Dick Sargent) continually down double martinis. When Darrin's boss visits during Santa's stay, he requests a triple. (This always was a hard-drinking sitcom.) *Bewitched*'s 1967 episode is less inebriated. Don Beddoe's Santa pays a visit there in order to soften the heart of one of Darrin's grinch-iest advertising agency clients.

It's again easy for Santa to seem bona fide in Steven Spielberg's fantasy anthology *Amazing Stories*. For Christmas 1985, Spielberg wrote the story "Santa '85," about a young boy who's keeping the faith when it comes to the Claus. This Santa is a part of the "modern, sophisticated world," check-ing weather readouts before leaving the North Pole and being warned by his wife, "Watch out for the 747s!" Yet Santa falls into a high-tech trap when he trips the alarm system at the boy's house, which alerts the cops, who order, "Drop that bag and raise those mittens!" Top cop Pat Hingle is a bit-ter man, brought up in a Depression-era orphanage, where he never got the Buck Rogers ray gun he wanted. He's only too happy to throw Santa in the slammer. With the sleigh idling in his backyard, the boy jumps in and busts Santa out of jail by tossing a rope around the bars and having the reindeer pull. They lead the sheriff on a merry chase through the snowy town—"Pull that sleigh over!"—until Santa drops off the boy and takes flight once more. He has, of course, left behind a present for the sheriff: that Buck Rogers ray gun, with a card signed "Santa '85."

Santa might as well be authentic on cartoons, too. In the 1964 holiday episode of ABC's prime time hit *The Flintstones*, Fred Flintstone—the Stone-Age approximation of lovable *Honeymooners* working-man Ralph Kramden—is earning extra money at the Macyrock store by gift wrapping, stocking shelves, and finally serving as an emergency Santa. Fred falls asleep in the store's dressing room on Christmas Eve, and awakes to elves asking that he accompany them to the North Pole. Santa needs Fred's delivery help since "this cold I have has spoiled everything." But "how can we deliver presents all over the world in one night?" wonders Fred. Elves Blinky and Twinky have the answer: "We don't take coffee breaks." Soon Fred is parachuting presents into chimneys and shouting holiday greetings in countless lan-guages. He's too busy to make a delivery stop at his own home in Bedrock. But the authentic Santa has taken care of that. "You were so real!" enthuses wife Wilma. Fred will never tell.

But Mister Ed will. The talking horse of one of those fantasy sitcoms so popular in the 1960s spends the 1963 holiday of CBS's *Mister Ed* confiding to owner Alan Young ("Willlllbuuuurrrr") "the real Christmas story—the one Hollywood doesn't dare make!" In the rumbling voice of character actor Allan "Rocky" Lane, the arrogant Ed insists, "If it wasn't for a horse, there'd be no gifts from Santa Claus on Christmas Day!" His dream-sequence tale casts Wilbur's tough-talking neighbor as Scrooge Kirkwood of the North Pole Savings and Loan, refusing to lend Santa the money to make enough toys for all the kids in the world. After Ed bets the banker that Santa can make all his deliveries in one night, the horse then teaches his reindeer to fly ("Donner was a little chicken at first") and insists Santa save doorbell-ringing time by using chimneys instead. The episode ends in the show's improbably logical fashion: The palomino dons a red suit and beard to deliver gifts to his friends.

If a horse could be Santa in the 1960s, why couldn't a communist? At the height of the nuclear-standoff Cold War between the so-called free world and the Soviet Union's socialist bloc, TV retreated further into fancy than ever before. NBC's *The Man from U.N.C.L.E.* was a quintessential embodiment of the trend—a secret-agent romp that used international intrigue merely as a backdrop for adventures whose caricature made them essentially a modern western. This was a retreat from reality in which the good and bad guys were obvious, guns could blaze for days without anybody actually seeming injured, and situations that should have been complex were rendered at a flippant level of naive resolution.

What better setting for Christmas magic? Witness the nearly adorable spy play of the international justice organization U.N.C.L.E. in its 1966 yuletide outing "The Jingle Bells Affair," depicting a New York visit by the chairman of a vaguely alluded to "People's Republic." Backed by footage of the actual Macy's Thanksgiving Day Parade and Manhattan storefronts of the 1960s, Hollywood veteran Akim Tamiroff portrays a volatile communist who observes to his U.N.C.L.E. bodyguards that the American Christmas is "the time when the rich get richer and the poor get poorer." Robert Vaughn's fancifully named agent Napoleon Solo replies dryly, "That's not exactly the intent, but you probably have a point." Along the way, Tamiroff even gets to bang his shoe on a desk, à la Soviet leader Nikita Khrushchev's infamous 1960 United Nations tirade. His scorn, however, eventually turns to enchantment, as he partakes in holiday traditions after meeting a lovely blonde Salvation Army officer and enrolling in her "Santa Claus school." His infection with the Christmas spirit leads to him saving a sick boy who'd been dying of a mysterious ailment before Santa Chairman perked him up. By episode's end, the commie is irredeemably cuddly. "If I will lose my job over there," he asks U.N.C.L.E., "can I be a Santa Claus at Macy?" If the Santa spirit can "cure" a commie, it's got to be real.

BAD SANTAS

Other St. Nick incarnations are not so nice. *Bad Santa* the movie has nothing over TV. Long before Billy Bob Thornton was comedically outraging big-screen fans in 2003, the tube was offering a wide assortment of rude Santas, drunken Santas, crazed Santas, suicidal Santas, even Santa gangs and robot Santa clones.

Better that than a criminal Santa, of which TV has also seen many. Scalawag Santas steal family presents from under the tree in episodes of NBC's 1991 *Fresh Prince of Bel-Air*, CBS's 1987 *Designing Women*, and NBC's 1988's *227* (with future *Family Matters* dad Reginald VelJohnson as the sticky-fingered fat man). Street-corner St. Nicks mug passersby in NBC's 1976 *McCloud* ("It's been a bleak year at the toy shop") and Dabney Coleman's 1991 Fox half-hour comedy *Drexell's Class*. Santas are themselves being mugged in ABC's 1976 *Barney Miller*, sending Abe Vigoda's tired old detective Fish out into the street as an undercover decoy. "Cops dressed up like Santa Claus?" moans a perpetrator. "Ain't nothin' sacred no more?"

Sammo Hung pulls the same duty on CBS's 1999 *Martial Law*, the attempt to make an American hero out of a chunky, middle-aged martial arts master from Hong Kong cinema whose command of the English language was, to be kind, limited. Hung's embryonic enunciation was mostly so impenetrable that he was given little dialogue alongside costars like Arsenio Hall who carried the exposition. Everybody knows what Sammo is saying, anyway, when 1999's holiday episode dresses him as a department store St. Nick. He's out to catch a Santa-suited gang stealing toy deliveries in which they believe a missile chip has been hidden. One do-badder fires off a round and warns store patrons, "If I see you moving, I'm gonna have to shoot you, so be good for goodness' sake." Words have become entirely superfluous by the time the gang bursts into Sammo's store. He takes 'em on nearly single-handedly, using an on-sale trampoline to bounce after the bad guys, hanging from store fixtures to fight, and pouncing from a ceiling-mounted sleigh.

Santa gangs seem to be a go-to plot device. In 1994 on CBS's whimsical Canadian Mountie import *Due South*, movie-star-to-be Ryan Phillippe plays a kid whose ex-con dad has been forced into red-suited bank robbing by old criminal acquaintances. Crooks looking like St. Nick converge to rob armored cars in 1999's CBS *Walker, Texas Ranger*. It's banks again in 1998's *Melrose Place*, when the Fox soap's male cast members, out playing Santas for schools, get mistakenly thrown in the clink for the crime. Not that the bad Santa can't go it alone. He's back in the bank biz for 2002's *Sue Thomas F.B.Eye*, the PAX hour-long drama in which deaf actress Deanne Bray helps crack cases by reading lips. Sue and other investigators trace their hold-up artist from the store that rented the Santa suit to his house, where they discover his stolen loot hidden inside under-the-tree holiday presents.

Other series depict an even more evil character in Santa clothing. It's a rapist in ABC's 1991 *The Commish,* in which Michael Chiklis's sensitive title cop ("I'd rather think and talk than shoot") announces his arrest with "Merry Christmas, Santa." And the red-suited soul is a murder suspect on A&E's 2001 revival of *Nero Wolfe.* But in this 1940s period piece, the man wearing the Santa suit is surprisingly the irascible title detective recluse himself, as played by Maury Chaikin. "Christmas as celebrated is merely an excuse for wretched excess, aptly symbolized by an elephantine elf who delivers gifts to the whole world in one night," Wolfe has drolly told legman assistant Archie (Timothy Hutton). He only gets into Santa gear to secretly tend bar at a party where Archie intends to announce his engagement to a woman Wolfe considers bad news. After a partygoer is killed, Wolfe's fleeing Santa is fingered, but the egotistical gourmand won't cop to wearing the costume—"I will not unfold the morning paper to a disclosure of this outlandish masquerade"—so he has to solve the case to get the fat man off the hook. (Yes, the would-be fiancée did it.)

Playing Santa is murder again on NBC's Andy Griffith courtroom whodunit *Matlock,* in both 1986 (Pat Hingle as an apartment evictee with a dead landlord) and 1987. Future *Malcolm in the Middle* dad Bryan Cranston goes on trial in the latter as a noncustodial father whose rich and nasty ex-wife is killed at a party where all revelers are dressed as Santa, including the gotta-see-my-daughter dad. Not only does Griffith's folksy old attorney reunite dad and daughter by getting client Cranston off—doesn't Matlock always?—but he even manages along the way to thaw the cold heart of curmudgeonly judge William Schallert.

Of course, the red-suited rogues of these crime shows aren't really Santa Claus, merely pretenders who put on the garb for no-good situations. It's a handy way to turn a workaday script into a Christmas special. An ostensibly grounded drama would have a hard time persuading us to suddenly suspend disbelief for a week. That is hardly a problem with animation, however, and cartoons have often leapt into extremely elevated flights of evil fancy where it comes to the gift-giver from the North Pole.

It's a dastardly Santa vs. the good old good version in 2004 on *¡Mucha Lucha! ¡Gigante!* The WB's vibrant weekday afternoon romp depicts kids as masked Mexican wrestlers-in-training, using Latin themes and colorful *Batman*-type graphics to punctuate its moral conflict at holiday time. The heroic young *mascarita* trio loses the Lucha Xmas Megamatch to *rudo* opponents who cheated, but the skilled *tecnico* contenders can still look forward to the visit of "Santo Claus." As "the toughest *tecnico luchadore* of them all, he knows who's been *rudo* and who's been *tecnico.*"

Unfortunately this time, Santo lavishes the *rudos* with "new cheating devices" like poisonous blowfish. That's because, as clever Buena Girl discovers, "somebody's been messing with *Lucha* Christmas!" It's Rudo Claus, Santo's "no-good *rudo* twin brother," who's taken Santo's place and started telling kids to "lie, cheat, steal, be *rudo* to each other, and I will bring you tons of presents!" Once Buena Girl frees the real Santo from the sack into which Rudo has stuffed him, a winner-take-all match on the wrestling mat finally puts things right. " *Feliz Navidad*, chump!" reads the bold on-screen inscription of victory.

Futurama, the space-set Fox send-up from *Simpsons* creator Matt Groening, offered not one but two Christmas outings with a demented Santa, this time a badly programmed robot on a futuristic rampage. When the unit was built by the Friendly Robot Co., we're told in 1999 by know-everything Professor Farnsworth, "Santa's standards were set too high, and he invariably judges everyone to be naughty." Children know that if they go out after dark, he'll "chop off your head and stuff your neck full of toys from his sack of horrors." This is hardly the Santa remembered by twenti-eth-century human Frye, who after being accidentally frozen has suddenly awakened 1,000 years in the future. Not only have pine trees been extinct for 800 years (they use palms), but Santa (voiced by John Goodman) now ho-ho-ho's with ornament grenades and TOW missiles.

"In my day, Christmas was supposed to bring people together, not blow them apart," Frye observes in 2001's follow-up episode, where the frus-trated everyman decides to "deliver a gift of my boot up Santa's chimney!" Heading to the North Pole, Frye finds Santa trapped in the ice, so he seizes the opportunity to have his drunken robot Bender build billions of toys in Santa's "nonunion shop." Delivering them is another story. People expecting the evil Santa are on the attack. Some traditions simply can't be thwarted. After thawing out, the wicked St. Nick has a proposal: "If I don't complete my brutal rampage, well, it just wouldn't be Christmas. I guess what I'm asking is: Bender, won't you join my slaying tonight?" "Well," says Bender, "'tis the season." Frye is forced to conclude, "Fear has brought us together. That's the magic of Christmas!"

The actual Santa is a late arrival in Fox's 1995 cartoon rendering of Ben Edlund's hapless blue comic-book superhero *The Tick*. A bank burglar steals a Santa suit to make his escape, and then flees smack into a neon sign, whose electrical charge reproduces him into dozens of copies. "The streets will run red with Santas!" vows the crook, whose new minions function as a single "multiple Santa" in subsequent criminal enterprises. The dense and gushy Tick mopes, "We fried Santa!"—he's simple enough to still be a believer—until the gift-giving St. Nick journeys from the North Pole to Tick's shabby city apartment, proffering the gift of an in-the-egg egg scrambler. He inspires our hero to "get out there and save Christmas" from a "yule-tide" of evil Santas flowing down river from the hydroelectric plant. As it turns out, "their Achilles' heel is the noogie!" Static electricity saves the day by poof-ing them away. Edlund's witty Tick concept would later become a critically acclaimed Fox live-action series in 2001, delightfully starring dead-pan *Seinfeld* boyfriend Patrick Warburton. But with its run cut short at eight episodes, a holiday half-hour was not to be among them.

It's surprising how many other shows find a way to incorporate Christmas, though, even when their concepts seem ill-suited and their air dates don't overlap the holiday season. In April 2001, we got one of TV's most sinister Santa renderings ever, on one of its most unsparingly brutal dramas. Can you imagine Christmas with *The Sopranos*? Creator-producer David Chase did, and his curse-strewn HBO hit chronicled the holiday woes of street-level New Jersey mobster Tony Soprano and his hands-on wiseguys. As a TV drama veteran with credits from *The Rockford Files* to *Northern Exposure,* Chase was savvy enough to mine holiday closeness for its propensity to lay bare the sort of intimate emotions that earned his dark adult saga millions of fans and innumerable awards.

In *The Sopranos,* holiday horror lies not in Santa but in his suit. The red garb is unpacked by James Gandolfini's Italian mob lieutenants as these oh-so-Catholic thugs are hauling out their annual yule decorations. "Burn the fuckin' thing," Gandolfini curses. The costume was worn for years by Vincent Pastore's Big Pussy, the recently rubbed-out "family" turncoat; it's something no one wants to inherit (though Steve Schirripa's fat schlub Bobby Bacala eventually gets drafted). Its reappearance inspires haunting flashbacks to Pussy's Santa days amid suspicions that it probably helped conceal the wire Pussy was wearing for the feds. Yet "one thing you got to admit," drawls Steven Van Zandt's slicked-back Silvio, "he made a great Santa Claus." "In the end," says Tony Sirico's resentful Paulie, "fuck Santa Claus."

The tension on this show never lets up, not even for—especially not for—this holiest of holidays. Christmas is the celebration that most under-scores the centrality of family, however that word is defined. The tension behind those ties is enough to bring back the anxiety attacks with which Tony Soprano had started this acclaimed series. "Oh, the pressure we put on ourselves this time of year," observes Lorraine Bracco as his poker-faced psychiatrist. She has come to her own view of yuletide time: "I call it Stress-mas."

SANTA GETS STRESSED OUT

Few shows get anywhere near so grim for Christmas. Yet even sitcoms can find themselves reflecting the stress of the season. Comedy writers often employ the sentiment of the holidays to tackle unusually weighty subjects, though most do so in an ultimately lighthearted manner. What better way than to dress despondent people in Santa suits?

Men playing the part of St. Nick are determined to kill themselves in two ABC half-hours, 1985's *Growing Pains* and 1997's *Soul Man*. Alan Thicke's Long Island psychologist in *Growing Pains* frantically tries to talk down a patient who's threatening to hurl himself down the doctor's chimney, using a measuring tape and a calculator to make sure he'll fit. (He's an accountant.) After moping how he misses his dog, the patient comes around when Thicke's young son pleads up the living room fireplace from below, "If you don't kill yourself, you can have my puppy." Yes, sitcoms of the 1980s knew how to lay it on thick(e). The touch was a bit lighter on *Soul Man*, starring *Saturday Night Live* loon Dan Aykroyd as a much straighter minister. He has a crabby elf played by Mark-Linn Baker *(Perfect Strangers)* poised to jump from atop his church. "You said to drop by anytime," says Baker, "so in about five seconds I'm gonna be dropping by your left ear." Thanks to Aykroyd's counsel, of course, he doesn't.

The *Soul Man* elf was driven to drastic measures after "working crowd control" at Christmastime. And he isn't the only one. Working as Santa or one of his helpers is a common TV theme. Most times, it's just a handy trigger to set the story in motion, to set up a laugh or an irony. But putting a key character in Santa's shoes can also provide an opportunity for growth in shows that like to leaven their snickers with substance. On ABC's flashback coming-of-age half-hour show *The Wonder Years* in 1990, Fred Savage's adolescent student of the 1960s discovers his loathed school gym taskmaster is working as Santa at a suburban Long Island store—"the first time I had ever seen a teacher outside of school, and he had a pillow strapped to his stomach," as recalled by the kid's grown-up narrating incarnation (the voice of Daniel Stern). The boy learns that "knowledge is power" as he becomes teacher's pet to the man who doesn't want other students to learn he can also be a softie. The teacher, played by Robert Picardo *(Star Trek: Voyager)*, confesses he took the job for the employee discount at holiday shopping time. The bonus was that he learned along the way "kids like me when I'm Santa," he admits plaintively. His student, too, is gaining a mature new view, realizing the hard-nosed man is actually "a very lonely human being." Bit by bit each week on this uniquely insightful series, a boy was becoming a man.

A man becomes a boy on ABC's *According to Jim*, showcasing comedian Jim Belushi as a too-often-juvenile family man. In 2004, the Chicago hothead tussles with a mall Santa after the man backs into his car in the parking garage and provides fake insurance information. Jim, Santa, and store elves brawl their way through the entire Christmas display when Jim confronts him at work. "Santa punched him, and the cops came!" the kids report back to mom Courtney Thorne-Smith. Ever the reasonable sitcom wife, she insists he "make nice in front of Santa" to pacify the little ones' no-presents fears. But Jim's Christmas Eve plea that Santa try to find his better self and shake hands provokes the response "I'll find my better self at happy hour" and a punch in the nose. He finally corners contentious Santa back in the parking garage to buy the guy's Santa suit to reassure his kids that Santa still loves them. Wearing it home, Jim is touched to hear his son ask that Santa give some of his presents to daddy "'cause he had a fight with your helper, and I don't think he's getting anything." In the "awwww"-some style of ABC's live audience familycoms, a silly situation turns sentimental with a lesson to be learned. "You don't worry about your daddy," concludes Belushi's much-moved dad, "He's the luckiest man in the world."

Women can also come to new understandings playing Santa. The title comedian of ABC's *Roseanne* does it at the mall in 1991 to earn some extra money. (And she's awfully charming under the beard.) Then she gets an unexpected dose of information when a visiting child's mom turns out to be alienated daughter Darlene's vaguely alluded—to new "friend"—an adult in whom the unsettled adolescent confides instead of her concerned (and now offended) mother. Another stand-up comic, Monique, steps in on UPN's *The Parkers*, in 2001, after she finds a store Santa with flask in hand, asking, "Where are my manners? Would you like some?" She's determined to restore the Christmas spirit to a jaded world. Skeptical kids are more often the impetus for women to don the duds. They want to show the little one that Santa does too exist on NBC's *227* in 1988 (both lead Marla Gibbs and comic foil Jackee Harry, later joined by the entire adult cast), on UPN's 2002 *Girlfriends* (lead Tracee Ellis Ross for a friend's son), and on ABC's 2004 *Hope & Faith* (Kelly Ripa's spoiled soap star, who gets stuck coming down her nephew's chimney).

Santa can be simply silly, too, on sitcoms that have no interest whatsoever in sending a message. Take Fox's *Drexell's Class*, in which misanthrope teacher Dabney Coleman so needs the extra money of the red-suit gig that he goes to work in 1991 for an employer who brags of having a pimp Santa the previous year: "Not only did he have a list of who's naughty and nice, he had Polaroids." Kurtwood Smith's cantankerous dad on Fox's *That '70s Show* gets fitted for a charity Santa suit in 2003 by cheery but firm wife Debra Jo Rupp with this advice: "Remember, Santa is a cheerful, jolly fellow who never calls a child 'dumbass.'" (Her seasonal suggestion a year later when someone says a guy "needs a kick in the'nads"? "It's Christmas. At holiday time, we say 'he needs a kick in the sleigh bells.'")

Seinfeld turned to Santa in 1994, when NBC's proudly unsentimental comedy of self-absorbed Manhattan pals cast Michael Richards's gonzo neighbor Kramer as the ho-ho-host for store-visiting children. Working with dwarf pal Danny Woodburn as his elf, Richards's Kramer falls under the sway of friend Julia Louis-Dreyfus's new communist boyfriend. He starts telling children the store's toys "are assembled in Taiwan by kids like you," and then sold at "triple the cost.... These capitalist fat cats are inflating the profit margin and reducing your total number of toys!"

The more literally cartoonish Homer Simpson wasn't a much more effective store Santa in 1989 on Fox's very first half-hour episode of *The Simpsons* (billed as "The Simpsons Christmas Special" before the series went weekly the following month). Voiced by the comedically versatile Dan Castellaneta, a moonlighting Homer barely gets through the training program, listing Santa's reindeer as "Dasher, Dancer, Prancer, Nixon." (His stint did give problem son Bart his first chance to drop a catchphrase, while sitting on "Santa's" lap: "I'm Bart Simpson, who the hell are you?") Again desperate for extra money at holiday time 2000, Homer plays "prank monkey" for nuclear plant boss Mr. Burns. After hurling pudding at war heroes and acting up at the zoo in a panda suit, Homer finally draws the line at misbehaving while playing Santa in Springfield's Thanksgiving parade. Insightful daughter Lisa has persuaded him not to sell his soul, so it's Mr. Burns in a Santa suit who pelts spectators with fish guts from the float. *The Simpsons* always could make outrageous gags flow right into moments of emotional sweetness, striking a singular chord of tart absurdity. "Let's just say Lisa gave me an early Christmas present," he tells the family—"the gift of dignity."

That's not something often seen in two ABC sitcoms produced by Bruce Helford. The irreverent *Norm* vehicle for *Saturday Night Live* news spoofer Norm Macdonald actually shot Santa in 1999. Norm's social worker colleague Laurie Metcalf (*Roseanne*) has hated the holiday since childhood "when my mother tried to put her head in my EZ Bake Oven." Trying to restore her faith in Santa, friends climb in her apartment window to leave presents one night, but she fells the "intruder" with a gunshot. Next stop is the hospital, where a gaggle of kid carolers are treated to the would-be

St. Nick screaming in pain from his flesh wound. "To tell you the truth," confides Norm, "Santa's a bit of a drama queen."

Santa was no more popular on Helford's long-running *The Drew Carey Show*, in which blue-collar pals Ryan Stiles and Dietrich Bader often took holiday jobs at the Cleveland store where Carey toiled in a cubicle in charge of personnel. More than once, his friends worked as elves assisting the store Santa; the sight gag of the two gangly men in red tights, green tunics, and huge fake ears proved fairly irresistible. (This made a nice subplot in drama, too. CBS's *Family Law* takes the 2001 case of a six-foot-two-tall man claiming discrimination when a store won't hire him as an elf. The twist there was his going to court represented by dwarf attorney Meredith Eaton.)

On Carey's 1996 Christmas, Stiles and Bader find themselves tormented by a bad Santa who "woke up in the parking lot of the Capri Lounge in a bad way." Stiles snarls at the nasty St. Nick, "You kick me in the ass one more time and I quit!" Santa snaps back, "For 11 months out of the year, I'm just a fat old man. But for one month, I am king. This is my time. Now bring in another kid, and this time, no weapons." Santa's behavior does get the best of his health, though, and before long, he's no longer among the living. "He's still on the throne," Stiles tells Carey, "but we put the ropes around him so the kids can't get in. We told 'em Santa's having a little nap. With his eyes open. 'Cause he's always watching you."

Expired Santas are hardly uncommon. From a collapsed Kris Kringle on NBC's *St. Elsewhere* to Santa-suited corpses to investigate on NBC's *The Pretender* and *Homicide*, the fat man's demise can be quite dramatic. But it's also deftly played for laughs. A queasy-feeling Santa comes into the Bronx doctor's office of cantankerous Ted Danson in CBS's 1999 *Becker*, smoking a cigar and insisting "Hurry up, it's Christmas Eve and I'm Saint friggin' Nick." Then he quietly expires in the waiting room. Told he died peacefully, Becker tartly notes that it happened "on the floor in the Bronx wearing a humiliating costume with a kid pulling on his fake beard." Could things be worse? Becker heads down to identify the body at the city morgue, staffed by creepy *Bonnie and Clyde* costar Michael J. Pollard. "We got a load of Santas in today," sighs Pollard. "We got a Latino Santa, we got a Chinese Santa, we got a Santa with a really weird ear. Feel free to browse."

THE SICKEST SANTA SHOW

Yet for sheer outrageousness, nothing can top the first-season Christmas outing of Fox's impudent family sitcom send-up *Married … with Children*. The show's slovenly suburban Chicago clan debuted in 1987 at the height of success for *The Cosby Show* and its gentle comedy of conscientious parents raising their children right. On NBC's top-ranked hit, Bill Cosby's Brooklyn physician father of five always knew best. On Fox's satiric response, Ed O'Neill's shoe-selling sad sack Al Bundy never did. He was forever the foil for family members keen to talk back and greedily grab everything they could: Katey Sagal's trampy wife Peg; Christina Applegate's slutty, dim daughter Kelly; and David Faustino's scheming son Bud.

These subversive creations of writers Michael Moye and Ron Leavitt attacked Christmas with such merry ferocity that Fox ran an episode-starting disclaimer: "The following depicts a Bundy Christmas. It could be upsetting to small children and others." And no wonder. Son Bud lusts after a TV commercial for the new Lakeside Mall: "We've got six Santas, no waiting, and for you bigger kids, come to the Red Nose Bar and meet Santa's very special reindeer, Donna." Dad Al moans how the new stores are killing his, with "cheap, gaudy merchandise that only appeals to the tasteless, low-class shopper." Cue wife Peg, who enters weighed down with Lakeside Mall shopping bags. ("Peggy, I'm ashamed of you." "I know, Al.")

The new mall ups the ante by having Santa parachute in with gift certificates for a waiting crowd. "Let's trample the weak and get all we can!" cheers Kelly. But it's so late, they can only watch on TV. As the mall's Santa jumps from the helicopter, he drifts off course, his chute doesn't open, and then a thump is heard in the Bundy backyard. Cut to commercial, after which we see the Bundys calmly eating pizza as coroner Michael G. Hagerty retrieves St. Nick's body: "Did anyone actually see him fall?" "Oh, I wish!" chirps Bud. The coroner consoles him, "The real Santa would've never jumped out of a plane with a bottle of muscatel in each hand." He promises Santa will still find Bud's house for Christmas. "It shouldn't be too hard," notes the Bundy boy. "Just follow the buzzards." Mom Peg's enthusiasm remains unflagging. "Cheer up!" she tells everyone. "It could've been worse. He could've landed on the picket fence."

Married … with Children takes no prisoners. The coroner cacklingly takes his leave bouncing a gold ring in his hand: "Here's a little tip from me to you. Don't die with your jewelry on." The Bundys hear another thump—and gleefully glean that Santa's bag of gift certificates has made a delayed drop from a tree into their yard. "A moment of silence," intones dad Al. "'Cause we owe a lot to that jolly, flat man."

Santa Sleeps Around

Santa Claus can sure be a turn-on. Lots of women on TV lust after a guy in a red suit, beard, and big ol' belly. They don't always care who's under the getup. New York City staffer Heather Locklear makes a date with the city hall Santa on ABC's *Spin City in* 2001 without a clue what he actually looks like. Luckily, he's hunky Shawn Christian, later of The WB sun-and-surf drama *Summerland*. Peri Gilpin's randy radio engineer Roz is equally fortunate on NBC's 2002 *Frasier*. The Santa to her toy-drive elf turns out to be ex-Superman Dean Cain of *Lois & Clark*. Still, she doesn't like him nearly as much when he's an everyday investment banker. She's after "the jelly belly."

In some cases, women would rather not know what lies beneath. Kirstie Alley's Manhattan lingerie tycoon has the hots in 1998 for the Santa at Barney's on her NBC sitcom *Veronica's Closet*. Of course, she's just had four martinis and been taunted by business partner Ron Silver that she's "never had a purely frivolous sexual relationship." She confesses the next day to pal Kathy Najimy that "mommy did a lot more than kiss Santa Claus last night." Alley found out "he was good in the sack. I mean literally. Right in the sack. And under the tree, and in the sleigh, and in the housewares department." To her horror, Alley later discovers that inside the costume is Silver's "idiot stepson." Yet she just can't help herself: "Oh my god, I'm Santa's sex slave!" With Elvis Presley singing in the background, "Here Comes Santa Claus" takes on a whole new meaning.

And Rue McClanahan's flirty Blanche on NBC's 1986 senior-age comedy *The Golden Girls* can't help herself, either. Her most recent assignation out-rages Betty White's prim and proper Rose, who dresses down the Santa-clad suitor: "As long as you're in that uniform, the only thing that better be on your mind is giving people what they want for Christmas!" Acerbic roommate Beatrice Arthur has a ready retort. "He was trying to, Rose. I saw Blanche's list."

CHAPTER 8

All I Want for Christmas: Presents and Shopping

Only dopes wait until now. You'd be surprised how many dopes there are. I thought I'd never get out of that store today.

—George Burns on Christmas shopping,
The George Burns & Gracie Allen Show, 1951

Someone should remind her that Christmas is more than barging up and down department store aisles and pushing people out of the way. Someone has to tell her that Christmas is another thing—finer than that.

—Art Carney, *Twilight Zone*, 1960

Ask any modern kid what Christmas brings, and "the birth of Jesus" isn't going to be the first answer. "Goodwill among men" won't be second, either.

It's presents! From toddler time, children gleefully anticipate the annual December load of loot dropped by Santa Claus and all the adults around them. Among the many things it captured perfectly, Jean Shepherd's 1983 big-screen classic *A Christmas Story* starts by recalling its childhood holiday as "lovely, glorious, beautiful Christmas, around which the entire kid year revolved."

Shepherd's Depression-era kid just had to get a BB gun as his big present. Everybody has his or her own specific gift wish. Getting the giving just right is a perpetual Christmas concern in both real life and its TV approximation. Though rarely portrayed in vintage theatrical films, this seasonal quest seemed to rise to a primary concern as 1950s television ushered in a new and more commercial, consumerist, ultra-acquisitive American arche-type.

SHOP TILL YOU DROP

Laurie Metcalf: Is there anything even left on the shelves?

Sara Gilbert: Oh, tons. [Little brother] D.J.'s getting a thousand Q-Tips.

Roseanne: Well, at least you got himself something off his list.

—*Roseanne,* 1992

Then it hit with a bang. Shopping is the ne plus ultra of what may be series TV's first holiday masterpiece, the Christmas episode of CBS's 1950s stalwart *The Jack Benny Program. The* drawling title comedian had built a career in 1920s vaudeville and then 1930s radio out of his penny-pinching ways, so the shopping season was a natural for him to exploit. He did so first on radio, before transferring his aural persona—and many of his existing scripts—to the new visual medium in 1950. Benny's initial live holiday outings were variety-style shows that included monologues about present buying. But in 1954 he assumed the situation comedy format in a half-hour taking place in a department store as Benny dithers about his gift selections—and their prices.

This was a plot he had perfected on radio and altered little as he repeated it in TV form in 1957 and 1960, with virtually the same dialogue and the same repertory cast. Accompanied by his gravelly-voiced valet Eddie "Rochester" Anderson—who notes that last year's present from Benny was "a brand new dollar bill and a lecture on the evils of wine, women, and song"—the eternal tightwad stops first to look at wallets for announcer Don Wilson. Counter clerk Mel Blanc, the cartoon man-of-a-thousand-voices, shows him $1.98 merchandise, but Rochester points out the $40 cowhide model. Uncharacteristically, Benny springs for the top-of-the-line and writes a poem on the gift card: "This gift is from Jackie, oh golly oh shucks, I hope that you like it, it cost 40 bucks." ("Yeah," says Rochester, "it would've been tough to get a rhyme for a dollar ninety-eight.")

The episode then takes a turn to the bizarre. Benny considers a watch for wife Mary, which the saleslady promises is unbreakable crystal, proffering a hammer. "Here, try it out. Go ahead, hit it with the hammer," she urges, which he does—destroying it completely. When he protests to the store manager that she told him to, the clerk dismisses, "You walked in, lotus blossom; nobody dragged you." As Benny heads over to lingerie, that clerk asks Benny, "What size do you wear?" He refuses to touch the merchandise with his bare hands because it makes him "a nervous wreck. Especially the black ones." At yet another stop, clerk Richard Deacon of future *Dick Van Dyke Show* fame insists he's actually a store executive, but "I'm standing behind this counter because in a moment of wild enthusiasm, I sold my pants."

And throughout the half-hour, Benny keeps returning to Blanc's counter with second thoughts about that wallet gift. Initially helpful, Blanc becomes progressively more distressed and finally unhinged by Benny's demands. He's asked to unwrap the gift and, later, even fetch it from the delivery dock. Benny wants to insert a forgotten gift card (Blanc grumbles), change the wording on the card (he whines, "Oh, why did the governor have to give me that pardon?"), add his overlooked signature (he shrieks, "*Now what?*"), and finally change the gift itself. Rochester unfortunately has reminded Benny that it's the spirit of the gift, not the cost, that counts. "Don't tell me you're going to change the card again," weeps a completely disheveled Blanc when he spots Benny coming his way intent to substitute the $1.98 wallet for his $40 misstep. Blanc ultimately pulls out a gun and mopes away behind a wall until we hear an off-screen gunshot. "That's a shame. Such a nice young fella," opines Benny as customers cluster and he eases away from the crowd toward the cash register. "Let's see, a dollar ninety-eight from 40 dollars—I got some change coming."

Viewers can tell all along what's going to happen. We know Benny's stingy persona well. The episode (widely seen today in 1960's final incarnation) progresses like clockwork, honed over two decades of development to a perfect little routine. Benny's every hesitation and Blanc's every realization arrive with an almost delicious satisfaction. Its comedy is, in fact, dependent on the viewer's anticipating and savoring each little expectation. The experience is almost interactive, enveloping us in its gags with the kind of intimacy at which radio excelled and television too seldom succeeds. The entire episode takes place in the confines of one small store section, elaborating one simple notion, off an exceedingly familiar formula. Yet this *Jack Benny Program* bursts with a punch, vitality, and near dizzy lunacy that rewards repeated viewing of its oh-so-simple construct. It's a marvel, really, how the episode gets away with what might otherwise resonate as cruelty. There's even a potential death. And we laugh, and we love it, as it encapsulates the insanity of the modern Christmas shopping experience.

This would prove a hard episode to top, and few that followed with a shopping story would try. Subsequent expeditions almost never took place entirely within a store, for example. The search for the perfect present would become a part of a broader tale, more often involving parents on a quest to find "the" toy of a particular season to satisfy a kid's single-minded desperation (and thorough commercial indoctrination). In fictional representations of crazes along the lines of Cabbage Patch Kids, Tickle Me Elmo, and Furby, ABC's 1990 *Family Matters* wanted a Freddy Teddy, NBC's 1995 *Frasier* sought an Outlaw Laser RoboGeek, and Fox's 2001 *Grounded for Life* was after the Astro Jammer Battle Buggy.

Adults go bonkers seeking fad toys in hour dramas, too. CBS's 1999 *Martial Law* has parents, robbers, and cops chasing a stuffed armadillo named Armando, in one of which is hidden a stolen computer chip detailing stealth fighter technology. The Atomic Space Rat is the much-sought-after prize in a fanciful 1994 outing of ABC's *Lois & Clark*. The rat shoots stinky stuff that turns out to be "a highly sophisticated psychotropic mind-altering drug," as Teri Hatcher's crack reporter Lois Lane discovers. It turns all the adults of Metropolis into "gimme" children as part of a plot for "ruining Christmas" by disenchanted toymaker Sherman Hemsley. He reasons, "It's not as if we're foisting something on the public they don't want, are we? And in the meantime, if people become the scabrous, obtuse, jealous, greedy, nasty bunch of prepubescents they are anyway, well then, all the better."

When shoppers aren't jostling for the year's hot toy, they're scrambling for last-minute gifts. Some get locked in stores, like comedy star Monique in UPN's 2001 *The Parkers*. Some break into stores, like Patrick Duffy and Suzanne Somers in ABC's 1993 *Step by Step*. Some are forced to resort to the all-night corner drugstore, after no-presents pacts are suddenly broken on ABC's *Barney Miller* in 1976 ("Hey, you got the razor!" enthuses Ron Glass as detective squad colleagues pull products out of his plain brown grab bag) and on CBS's *Murphy Brown* in 1990.

The most novel shopping disaster could be that befalling Ted Danson's misanthropic doctor on CBS's 2000 *Becker*. Spotting an ornament on a store tree that matches one his Bronx diner pal Terry Farrell cherishes from her youth, Danson wades into an elaborate Christmas village display, but throws out his back when he reaches for it. The holiday hater—who's been preaching "no expectations, no disappointments"—ends up prostrate as part of the chirping, dancing, maddeningly repetitive display as a sour manager throws a blanket of fake snow over him till paramedics arrive. A scared boy calls him mean Mr. Angry Head, which makes Danson more incensed: "It's *Doctor* Angry Head." And the village train keeps circling around to smack into his head.

But for others, a Christmas shopping excursion provides a rare respite from the crush of everyday responsibilities. Especially if you're the president of the United States. In NBC's *The West Wing* in 1999, Martin Sheen's Jed Bartlet delights in being able to "sneak out every now and then. A couple of [Secret Service] agents, an unmarked black Suburban, they tell the manager, they clear the store, I'm in, I'm out." He wants Bradley Whitford's aide Josh to "take an hour and come shopping with us." Moans Josh, "An hour with you in a rare book store? Couldn't you just drop me off the top of the Washington Monument instead?" "It's Christmas, Josh," the president says cheerily. "There's no reason we can't do both." Sheen's former college professor is in his element, but nobody else's, savoring first editions of viviscalic poems translated from Latin and classical tales by freed slaves of Roman emperors. As John Spencer's chief of staff deadpans, "Nothing says Christmas like animal fables in iambic verse."

TOYS AND GOODIES ON HIS SLEIGH

In my house, we don't give gifts. No way. Every Christmas, my grandparents and I take something from each other and hide it. Then on Christmas morning, we look for it. And if we find it, we're so happy, it's like a gift.

—Merritt Buttrick, *Square Pegs*, 1982

By this time tomorrow, millions of Americans knee deep in tinsel and wrapping paper will utter those heartfelt words: Is this all I got?

—Kelsey Grammer, *Cheers*, 1987

The perfect gift. Everybody wants to give it, and everybody wants to get it.

So how come so many TV characters end up getting burial plots for the holidays? It happens on ABC's *Ellen* in 1995 as Ellen DeGeneres rushes her parents to the airport. The bookstore owner is already feeling down because they're going on a Caribbean cruise instead of holding the usual family celebration. And now their last-minute gift to her turns out to be Section C, Row 7 of—Forest Hills cemetery? "Right in the heart of Sherman Oaks, minutes from the freeway," promises mom, inspiring Ellen to moan, "I'm gonna spend my Christmas Eve working on my will."

The graveyard is only hallucinatory in CBS's *Yes, Dear*, but it's a good deal more sinister. This sitcom about two distinctly different sisters and their young families—one professional, one working class—compounds the chaos with two sets of grandparents visiting for Christmas 2001. Husband

Anthony Clark's folks announce that although they're separated, they've purchased the plots around theirs in the cemetery for their kids. After Clark shocks himself installing a lighted Santa figure, he dreams he's trapped in a coffin with all four warring parents-in-law. Relieved to awaken in his own home, he's blindsided again when they tell him they're no longer competing with each other for the grandchildren's affections. "That's why we decided," says grandma Vicki Lawrence, "we're all going to be buried together."

Nonplussing presents are a TV staple. So are nonmaterial ones. On ABC's *8 Simple Rules* in 2002, mom Katey Sagal gets a much-wished-for church choir solo, daughter Kaley Cuoco gets to have her boyfriend over, and dad John Ritter gets to have the best decorated house on Oakdale Avenue after his family finds a way to blow out the lights on the rival Doyles' house. ABC's *Family Matters* in 1990 finds Jaleel White's teen nerd Steve Urkel pining, as always, after uninterested neighbor Laura. When he's finally invited next door for the holiday, he's gotten his wish, "to spend Christmas with my favorite people in the world, the Winslows." In NBC's 1982 *Taxi*, Judd Hirsch's cab driver Alex feels stuck with morose ex-wife Louise Lasser until she announces, "About New Year's Eve—you don't have to see me. It's my Christmas gift to you." A similar sentiment on Fox's ruthless *Married . . . with Children* gets twisted in 1989 on the way from lazy wife Katey Sagal to sad-sack husband Ed O'Neill: "Oh, honey, I know what would make you feel better. But I'll never leave you, not in a million years." On ABC's *Soul Man* in 1997, minister Dan Aykroyd facetiously tells his kids he'd like "peace on earth, goodwill toward men, and one less child. I'll let you work that out among yourselves."

Robin Williams's naïve alien Mork from Ork ends up giving spiritual gifts on ABC's 1978 *Mork & Mindy* after his homemade crafts fail to impress (like a portrait of Liberace made out of old bubblegum: "I painted each wad myself"). When Pam Dawber's Mindy explains it's the thought that counts, Mork realizes, "I should have given you one of those for Christmas." And he holds a hand over Mindy and each of her family members to envelop them in a wonderful memory. Mindy's dad Conrad Janis savors his: "You just made me remember the first time I held my newborn daughter. My hands were so large and clumsy, I just couldn't believe anything so tiny could make me so happy. Thank you, Mork."

Life itself is a powerful present. Even when it's a schmaltzy one. On CBS's long-running half-hour heart-tugger *Lassie*, the title collie is hit by a car at Christmas 1958, leaving child owner Jon Provost to pray for her recovery as hymns swell in the background and his farmer parents issue a radio appeal for a veterinarian to come help. As if that isn't enough, the children of their rural town gather outside the family barn with their own animals—goose, rabbit, cat—until Lassie awakens after surgery. "You did it, Dr. Watkins," gushes Provost's little Timmy. "You made her well. That's my best Christmas present. You're a real Santy Claus."

Combining sentiment and surprise does the trick in 1966 on CBS's city/rural culture-clash comedy *Green Acres*. Eva Gabor's urbane wife gives farmer husband Eddie Albert a taste of the old-fashioned Christmas for which he longs. As Pat Buttram's Mr. Haney wonders, "City folks sure are peculiar—a wife giving her husband a bag of soap flakes for a Christmas present?" the wheeler-dealer sits on the roof throwing the flakes down past the window, and Albert gets his holiday "snow."

But it isn't always that easy to know what your friends and family members would like to receive for Christmas. "Frasier, you're always giving people things that you think they should like, instead of things that they really like," points out John Mahoney's just-folks dad to Kelsey Grammer's high-toned title character on NBC's 1995 *Frasier*. All of dad's gifts from recent years are still in their original boxes. "It's like when you were a kid, remember, I wanted you to love baseball. I wanted to get you a bat and glove, everything for Christmas, but you had your mind set on a microscope, so that's what I got you." ("And then when dad took us to a game," observes brother David Hyde Pierce, "you spent the whole time looking for rodent hairs in your hotdog.") As it turns out, what Frasier really would like for Christmas is the year's hot Outlaw Laser Robogeek toy to give to his son—and luckily, that's what Martin gives him.

Faith Ford's supermom on ABC's sitcom *Hope & Faith* tries implementing guidelines for her family's secret Santa exchange in 2004. It should be "a present the person needs but doesn't know they need, a present the person wants but doesn't know they want, and finally a present the person doesn't have but thinks they do." Argues more footloose sister Kelly Ripa, "I know you mean well, but nobody wants to pick a present the person thinks they have but don't. Nobody knows what that means. That's why it's always batteries!"

Some characters take personally the gift-giving mistakes they've experienced. "I don't wanna be cheap like my dad was when I was a kid," says hardscrabble family man Mike O'Malley on *Yes, Dear* in 2000. "Instead of buying me a Lionel train, he made me one out of his old cigarette cartons. Called it the low-tar express." Roseanne isn't all that thrilled with what she gets, either, on ABC's 1992 *Roseanne*. Grandma Shelley Winters coughs up only a salad spinner and a cutting board in the shape of a rooster. "Well, I don't mean to sound ungrateful or anything, but these gifts suck," squawks the cranky comedian, who notices her cousins seem to be getting some good stuff. Winters argues, "Eventually, I'm gonna have to go live with somebody. They got a pool." Deadpans Roseanne, "Just promise us that you'll linger long enough to be a huge burden."

The meaning behind the present can also be the problem. When Alexis Bledel's brainy high schooler in The WB's 2000 *Gilmore Girls* buys Kafka's *Metamorphosis* for her would-be boyfriend, her best friend warns "a book sends the wrong message." Tony Danza's slick lawyer on CBS's *Family Law* buys beef filets for the woman he's romancing in 2001. "You don't send a person that you're sleeping with meat," scorns girlfriend Salli Richardson. "They're free range," insists Danza—who turns out to be right. "It's unbelievable," Richardson later gushes to a colleague, whose taste-test reaction is "Jesus, Mary, and Joseph! The man loves you."

Even the charity donation-in-your-name strategy can rile some recipients. "I got him Yankee tickets, he got me a piece of paper saying 'I've given your gift to someone else'!" seethes Jason Alexander on NBC's 1997 *Seinfeld*, way too exercised about receiving such a charity notice. "Don't you see how wrong that is!" he fumes to pal Jerry Seinfeld. Alexander makes up his own "charity" called the Human Fund to get out of his gift obligations, but this being *Seinfeld* and him being schlub George Costanza, his "fake Christmas gift" efforts backfire.

The idea that gift giving should somehow always be equal fuels the 1995 holiday for NBC's radio station office sitcom *NewsRadio*. Owner Stephen Root gives his staff members each a sports car—except for forlorn screwup Andy Dick. "I remembered that you once mentioned you liked old-time radio comedies," says Root. "Well, I got you the best old time radio comedy of them all, *Fibber McGee and Molly*." After Dick sulks with his box of *Fibber* tapes, it turns out Root gave him not tapes of the show but the show itself, "the rights to the show and all the characters in it." Not quite so cheesy.

The scales of gift giving never do seem to balance on CBS's *The King of Queens*, in which cameras cause conniptions in 2000. After Kevin James gets one for wife Leah Remini, her boss gives her a better one. So they give the cheaper one to a friend—but that angers her husband, who gave her one even cheaper than that. "This camera's bitten me in the ass twice!" gripes James. "I'm out of ass cheeks!" The gift round revolves again in 2002, as Remini gets dad Jerry Stiller a cruise instead of the "old man cap" she usually buys. When Stiller finds out, "damn her, now I'll have to get her a nice gift, too," instead of the chopsticks he lifted from the Cantonese Hut. But then Remini needs money to buy something for a friend she thinks is getting her something expensive: "How's it going to look when she hands me a leather jacket and I hand her a Lady Gillette gift pack?" So she has to cancel her dad's cruise. Now he's gotten her something great. And her friend didn't get her anything so pricey, after all. Nobody's gift giving came out even.

But those are minor discomforts compared to the gift that gets James Gandolfini's New Jersey mobster Tony Soprano worked up on HBO's *The Sopranos* in 2001. Gandolfini has spent the holiday episode haunted by memories of Vincent Pastore's late friend and fellow wiseguy Big Pussy, whom Soprano's crew rubbed out for squealing to the feds. Pussy had always played Santa. But he has also previously tortured Tony in hallucinations, when his voice seemed to emanate from dead fish at the market after his body was sent "to the fishes" off a boat in the Atlantic. So what should Soprano's loving daughter buy for her dad as a Christmas gift? A Big Mouth Billy Bass, one of those singing mechanical fish that wriggles on a wall plaque. "It's cute" is all he can choke out. "Thanks, honey."

THE AGONY OF GIVING

Contemptuous kid in toy store: The Living Brain! What kind of dork wants that?

Kelsey Grammer: With any luck, the kind of dork who'll be operating on your prostate someday.

—*Frasier*, 1995

The all-time series champ for gift-giving agony has to be CBS's long-running *Everybody Loves Raymond*, that hilariously incisive saga of Long Island family man Ray Romano, long-suffering wife Patricia Heaton, and his parents and brother who barge in from across the street. Its 1996 first-season episode finds Ray distressed to discover his childhood Mickey Mantle–signed baseball isn't authentic, though it turns out his dad knew he wanted it so badly that he went to great lengths to give it. Two seasons later, his parents actually take Ray's present of a toaster back to the store, neglecting to notice how he'd gone to the thought and trouble of engraving it to them.

But *Raymond*'s sharpest gift scenarios were its next two. "The Christmas Picture" in 1999 worked Romano up to a frenzy in his attempt to get the entire clan to sit for a family portrait. When his wife's parents show up, never-happy mom Doris Roberts starts her passive-aggressive pouting. "You had to know that my mom would go all *Dog Day Afternoon* on us if your parents were in her picture," he rages to Heaton. "This is so typical of your mother," she snarls back, "it's either her way or no way.... Well, guess what? Not this time." Romano is about to burst a blood vessel: "This is the first gift I'm getting her that even has a chance of working. Remember the toaster, huh? The aquarium? The fruit of the friggin' month club? Don't you see? I thought she would like this because she told me she would!" Romano races among them all, trying to coax, cajole, and implore, until he throws what brother Brad Garrett calls "a hissy fit"—the only thing the entire family can agree upon, finally uniting in laughing at Raymond's predicament.

"Christmas Presents" in 2000 has him buttering up Heaton with a fancy Cuisinart set so she'll agree he can golf with his pals while she cares for the kids. But she gives him an expensive DVD player, and pampers him for the holiday. "What is she up to? What's she sucking up to me for?" he obsesses, finally confronting her: "I want to know what's going on with the kissing and the marshmallows and the letting me play golf and the big expensive DVD player." "You think that I got you that DVD thing because I want something?" "Noooo," he counters sarcastically, "because you lovvvve me. Come on, what is it? What do you want?" She finally figures, "Have you ever gotten me a present without expecting something in return? You know, the worst part isn't that you're a manipulative jerk, it's that you think I'm like you!...Do you know how close you are to the end of your life?"

Ray outsmarts himself, however, by telling her she's a martyr. "Why, after years of complaining that all I do is lay around and watch television, do you buy me a device that is designed to make the television watching experience even better? We must ask ourselves, whyyyy?" But she agrees: "What is wrong with me?...I work too hard. I don't need to be a martyr." Suddenly, golf is going down the drain. "How can I not think of myself as a martyr," she asks, "if I'm stuck at home with the kids by myself while you're out golfing with your buddies? Thank you. 'Cause you really helped me. This was a great Christmas."

It's the "credit" for the present that causes consternation in 2002, when the brothers share paying for mom's gift in unequal portions. That debate evolves into another tussle when their wives think their husbands gave them gifts less thoughtful than mom's. Finally, Ray's 2003 presentation to his dad—jazz CDs to replace record albums damaged decades earlier—opens up old wounds about how the records got ruined in the first place. Maybe it wasn't Ray's fault, as he's been led all his life to believe. *Everybody Loves Raymond* always had an incisive feel for portraying the way Christmas magnifies family ties (and trouble), the way it lays bare resentments, the way even the sharing and caring of gift giving becomes a divisive barometer used to measure where we rank in our loved ones' affections. *Raymond* knew how to make us see ourselves in this sorry syndrome—and laugh at it, anyway, all the harder. That was probably the most precious gift of all.

Gift of the Magi

O. Henry's short story "The Gift of the Magi" isn't quite a TV-knockoff favorite on the level of A Christmas Carol or It's a Wonderful Life, but it remains a familiar source for plot lines. The 1906 tale of a husband who sells his watch to buy combs for his wife's exquisitely long hair—and a wife who sells her hair to buy him a chain for his watch—offers a twist ending that tugs at the heart as much as Scrooge's epiphany or George Bailey's renewed gratitude.

It provides a tearjerker and a half in the first season of Michael Landon's NBC pioneer-family period drama Little House on the Prairie in 1974. For the first Christmas in their new frontier homestead, the three girls of the Ingalls family are determined to give memorable gifts to hard-working parents Landon and Karen Grassle. "We don't have money to buy presents," cautions mom. "If it's going to be special, we're going to have to make it that way ourselves." So middle daughter Melissa Gilbert sells her beloved pony to a grasping neighbor girl to buy her mother a stove. Meanwhile, dad Landon is hiding his present to "half-pint": a saddle for the pony. The rest of the brood, too, works late and long to make or trade for simple gifts that represent much more in their hardscrabble lives than the mall-bought holiday hauls taken in by celebrants today. The Ingalls's yearnings resonate because they're emotionally grounded, intensely meaningful, and expressive of the life and love at the heart of the religious holiday.

Plain presents make a modern personal statement in The Honeymooners, the sketch concept that debuted on Jackie Gleason's live 1950s variety hour and later aired as a CBS situation comedy for one season, yielding the "classic 39" filmed episodes that repeat to this day. Gleason's bus driver Ralph Kramden sells his bowling ball to buy wife Alice a present for Christmas 1955, while Audrey Meadows' Alice has bought him a bag for that prized new ball. The "Magi" connection isn't quite complete: He gives her an orange juicer shaped like Napoleon's head, "and the juice squirts out his ears," as Ralph announces. But the ironic sentiment is there. Gleason's pride is palpable as the cash-strapped everyman finally comes up with what he thinks is an amazing gift, after having first stumbled in buying a mere trinket he was hoodwinked into believing was an Asian objet d'art.

A couple that wasn't married and wasn't even a couple goes at the "Magi" angle, too. ABC's 1986 Who's the Boss? has executive Judith Light searching for a baseball card depicting housekeeper Tony Danza in his brief sports career. She thinks he doesn't have one, but only because he told an inquisitive friend he didn't, in order to hang onto it. Now that she's promised a card dealer she'll pay $325 for it, the dealer calls Tony, who sells it to get enough money to buy her an expensive Tiffany's vase. He gets the card back from her, of course, and she's moved at his effort: "I didn't realize how beautiful this vase really is."

Gene Anthony Ray's dancer Leroy on the syndicated performing-school drama *Fame* tries to impress his devoted little poor niece when she comes to visit in 1986. "All Tina knows about Christmas is seeing everybody else have a good time," he tells a friend, who's amazed he's trying to buy her a $300 dollhouse. But Leroy works so hard to earn the money that Tina never gets to see him. "I just wanted to do something special for you for Christmas," he tells the sad child, who explains, "You're the only special thing in my life, and I'm not even enjoying that anymore." He asks her forgiveness for forgetting "the most important thing to me."

The two most important things to *Sesame Street* Muppet pals Bert and Ernie are at the heart of a true "Magi" twist on public TV's 1978 family special *Christmas Eve on Sesame Street*. All the urban neighborhood characters from the preschool education series are preparing for the holiday in separate sequences—Big Bird wondering how Santa gets down those "skinny chimneys," Cookie Monster trying to write to Santa (but he gobbles up his pencil and then his typewriter). That's when each of the Muppet roommates has a brainstorm about the other's holiday present. Bert thinks, "I'll get Ernie a soap dish to put his rubber ducky in!" while Ernie decides, "I'll get him a cigar box to keep his paper clip collection in!" But that's easier said than done. Shopping at Mr. Hooper's, Ernie tells the store keeper, "I don't have any money, but suppose I gave you rubber ducky here for that cigar box." Bert is "prepared to trade you this terrific paper clip collection for just one small soap dish, color pink."

So what happens when they exchange presents? Luckily, Will Lee as Mr. Hooper arrives with presents of his own—a paper clip collection for Bert, a rubber ducky for Ernie. Bert worries, "We didn't get Mr. Hooper anything." "You're wrong, boys," says the old man. "I got the best Christmas present ever. I got to see that everyone got exactly what they wanted for Christmas."

CHAPTER 9

An "Old-Fashioned" Christmas: Yearning for Simpler Times

The tawdry trivialization and cheap commercialization of perhaps the most sacred moment in human history indeed typifies the decay and decline of Western civilization as we know it.

—John Hillerman, *Magnum, P.I.,* 1983

Enrico Colantoni: Christmas, it's depressing. It's gotten so commercial, it's lost all its spiritual meaning.

David Spade: No, it hasn't. This is such a cliché.

George Segal (arriving): Check it out! Lollipops in the shape of Jesus!

Colantoni (reading label): 'My Sweet Lord.' Somebody's going to hell.

—*Just Shoot Me,* 1998

Christmas has gotten too commercial. We hear it all the time. But since when is this terrible shift supposed to have taken place? Characters in TV's earliest days were already decrying the gift-grabbing, tinsel-obsessed culture of the modern holiday.

In 1954's first-season holiday outing of *Father Knows Best* on CBS, Robert Young's otherwise understanding dad gripes about wife Jane Wyatt keeping a gift list in order to give only to those who give them presents. "It seems to me it's just becoming a matter of bookkeeping," he moans. "Why can't we have Christmas the way it used to be? Quiet. Simple. A few friends of the family sitting around the fire, the kids hanging their stockings over the fireplace, church bells ringing on Christmas Eve, carolers singing."

The only street carols he hears are the ones booming from a van loud-speaker as son Bud hawks "Big Steve's Used Car Lot, your used car Santa Claus." "Selling stuff is not the purpose of Christmas," Young insists. He's also not happy that teen Betty wants a pink tree, while nine-year-old Kathy wants purple. "My dad used to take me up into the hills and we'd cut down our own Christmas tree," he maintains. So that's what the family clambers into the car to do.

But they run into a snowstorm, of course, and seek refuge in a mountain cabin, where they find a forest hermit with a white beard (of course) named Nick (naturally). As Betty mopes about missing a holiday party, Kathy tear-ily moans, "It's Christmas Eve, and Santy won't ever find us up here." Bud heads out with Nick, played by Wallace Ford, to chop the family a truly fresh tree, which inspires knowing-best father to wonder, "Nick, do you have magazines we can cut up, or corn to pop? We'll make our own decora-tions, the way we used to!"

The family rallies round, even as the local ranger arrives to confide to Young and Wyatt that Nick is actually a squatter in someone else's lodge. Father knows enough to pay his bills for him, while asking the ranger to keep quiet that they know. "We'd like him to still think that he's our host." When sleepy young Kathy spies Nick out back with a sack slung over his shoulder, petting a deer while standing near a sleigh, she's convinced she's seen Santa Claus. "Oh, Daddy," she cries, her voice breaking, "I feel kind of all shivery inside." "That's all right, baby," hugs Young. "You know some-thing? So do I."

It's schmaltz, all right. But schmaltz in a time that seemed made for it, in black and white—both literally and figuratively—with background music ever swelling to touch those heartstrings. The story is told simply and sincerely by writers Roswell Rogers and Paul West, and the cast plays it so directly that its emotional tug endures decades later. The same tale certainly endured in its own decade. A similar script of "a simple, old-fash-ioned Christmas" in the mountains had been used in 1953 on radio (where Young had been doing *Father Knows Best* since 1949 with a different sup-porting cast). The 1954 TV episode was repeated in subsequent seasons as a holiday flashback.

Other 1950s families were similarly nostalgic. The title mom is appalled in ABC's *The Donna Reed Show* in 1958 when she hears her kids parsing how they'll give what to whom. Teen Shelley Fabares doesn't know whom to buy for because she doesn't know who's bought for her. Younger brother

Paul Petersen grumbles that a friend got him a "crummy" present "for 35 cents! I spent a dollar on him." As Donna sighs to Carl Betz's husband Alex, "Mary has to be sure she'll get before she gives, Jeff keeps a profit and loss ledger.... Was Christmas always like this?" As far away as Morocco on 1955's syndicated kids' adventure *Captain Gallant of the Foreign Legion,* officer Buster Crabbe's real-life son Cullen goes on about the presents and tree that to him represent Christmas. "It's a lot more than that," corrects Crabbe. "It's peace in the hearts of men of goodwill everywhere."

Even that beacon of holiday spirit, CBS's 1965 animated classic "A Charlie Brown Christmas," finds its hero depressed about the season. "'Find the true meaning of Christmas,'" he reads from a flyer being distributed by Snoopy. "'Win money, money, money. Spectacular, supercolossal, neighborhood Christmas lights and display contest.' Lights and display contest! Oh, no—my own dog gone commercial." Speaking of which, NBC's late-1960s quick-cut lampoon *Rowan & Martin's Laugh-In* kept viewers informed in a screen-bottom graphics crawl when they'd reached the point of only "34,000 commercials till Christmas."

Eddie Albert's character was already grousing about "an old-fashioned Christmas" even before he and city wife Eva Gabor decamped to rural Hooterville in *Green Acres,* CBS's famously surreal 1960s sitcom. As seen in a 1966 holiday episode flashback, the chic urban couple had been Christmas tree shopping on the streets of Manhattan when Albert's well-to-do attorney expressed outrage about paying $42 (then a week's pay for a working man) for a tree that was, even more offensively, colored white. "Oh, you want a green one?" offered the seller, pulling out a can of spray paint.

"These trees are a travesty on Christmas!" declaimed Albert, noting that in the "real" world, "Farmers are going out into their own fields, chopping down their own trees. In the kitchen, the wives are baking fruitcakes and stringing their own popcorn. These people are having a real old-fashioned Christmas!" The seller had to ask Gabor, "He's been hitting the eggnog a little early, isn't he?"

Much of America would have agreed. Nostalgia for the "traditional" Christmas already ran strong in holiday hearts, as it continues to in the twenty-first century. But most celebrants then as now were enjoying a much more modern yule, with plastic this, artificial that, the newest/latest of something else. And happily so. The 1966 Christmas episode of *Green Acres,* for all its loopy meanderings, beautifully encapsulates both sides of this perpetual debate: the wistful yearning for down-to-earth customs that may never have existed so pervasively in the first place, and the other-hand delight in the wonders of modernity. The "simple" country folk of

Hooterville can't fathom Albert's backward thinking, as expressed by Pat Buttram's hard-sell peddler Mr. Haney when he discovers the citified farmer outdoors dutifully cutting his own Christmas tree. "Doggone," squawks the drawling hillbilly, "you sure go out of your way to make folks think you're addled."

Mr. Haney's idea of Christmas joy is the transistorized necktie/radio he's selling: "If anybody says your tie is too loud, you can just turn it down." The Hooterville store doesn't even carry those "old aluminum trees" anymore, preferring the new ones that come with "genuine spruce spray" for "automatic oozers" that "ooze imitation sap." Their popularity in the sticks eventually confuses Arnold Ziffel, the school-going pig who goes everywhere with parent-owners Fred and Doris Ziffel. "Oh," Doris explains when Arnold starts nuzzling the Douglases's real pine, "he thinks all trees are squirters."

Albert's 1960s yearning for old-time festivity was updated into an insistence on a soulful "old-school Christmas" two generations later in Fox's thoroughly contemporary *The Bernie Mac Show*. The 2003 holiday outing of the stand-up comedian's sitcom finds him bemoaning the gift lust of the nephew and two nieces he's taken into his Hollywood mansion due to his Chicago sister's drug woes. "When I was your age," the Mac-man rants, "we didn't have malls, we didn't have no walking cell phones, Jesus didn't have six pockets on swaddling clothes," like the window display at the mall. "They didn't have no fleece in Bethlehem!" For him, as for Robert Young 50 years earlier, "the old-school Christmas is about tradition. It's about all of us going to pick out our own tree, making our own ornaments, then on Christmas Eve going to see the lights on Candy Cane Lane and come home to a family dinner."

"When I think about it," Bernie reminisces with the audience in one of his in-the-den chats directly to the camera, "I don't remember the gifts, I remember the times. That's what sticks with you, America. That's what I gotta show them kids." Easier said than done. They're much more into providing him with model numbers to receive the exact presents they want. "Christmas is just one big-ass commercial!" he roars. With the kids bored by their guardian's entreaties to make a gingerbread house, trim the tree and drink eggnog, Bernie eventually dumps their presents unwrapped in their room, takes down all the decorations and announces "Christmas is canceled!" But while Bernie and his wife are out looking at lights on Christmas Eve, the kids put the decorations back up, patch together his broken gingerbread house and even cook up their own eggnog ("tasted worse than milk of magnesia," he reports). When Bernie arrives home to a delayed display of his desired enthusiasm, he's bearing the hamburgers that nephew Jordan had earlier requested for Christmas dinner. "It'll be our new Mac tradition," he says, having in turn adapted his old-school to the kids' new-school yule.

If kids seem to be getting more cynical about the holiday, it's not just because they're so excited about the trappings, à la *Father Knows Best* or *Bernie Mac,* where they simply overlook the holiday's "real meaning"—which itself is often just another modern symbol to which the grown-ups have built up a personal attachment (perhaps a fresh-cut pine). No, these kids are hip to the business into which Christmas has evolved. As poor little rich boy Butch Patrick declares to his rock and roll babysitters on NBC's 1967 yule with *The Monkees,* "I've always felt that if one stripped away all the tinsel of Christmas, underneath you'd find nothing but more tinsel." On Fox's 1991 schoolroom send-up *Drexell's Class,* venal teacher Dabney Coleman hears from a student that the holiday has been "created by desperate merchants to boost year-end profits in even the most sluggish of economies." The caustic wit of The WB's 1999 high school satire *Popular* is encapsulated in another classroom yuletide diatribe, from Tammy Lynn Michaels's spoiled trend-chaser Nicole: "It's the time of year when the suicide rate is highest, when lonely, deluded people pretend to feel comfort and joy and then crash two weeks later because all they're left with is credit card debt. Christmas is just a silly holiday kept alive to bolster the national economic index and relieve a little guilt."

But none of these cut as deep as the ruminations of Kevin Anderson's activist young Father Ray on ABC's 1997 parish drama *Nothing Sacred.* As his staffers bustle about, decorating the tree and arguing over who preaches at midnight mass, Ray is in a funk about it all. "What if we celebrated Christmas like the first one? No expectations, no plans. Just like Joseph and Mary, making it up as they go along." Replies his Jewish business manager, "You know, deforestation seems like an odd way for God to want His birth to be celebrated." Says Ray, "There were no Christmas trees in the first Christmas." "Trees aren't part of the story?" "And neither were the pre-Christmas sales, and the post-Christmas sales, and the competitive gift giving, or the tinsel.... And there were no homilies," he reminds the I-want-to-preach combatants. They include an agitating nun, who is told by another priest that only "ordained persons" can do that. "And there were no ordained persons," adds Ray, taking Christmas back to its true basics—the originating ones.

Celebrating the Commercial Spirit of Christmas

Not everyone thinks Christmas is too commercial. The four self-obsessed third-graders at the heart of Comedy Central's scathingly adult animated satire *South Park* despair that "the commercialism has been sucked out of Christmas" in their scatological 2000 holiday outing, "A Very Crappy Christmas." When their annual visit from Mr. Hankey, the talking piece of Christmas excrement, fails to materialize, the boys track him down in the sewer, where he's moping with his drunken wife (and the little "nuggets") that "it's like Christmas doesn't matter anymore." Even TV anchormen are announcing "it appears that everyone is officially sick of Christmas." So green-capped pal Kyle suggests, "We can get everyone back into the Christmas spirit by making our very own animated Christmas special." Pipes up blue-hatted Stan, "We can call it 'The Spirit of Christmas'!"

That, of course, is an inside joke: Series creators Trey Parker and Matt Stone got the gig when Comedy Central execs saw their wickedly irreverent five-minute "video Christmas card" by that name, in which Christmas claimants (and South Park residents) Jesus and Santa battle it out in front of the greedy little boys to "settle" their rivalry. The two icons eventually reconcile (after much cartoon brutality), by which time the boys have come to see, as their self-made special also proclaims, that "Christmas is about something much more important—presents."

"That is the spirit of Christmas—commercialism," realizes Stan's dad Randy, visibly moved by the boys' celluloid sentiments. "It's what makes our country work." Agrees teacher Mrs. Choksondik, "We got so caught up in the little things of Christmas, like love and family, that we almost forgot, it's buying things that makes our economy thrive." The guys behind *South Park* should know. Their little cartoon continues to be a multi-million-dollar TV/DVD/merchandise empire.

Vivian Vance, Lucille Ball, Desi Arnaz and William Frawley all play Santa on CBS's 1956 holiday episode of *I Love Lucy*. *CBS/Photofest*

Danny Thomas cuts up with TV kids Sherry Jackson and Rusty Hamer on ABC's *Make Room for Daddy* in 1956. *ABC/Photofest*

The Nelsons—Rick, David, Ozzie and Harriet—as themselves in ABC's long-running '50s-'60s sitcom *The Adventures of Ozzie & Harriet*. *ABC/Photofest*

Elizabeth Montgomery's witchy character conjures up the real Santa Claus on ABC's 1960s hit *Bewitched*. *ABC/Photofest*

Even (talking) horses
celebrate the season
on CBS's whimsical
'60s favorite *Mr. Ed*,
with Connie Hines
and Alan Young.
CBS/Photofest

Jon Provost plays
with the collie star of
CBS's half-hour drama
Lassie in 1958.
CBS/Photofest

Art Carney stars in CBS's 1960 *Twilight Zone* episode "The Night of the Meek" as a down-and-out department store Santa who discovers a magic bag of presents. *CBS/Photofest*

The Cartwright clan of NBC's 1960s western smash *Bonanza* includes Dan Blocker, Pernell Roberts, Lorne Greene and Michael Landon. *NBC/Photofest*

Christmas animation arrives in prime time in 1962 with NBC's musical hour "Mr. Magoo's Christmas Carol." *Photofest*

"Rudolph the Red-Nosed Reindeer" becomes a holiday perennial in 1964 as Burl Ives narrates NBC's stop-motion saga. *Golden Books/Photofest*

Charlie Brown and Linus assess their sad little tree in CBS's touching 1965 half-hour "A Charlie Brown Christmas." *United Feature Syndicate*

Bing Crosby's real-life family made yule appearances through the '60s and '70s in specials and variety series like ABC's "The Hollywood Palace." *ABC/Photofest*

"The Judy Garland Christmas Show" on CBS in 1963 was a homey hour with kids Liza Minnelli, Joey Luft and Lorna Luft. *CBS/Photofest*

Andy Williams and wife Claudine Longet gathered their kids and family annually for TV yules like this 1971 event, staged after the couple separated. *ABC/Photofest*

Variety shows were a dying breed by 1977, when old-time crooner Bing Crosby and glam rocker David Bowie teamed for an unlikely duet. *CBS/Photofest*

Bob Hope's NBC specials endured into the '90s, with Reba McEntire. *NBC/Photofest*

Variety reborn: Eddie Murphy sends up both Christmas and kids' show host Mister Rogers in '80s skits on NBC's *Saturday Night Live*. *NBC/Photofest*

One of series TV's best *Christmas Carol* salutes: Tony Randall and Jack Klugman on ABC's *The Odd Couple* in 1970. *ABC/Photofest*

Tim Reid's Venus Flytrap makes an unusual St. Nick in 1979 for CBS's rock 'n' roll sitcom *WKRP in Cincinnati. CBS/Photofest*

Dennis Franz's cantankerous Andy Sipowicz is drafted to serve as Santa in ABC's gritty 1993 *NYPD Blue. ABC/Photofest*

Christmas always brings commotion for Ray Romano's fractiously funny family on CBS's *Everybody Loves Raymond*. *CBS/Photofest*

Flights of fancy and fantasy: John C. McGinley gets Grinch-y on NBC's *Scrubs* in 2001. *NBC/Photofest*

The Simpsons actually premiered as a half-hour Fox series in December 1989 with a Christmas episode.
Fox Broadcasting/ Photofest

David Schwimmer's attempt to interest his son in Hanukkah on NBC's Friends in 2000 ends with him playing the holiday armadillo.
NBC/Photofest

Chrismukkah is the 21st century holiday of Fox's *The O.C.*, celebrated by Adam Brody and Rachel Bilson. *Fox Broadcasting/Photofest*

CHAPTER 10

O Come All Ye Faithful: Faith, Charity, Babies, and Miracles

Everybody says we should fight to keep Christ in Christmas. Well, Leo, I'm not so sure about that. What if we gave the whole thing over to the retailers, lock, stock, and barrel, and we'd find another day to celebrate the birth of Jesus?

—Kevin Anderson, *Nothing Sacred*, 1997

"The reason for the season" is no new point of concern. TV's earliest holiday episodes in the late 1940s and early 1950s often revolved around the way our material society was neglecting the spiritual ideals of Christmas—those based in contemplation of Christ's birth, future hopes, helping those less fortunate, and renewing our faith in both God and our fellow human beings.

At a time when the term *multicultural* wouldn't be heard for decades, when America was widely accepted to be "a Christian nation," the story homilies presented on early TV were actually less religious than simply openhearted. A staple on the family sitcoms that dominated the day, they often centered on the "less fortunate" element of the Christmas equation—perhaps to remind a country basking in unprecedented postwar prosperity that not every American was equally privileged.

On ABC's *The Ruggles* in 1950, the father played by Hollywood character actor Charlie Ruggles decries how people seem to "neglect our duties
through the entire year and [try to] make up for it at Christmas," though at
least the holiday serves "to remind us to do the things that we should do."
His wife's urging to "share our blessings" leads the family to share their
Christmas bounty at the home of a girl whose father has just died.

America's "favorite family," the real-life clan of *The Adventures of Ozzie &
Harriet*, echoes the sentiment in their 1954 ABC holiday. "Doesn't it seem
to you as if the boys are missing the real spirit of Christmas?" wonders dad
Ozzie Nelson. "All they seem to be interested in is the number of presents
they receive." Harriet assures him it's "normal for boys their age," but David
and Ricky turn out to be more grown-up than their parents expect. When
the family can't find the catcher's mitt they know a store was supposed to
deliver (and for free, back then!), they suspect it wound up across town at
the home of a Nelson family with whom they're occasionally confused. The
father has died here, too, and there is, horror of horrors, peeling paint on
the doorjamb —clear signs to Ricky that "they don't have hardly anything."
"Maybe we can do something for 'em," pipes up David. The boys collect
toys from neighbors to give to the widow's kids. "The nicest part of all this
is that it wasn't our idea, but David and Ricky's," muses Ozzie. Even when
Ricky's mitt is "miraculously" found under the tree, the boy wants to give
it to the widow's son: "The way it turned out, it just doesn't seem that it
belongs to me."

The sheer simplicity and utter sincerity of the *Ozzie & Harriet* approach
would for years afterward be considered synonymous with a syrupy simplistic view of American family life. But retrospective viewing reveals an
episode like this to be genuinely, if quaintly, moving. Nelson's tale (he also
wrote and directed most episodes) never overreaches, seeks to be "smart,"
or pretends to be anything more lofty than one plain anecdote from an
ordinary life.

The same could be said for its ABC Wednesday night lineup-mate *The
Donna Reed Show*, though the star's TV spouse was a physician perhaps
higher up the career ladder. (TV Ozzie's occupation was never quite clear.)
Their family's 1958 holiday is a whirl of gift-buying and tip-giving that has
Donna chagrined. "Christmas should be warm and friendly and peaceful,"
she muses, a sentiment shared by the longtime handyman at her husband's
hospital, who annually fixes toys to be distributed at the children's ward. "I
love to watch children at Christmas," says silent film legend Buster Keaton
in a memorable twilight role. "It's a shame we took it away from them." So
they give it back. Reed and Keaton take it upon themselves to get the kids

a tree and presents, with Reed then deciding to "do something nobody's ever done before." She gives Santa—Keaton—a present. "Found the real Christmas?" husband Carl Betz asks at episode's end. Says Reed, smiling, "I knew it was somewhere."

As sitcoms broadened their scope beyond the nuclear family and the adult point of view, CBS's *The Many Loves of Dobie Gillis* presented the teen perspective. In 1961, glib title star Dwayne Hickman's college class has entrusted the money raised for the Christmas dance to Bob Denver as Dobie's beatnik pal Maynard G. Krebs. Too bad the soft-touch kid takes pity on a shoe-shine boy outside the bank. "You probably got like eight or nine little brothers and sisters just like you out there workin' instead of being home getting ready for Santa Claus," Maynard babbles at the Spanish-speaking boy, giving him tips until all the money is gone. Warns Dobie, "You'd better find a way to pay it back before Christmas or what the kids in class hang on their tree is gonna be you." The class comes around, though, once a Spanish-speaking student clarifies the situation. Their party is provided by the poor boy's Mexican family using its musical instruments and piñata. Admires Frank Faylen as Dobie's hot-tempered, Maynard-loathing dad, "That Maynard is a soft warmhearted boy—who is a dimwit."

So is Tommy Smothers on CBS's *The Smothers Brothers Show* in 1965, costarring with brother Dick, the one mom "always liked best." When the hot nightclub comedy duo came to TV in a sitcom casting Tom as an angel and Dick as his still-alive sibling corralled into aiding his heavenly schemes, their holiday was spent trying to miraculously fill those charity Toys for Tots barrels. Even small children like 10-year-old Anissa Jones's pig-tailed Buffy on CBS's 1968 *Family Affair* know it's better to give than to receive: Her custodial Uncle Bill (Brian Keith) stages a sentimental early Christmas for a dying classmate who won't live to see the holiday.

By the 1970s, such open sentiment would often be couched in more ironic, even mocking scripts—a nod to the notion that viewers were now hip to all of TV's sentimental Christmas tricks. Teens were the coolest of all. And the most cynical. The rebel-student Sweathogs of ABC's *Welcome Back, Kotter* classroom spend the 1976 holiday kidding their Brooklyn neighborhood's local bum ("You guys are as funny as a pork chop at a bar mitzvah"). So Gabe Kaplan's ex-Sweathog teacher Kotter invites the object of their insults to tell the class how he came to live on the street. The guys then pool their Christmas present money to buy him a new suit. Which he promptly takes off. "The snazzy looking guy in the mirror," he says, "it wasn't me." They learn to respect him for who he is, while also learning the joy of helping others. The popular kids and the misfits of CBS's *Square Pegs,* the dry high school social satire from *Saturday Night Live* writer Anne Beatts, work together in 1982 to bring a Guatemalan children's choir to town. But when Jami Gertz's officious organizer Muffy senses that not every classmate embraces her brand of Christmas overdrive, she scolds, "If the baby Jesus had an attitude like that, we'd all be Hindus!"

Kids are entirely too jaded by 1992, when ABC's *Home Improvement* has sons Brad and Randy collecting door-to-door for charity. Counting the $90.24 they've raised, they realize they'll have enough to buy themselves a new Nintendo GameBoy. "I'm just taking a little bit out for business expenses," explains Jonathan Taylor Thomas's Randy. But when mom Patricia Richardson finds their new-bought toys, she lets them have it: "You stole money out of the hands of kids who have next to nothing for Christmas." Down they're taken to the local homeless shelter, which turns around their attitude and has them gathering up their own playthings to donate. The episode adds edge to its ultimate sweetness, resulting in a more satisfying contemporary impact.

Yet other familycoms remained straight-ahead saccharine. One of the *Family Matters* kids brings a homeless man home for Christmas in 1994 (and he turns out to seemingly be Santa!). Similar themes could be seen in the show's ABC Friday "TGIF"-mates: The gift-obsessed girls of *Full House* learn about giving in 1992 when they visit a homeless shelter; *Boy Meets World*'s Ben Savage feels generous toward his best friend in 1993 after the boy's father is laid off his job.

Shows like those often used Christmas as a setting for a "very special episode," more serious than usual and more socially relevant in its message-delivering scope. So did that rare drama that truly embraced the child audience. CBS's long-running early Sunday evening half-hour *Lassie* (1954–71) explained "the less fortunate" in kid terms in 1960. Ten-year-old Jon Provost as dog owner Timmy meets a sad little girl at the candy store of his farm town and later discovers her impoverished family has been living nearby in an abandoned tool shed since their car broke down on the way to California. "People should always try to help each other," counsels mom June Lockhart as she takes food to the family. "We are not objects of charity," scolds the girl's dad, turning them away. "It must be terrible to be hungry at Christmastime," Timmy tells Lassie as he sends the faithful collie to their shack pulling a toy wagon carrying a food basket. "It must be pretty tough not to have a regular Christmas. Think how we'd feel. We'd feel pretty awful, even if we tried not to show it." Timmy dresses as Santa to collect money for their expenses at a street-corner kettle, and his dad finds the girl's father a job and a place to live.

"Well, dear," Lockhart says as they all decorate the tree together, "it's a time of joy and true religious expression." The episode ends with Timmy saying grace for their joint Christmas dinner. It's one of TV's rare direct acknowledgments of religious faith. But *Lassie* doesn't make a big show of it. It's simply an ingrained part of these people's lives.

Adult-aimed programs would be lucky to equal such grace, dignity, and unaffected charm. And few do when it comes to showcasing holiday benefi-cence. More often, they're too-obvious depictions, like the 1980 episode of ABC's *The Love Boat*. One of that yule cruise's several passenger tales focuses on abused-boy stowaway Meeno Peluce, who's essentially adopted by reformed-grinch stranger Dirk Benedict before the hour is out.

A few grown-up shows do manage to balance holiday help, heart, and humor with aplomb. One of the least expected is CBS's insult-laden sitcom *The Jeffersons,* which in 1977 delivered one of its most finely shaded outings at Christmastime. As wife to strutting Manhattan entrepreneur Sherman Hemsley, Isabel Sanford discovers her loud-mouthed husband has been sending an employee to an address in Harlem every month with an enve-lope full of cash. Fearing this means cheating or worse, she follows as her husband makes a personal delivery—and confesses "I used to live here." It's a rare moment of vulnerability as he explains this anonymous charity to his childhood apartment's current inhabitants: "There were a lot of bad times in this apartment, and you know, sometimes we didn't have presents or a tree or nothin'. I mean, now you know how that makes a kid feel. So I made a promise that if I ever made it big, there would never be no more bad Christmases in this apartment.... It's not that it's a gift or anything. It's just something that I owe. Look, just because you get out of here don't mean you forget the place. I mean, you gotta put something back." It's all the more effective for showing such an unexpected side to his character.

Similar surprises pop up in the Korean holiday of CBS's 1980 *M*A*S*H*. The Army medical unit's most annoying doctor, David Ogden Stiers's snooty Major Winchester, won't join in donating food to the local battlefront orphanage because, Jamie Farr's Klinger excoriates, he's "a cheap, selfish skunk." But au contraire, as the aristocratic Bostonian might phrase it. "To be a true act of charity, the gift must remain anonymous," insists Stiers as he upholds his wealthy family's tradition in delivering his largess to the orphanage personally, but unobserved.

Not everyone's bigheartedness goes so smoothly. More than a few gener-ous gestures backfire. Laura San Giacomo's campaign to help the janitor at her magazine's offices in NBC's 1997 *Just Shoot Me* only leads to his using the donations to buy presents to impress the woman on whom he's got a secret crush—her. And on CBS's 2001 *Becker*, Ted Danson's Bronx cynic gets turned around, from scorning any response to poor kids' letters to Santa—"Twenty years from now, they're gonna be bitter 'cause some do-gooder didn't fix the rest of their lives"—to munificently driving a desired toy to a poor boy's home. On the way, he picks up a hitchhiker—who steals the gift.

Yet Becker gets a thank-you letter from the kid's mom. Could it be—a miracle? The hitchhiker was, after all, on his way to see two college pals. "Three wise men!" marvels a Becker cohort. "Was there a star burning in the east?" inquires another. "There was a Buick on fire, and in the east-bound lane." But actually, Becker's nurse bought and sent the toy because she figured her misanthropic boss would fail to. "So all that really happened here was I did a good deed for some guy on Christmas Eve, and he turned around and robbed me," concludes Becker, excitedly adding, "It's wonder-ful! I always thought Christmas sucked! Now I have proof!"

AWAY IN A MANGER

> *Roseanne (arguing with her agnostic mother):* I've been through stuff, you know, but I still believe in God. I'd like to believe that all of the horrible, hideous crap that I have to wallow through every single day of my life, at some point I will find out the meaning to and the reason for. There just is a God, there is. I swear to God there's a God. And if there ain't, I've been screwed.
>
> *Laurie Metcalf (upset):* Why are we talking about this? God and heaven and everything? It's Christmas!
>
> —*Roseanne*, 1992

More often, the wise men, the star, and other nativity symbols based in Biblical tales of Jesus' birth are employed not for punch lines but for narrative power. It can be as simple as a line of dialogue at a church food kitchen in NBC's 1989 *The Golden Girls*, when the pastor says in passing, "We promise to turn away no one, remembering how Mary and Joseph were turned away at the inn."

Or it can be as involved as ABC's *The Commish* in 1991, when Michael Chiklis's softhearted police commissioner spends the hour sticking up for a destitute woman who's taken up residence in a public manger scene. "It's supposed to beautify the square," says the businessman who built it, "except it isn't beautiful to find some homeless person bunking next to the baby Jesus." Chiklis takes his leave-her-alone crusade all the way to the town council: "You know, Mary and Joseph were homeless, too, if only for that one night. Shouldn't we let the spirit of the season guide us instead of the letter of the city ordinance? We have an opportunity to offer shelter to a woman who needs it. And in this case, what more appropriate shelter could we have to offer?"

That question is yet more provocatively asked in an inner-city Catholic church in ABC's hot-button drama *Nothing Sacred*. Created to present complex consideration of diverse views on oft-simplified issues of faith, the parish saga drew fire from conservative Christians even before its 1997 premiere. Why would its Christmas episode be any less challenging? Even the parish children's nativity pageant confirms that religion is no strictly G-rated enterprise of clean simplicity. "Don't let those Christmas carols fool you," says Kevin Anderson's parish pastor Father Ray. "It's a tough story. A couple is forced by politics onto the road. When it comes time for the girl to give birth, they're homeless.... The king, he wants the child dead, and when his men can't find the child, he kills all the children under the age of two." Yet parish staffers bicker at high volume over who's in charge of the pageant, the Christmas homily, and other matters of rivalry. Already despairing of a holiday hijacked by "the pre-Christmas sales and the post-Christmas sales and the competitive gift-giving," Anderson shouts them down by insisting "Let's all just take a deep breath and let's pray that God shows us the true meaning of Christmas."

In rush a refugee couple from Guatemala, earlier shown protesting with the street slogan "Joseph and Mary were undocumented." Pursued by the authorities, they seek sanctuary, "an ancient privilege of the church to harbor the innocent." Suddenly, observes Bruce Altman as the parish's sardonic Jewish business manager, "This isn't Christmas, it's Hanukkah, and we're the Maccabees." After the couple explains being "called communist for telling people that their suffering is not the will of God," the staffers find a way to whisk the refugees secretly out the back of the church. In a way, Anderson's Ray has gotten his wish to revisit the essence of Jesus' emergence. He had started the episode by asking, "What if we celebrated Christmas like the first one—no expectations, no plans? Just like Joseph and Mary, making it up as they go along."

That "true meaning" of Christmas isn't just practical, it's miraculous, as we're also reminded here by series creators David Manson (who directed) and Bill Cain (cowriter, and a Jesuit priest himself). That's addressed within another swirling current of the parish: Ann Dowd's desire as Sister Maureen to deliver the Christmas homily, which only "ordained persons" can do. And women can't be ordained. Mo finally speaks at the midnight service when the parish's priests are otherwise detained, in jail, over the refugee skirmish. (She stresses to the flock, "This is a prayer service; this is not a mass.") The convenient exception allows a stirringly fresh, female perspective on the specific wonder that underlies so much Judeo-Christian teaching. "Abraham and Sarah wanted to have a child, just as for the Virgin Mary having a baby was impossible," proclaims Dowd with a luminous fervor. "I believe in the virgin birth. It means everything to me," she marvels. "Is anything, is anything, too wonderful for God?"

These seasonal invocations are delivered passionately, as beliefs so deeply internalized that they've been personalized into palpability. The series's clear-eyed drama richly explored the doubts and temptations afflicting those of faith, even (or especially) the clergy. The stories refused to spout any official line, or to harshly judge those who refused to hue.

TV seldom touches the third rail of explicit religion quite so directly—evidently, for good reason. Under fire from all sides in the religious debate, ABC canceled *Nothing Sacred* after airing just 15 of its 20 produced episodes. Generic references are much less likely to provoke accusations of disrespect or sacrilege from those claiming to speak for specific creeds. In the end, religious activists make it harder, not easier, for TV to "put Christ back in Christmas," as they say they seek. It's safer to poke fun than to represent faith that may not be depicted exactly the way some other believer thinks it should be it depicted.

Animator Seth MacFarlane's gleefully flippant Fox satire *Family Guy* went for that throat in its 2001 Christmas cartoon. Its boorish suburban dad hosted the town nativity pageant by proclaiming "Christmas is that mystical time of year, when the ghost of Jesus rises from the grave to feed on the flesh of the living, so we all sing Christmas carols to lull him back to sleep."

"How dare he say such blasphemy? I've got to do something," rages one onlooker, whose friend replies, "There's nothing you can do." "Well," deadpans the objector, "I guess I'll just have to develop a sense of humor." MacFarlane isn't being irreverent just for the sake of mocking religion at Christmastime. This is par for the course on a show in which family baby Stewie is a homicidal maniac who talks with a clipped British accent and agrees to play Jesus in the pageant only because he hopes Santa will reward him with fissionable materials. Stewie isn't only speaking of Santa when he declares to pageant-goers that humans spread goodwill at Christmas only because "we are being watched. And so we unselfishly think of others, assured that our good behavior will be rewarded, with love—and plutonium!"

TV's skittishness around religious piety can lead to faith being peripheral even in a clergy-based series like the BBC sitcom *The Vicar of Dibley*. Dawn French's witty title character serves as more of a handy town counselor for the oddballs of her rural English congregation. Before the Britcom's 1999 nativity presentation on a local farm, French does retell the story of Jesus' birth in rehearsals with her parishioners. But the actual reenactment is characterized by her pregnant pal's onset of labor while playing Mary. "It's very realistic, isn't it?" asks one audience member. When the daft new mother wonders, "Have I actually given birth to the son of God?" the vicar indulgently reminds, "Apart from anything, she's a girl, isn't she?"

Things were simpler back in TV's early days, when NBC's half-hour cop drama *Dragnet* presented its 1953 tale of a manger scene's Jesus statue being stolen from a mission church in the Los Angeles barrio. Director–star Jack Webb had told the story on radio, and he would tell it again in NBC's 1967 TV revival. His police detective Joe Friday is shocked that the church's priest would just "leave it wide open so thieves can walk in." But the church welcomes "particularly thieves," stresses the priest. Police search for the humble treasure but get nowhere. When Friday returns to tell the priest he's had no luck finding the statue, in walks a little boy who had prayed to get a red wagon for Christmas. Having gotten his wish, he figured the baby Jesus deserved the first ride. "Paquito's family, they're poor," explains the priest. "Are they?" asks Friday, in his legendarily terse *Dragnet* kind of way.

Such simple acceptance of Christmas as something inspirationally fulfilling for all—even hard-nosed police detectives—was precisely what Americans were missing when the "inclusive" political correctness of the 1990s started making people think twice about even simply saying "Merry Christmas" to someone. In line with many businesses, boss Max Wright on ABC's *Norm* tells contrary star Norm Macdonald in 1999 that Christmas displays can be discriminatory. But Norm figures, "No one can be offended as long as I've accommodated all cultures. That's why I've included the bogus holidays of all the other religions," cramming the office to the ceiling with varied decorations—inanimate and otherwise. "I see we're ready for the goat sacrifice," he deadpans. Still, Wright insists, "I'm not gonna risk a reprimand for you to turn this office into an orgiastic religious petting zoo."

That's pretty much the sentiment in 2001 when Kathleen Quinlan's law firm head on CBS's *Family Law* decrees, "I don't want any religious symbols. I don't want to alienate clients." Which puts Dixie Carter's partner in a lather: "You do realize there's a reason they call it Christmas instead of secular evergreen-mas?" A plain tree is put up. And "religious symbols" keep materializing under it: a menorah for Hanukkah, the Kwanzaa cup of togetherness, lentil soup for ending Ramadan. "Every time I get rid of something," argues the receptionist, "two more things just show up." The staff wants to celebrate the season. And by hour's end, Quinlan is with them. She's so fed up with combative clients standing on ceremony over who gets the kids for the holidays, and other bitterness, that she's finally the one who decorates the entire office in holiday regalia. It's as if we all need a little of the warmth of Christmas—in whatever way we choose to make it.

MARY'S BOY CHILD

Babies are a big commodity in TV Christmas-land. They tend to be born to traveling parents with names like Joe and Mary who've been forced at birth time to take shelter wherever they can. On CBS's *The New Dick Van Dyke Show* in 1972, a pair with those names has "been traveling all day, but we couldn't find a place to stay." So they show up at the desert jail where Van Dyke is behind bars for Christmas Eve speeding. Luckily, Joe has brought his guitar to lead them in performing "Joy to the World." He explains, "Every year, we go around and remind people what the real spirit of Christmas is all about" by singing at hospitals and orphanages. Another police-related incident is found in comedian Rowan Atkinson's 1995 BBC cop comedy *The Thin Blue Line*, in which a pregnant hippie couple takes refuge at the station, having "arrived from far away with nowhere to stay for the night? Did you ever hear of such a thing?"

The American military gets into the act for the 2002 Christmas of CBS's Naval legal drama *JAG*. After being incorrectly ousted from base housing, a Marine named Joseph and his about-to-give-birth wife Mary are seeking counsel when labor time arrives. The admiral forced to deliver their new son, Jason, just happens to be awaiting a visit from three Kuwaiti military guests, who then honor the baby with gifts, one of which is a nearby apartment. On HBO's imaginative farce *Dream On* in 1993, Wendie Malick's character isn't named Mary, but she does give birth in the presence of frantic ex-husband Brian Benben, in a barn, in Bethlehem (Pennsylvania), to her saintly new husband's son.

Another baby tale actually features an inn without a vacancy. It's 1982's first-season Christmas on CBS's *Newhart*, where deadpan stand-up Bob Newhart runs a rustic Vermont sleepery. It's been completely booked by a ski club and so can't accommodate a couple stranded by blocked roads after a huge snowfall. "Let me get this straight," begins Newhart in his monotonic style. "This is Christmas Eve, and you show up with a pregnant wife and there's no room at the inn.... On behalf of innkeepers everywhere,

I think we owe you one." The baby is born, and later a motorist named Alan Wiseman and his two brothers are stuck in the snow. "When you talk about authentic old-fashioned Christmases," says Newhart, "this is about as close as you're going to get."

Not quite. Lifetime's *Strong Medicine* offers up a virgin birth just before Christmas 2004. A college student serving as a surrogate mother admits to clinic doctor Rosa Blasi, "I'm having a baby when I've never even, you know, had sex." But she's still more mature than the money-paying parents—Joe and Meredith, of course—who take a pass when the newborn boy turns out to have developmental problems. "Can they do this, just return him like he's some sort of defective product they bought at a store?" asks mom Yareli Arizmendi. She lacks resources to care for the child, yet she finally realizes, "I still feel like he's a part of me. I'm just not the kind of person who could leave a baby like this, especially when he needs so much." Blasi calls in a judge, his clerk, and a children's advocate for an instant bedside holiday adoption: "You are three very wise men."

Occasionally on Christmas, the baby is *the* baby. That seems to be the case in 1996 on, of all shows, *Hercules—The Legendary Journeys*, syndication's mythological action hour starring Kevin Sorbo. "Where am I going, Hercules? What am I supposed to achieve in this life?" questions Michael Hurst as sidekick Iolaus when their wanderings take them to a new realm. There, an oracle's prophecy has led the king to round up all male infants to ensure none threatens the succession of the royal family. Iolaus endeavors to thwart the scheme, joining forces with two other "wise" men who have had the same action-inspiring "dream" as he. Its meaning crystallizes when they feel drawn to a star in the sky, which illuminates a cabin in a distant field. "This is what the dream was all about," says one. "It's a sense of calm and peace," says another. "It's just a hunch," Hercules tells Iolaus, "but somehow I believe that what you're about to witness is bigger and more important than anything we've ever done."

Finding an infant at Christmas and feeling warmed by its presence, even in dire circumstances, also pops up as a popular plot. *Moonlighting* combined its trademark screwball repartee and private-eye sleuthing with holiday heart in its 1985 ABC outing "'Twas the Episode before Christmas"—the title just one more wink in its self-aware arsenal. Joseph is a former crook in the witness protection program who's been taken out by thugs as wife Mary fled through their apartment building with her infant. Allyce Beasley's mousy investigation firm receptionist finds the tot in her laundry-room basket, which draws interest from three justice agents named King. "A woman named Mary, a baby, three kings!" waxes Bruce Willis's droll detective. "Confidentially, I'm worried, Maddie," he tells Cybill Shepherd, his more uptight partner in both business and banter. "I think we're trapped in an allegory. I'm telling you, we got everything in this story except a camel." "Anybody care for a smoke?" asks Mary. The breezy approach acknowledges its own clichés, sends them up, and wallows in their ritual role, all at once.

Such zesty treatment can be bracing when so many other shows take their allegory seriously, even in fantasy presentations. Fox's oft-humorous *Ally McBeal* let supporting player Jane Krakowski get sentimental over finding a live baby in a 1999 Boston manger scene. (Her law firm's loopy partners were seen dancing through their unisex restroom with the tot.) Daytime dramas pull hardest on the heartstrings with this concept. ABC's daytime drama *All My Children* gives unhappily pregnant young Bianca (Eden Riegel) a "magical mystical adventure" in 2003 after she finds a baby at a church—except, as it turns out, the priest she encountered doesn't seem to actually exist and the child curiously resembles the Christ child doll from their nativity scene. The fantastic encounter eases Bianca's grief and enables her to move forward. "I was looking for an answer," she beams, "and I found it."

FAITH, LOST AND REGAINED

Answers can indeed be found in the most unlikely places and times. Those who've turned their back on faith frequently regain their regard for God and church amid the cheer, brotherhood, and forgiveness inspired by the holiday season. Bess Armstrong's young mother on ABC's acclaimed teen-identity saga *My So-Called Life* tries to persuade her reluctant husband to attend church with their daughters for Christmas 1994: "I know that it hasn't been a part of our lives, and it certainly isn't part of the girls'—but the thing is, I want it to be." Sharon Gless as a divorced lawyer on CBS's drama *The Trials of Rosie O'Neill* visits her mother and sisters in 1990 but refuses to attend their usual midnight mass because her ex and his new wife will be there. Watching *It's a Wonderful Life* on TV and pouting, she finally heads home in a rainstorm, almost hitting a pedestrian. She then gives the man a lift to church. "Christmas Eve is a lousy time to be alone," he says soothingly, encouraging her "never to miss an opportunity to celebrate the greatest gift we have—being alive." And she naturally ends up walking through those church doors herself.

Ed Flanders on NBC's 1985 *St. Elsewhere* also tells his college daughter to go to church without him. "The holidays are something I endure, not enjoy," the widower says, brooding over hospital bureaucracy and his autistic son. But his daughter's boyfriend's excitement over spending time with their close family forces him to see the good in his life, too, which leads him to belatedly join them at midnight mass. Such a turnaround is not fated, however, for William Daniels's caustic surgeon, who's agonizing over the recent car-crash deaths of his son and daughter-in-law. Hosting his annual wassail party, he grits it out until announcing to his guests "Let's not forget that we are celebrating the birth of Christ, God's only son—" Which shakes him. He shows the revelers how his Christmas tree is "an archive of my family's history," hung with ornaments dating back to the time of the eighteenth-century Continental Congress, "handed down from one generation to the next. Now we'll skip a generation." When Daniels breaks down weeping alone in the kitchen, wife Bonnie Bartlett reassures him, "We'll say a special prayer tonight at the midnight service." "Oh, no," he snaps. "I'm not going. I can't sit there celebrating the birth of a God who is so arbitrary and so mean-spirited, who asks you to serve Him without question, who could take away my boy." The episode ends as he walks past the church, and continues past it, unmoved.

It's the hospital grind itself that wears down Donald Faison's young intern Turk on NBC's daydream-and-drama-tinged comedy *Scrubs*. Working the 2001 Christmas, he encounters calamity after calamity to the montage tune of "The Twelve Days of Christmas"—"12 beaten children, 11 drive-by shootings, 10 frozen homeless"—and insists at the end of his shift that he, too, will skip mass: "I'm not going, ever." The decision fazes Zach Braff as his intern pal J.D., who realizes, "I never really thought of faith as important. But without his, I don't know, Turk kind of seems like he's fading away." Moping on the hospital roof, Turk tells nurse girlfriend Judy Reyes that he feels abandoned. "All my life I believed that God listens to our prayers and that he cares for us and that he watches over us. And last night there were so many people that needed to be watched over. How am I supposed to believe in someone that is willing to let innocent people suffer?" But Turk is also watching over things and suddenly spots a pregnant woman delivering her baby under a tree in the adjacent park. He rushes down to help and feels renewed: "A baby can stir something deep down inside you [that] you didn't even know was there." J.D. finds his own faith boosted: "Miracles do happen. I think you just have to be willing to look for them."

MIRACLES ON TV STREET

There's always something amazing about a baby being born. But when it happens on the day we celebrate the birth of the most amazing baby ever born, it becomes something you'll never forget.

—Billy Ray Cyrus, *Doc*, 2001

TV viewers don't have to look far. In Christmas episodes, miracles are strewn all over the place. After baby-of-the-family Susan Olsen asks Santa for some help in ABC's 1969 *The Brady Bunch*, mom Florence Henderson's laryngitis inexplicably clears up just in time for her church choir solo on "O Come All Ye Faithful." Sally Field's spunky title character in ABC's *The Flying Nun*—the aerodynamic headgear of her particular order's habit lifted her into the Caribbean air—finds a way in 1967 to fulfill a dying Norwegian nun's wish to see snow in Puerto Rico, by seeding the clouds above their convent with dry ice.

Other amazing happenings are more consequential. On The WB youth suspense drama *Roswell*, Jason Behr plays a New Mexico teen who's actually an abandoned alien keeping quiet about his empathetic superpowers. He doesn't use them at Christmas 2000 to save a man he sees hit by a car and is subsequently haunted by a vision in which the victim asks, "How could you let me die?" When a friend cries about a five-year-old dying of cancer, Behr visits the child's hospital ward and lays his healing hands on each of its ailing patients. "How can I not use my gift?" he implores earthling girlfriend Shiri Appleby. "As beautiful as that is," she responds, "you can't keep doing it. I know it seems like there's no reason for those kids to have cancer.... But maybe there is, maybe there's someone or something out there that's planning all of this. And maybe you have to respect it."

Miracles became almost an annual occurrence on NBC's hospital drama *ER*, in which doctors already dealt with so many life and death decisions every day. In 1997's "Do You See What I See?" a homeless blind man suddenly regains sight on Christmas Eve after Eriq LaSalle's Dr. Peter Benton touches his forehead while treating him. "Hey, St. Peter," Noah Wyle's Dr. Carter soon calls, "I heard about your miracle." Before long, another homeless man in a wheelchair is begging, "I want to walk again. You cured him; I want you to cure me." But the blind man returns later that day, blind again: "I can't see no more! You have to touch me again." Tests reveal the man has such a large brain tumor that, as the consulting specialist says, "There's no way this man has seen anything for five or six years." Except that he enthuses what a great day he had playing by Lake Michigan with his guide dog, seeing snow fall lightly on the trees, watching the steam rise from the water.

Carter gets his own *ER* miracle in 1998, when he tries to resuscitate an 18-year-old boy without a heartbeat whom George Clooney's Dr. Ross has just declared dead. Carter and Kellie Martin's resident Lucy Knight have been debating the existence of God. "Sometimes," she says, "I can't help but think God is just this comforting illusion. We all want everything to mean something so we create this all-knowing puppet master in the sky when really everything is just arbitrary." But Carter has just received a letter from a grateful patient calling him "the Lord's instrument on earth," and he won't let the boy with no heartbeat go. "You got some reason to keep flogging this kid?" asks Ross. "He's 18," says Carter, "he's his mother's only child, and it's Christmas." Ross shakes his head: "You looking for a miracle? He's been down for 40 minutes." "So what's 5 more?" One last jolt with the paddles brings the kid around.

But now he's brain-dead. And it turns out that this may be the real miracle. A teenage girl is soon brought in with liver failure. Carter had given up hope of transplanting the boy's organs because of his rare AB blood type. But it happens to match the girl's. "Two kids come in on Christmas Eve," he tells Lucy, "one is brain-dead, the other needs a liver, and they both have AB blood. Tell me that's not a godsend."

But not all TV characters are so eager to buy into the holiday miracle symbolism. Richard Belzer's acerbic Munch on NBC's *Homicide: Life on the Street* isn't having any of it. "How come all the miracles that happened happened in the past?" he scoffs as the Baltimore police squad trades musings while killing time on 1994's Christmas night shift. "Name one miracle that happened in your lifetime," he challenges.

We've got one: the way we're all such suckers for TV's unlikely Christmas miracles year after year after year.

CHAPTER 11

Christmas with a Conscience: Time for Social Statements

It's tempting to say that TV's holiday season episodes first got truly serious along about the "relevance era" of the early 1970s, when CBS's *All in the Family* began mining comedy from Vietnam War–era cultural conflict and when dramas tried taking a *Mod Squad* look at social issues.

But that approach had been around, to at least some extent, from the medium's very beginning, even as critics were deriding "the boob tube." CBS's half-hour drama *Racket Squad* hit modern holiday crime head-on in 1952, depicting a lonely old tenement resident who works as a street-corner Santa, thinking he's collecting donations for charity. The actual beneficiaries are two con men—until the old Santa helps the title police team take 'em down. It's a schmaltzy story—right down to the little handicapped neighbor child the old man befriends, not to mention the head cop letting the old man buy presents with some of the ill-gotten proceeds. Yet this episode's sentimental approach tackles a real-life problem and delivers a straightforward warning to citizens of an era considerably less wary than later decades.

Christmas was even used to make political statements in that same rabidly anticommunist decade. The 1956 Hungarian uprising against occupation by the Soviet Union formed the basis of a 1957 episode in the ABC drama anthology series *Telephone Time* sponsored by the Bell System. "A Picture of the Magi" had a little Hungarian girl spotting three petty smugglers who looked to her like a book's drawing of the three kings visiting the baby Jesus. They'd end up behaving as "three wise men" when authorities sought the girl's family thanks to her brother's anticommunist "free radio" activism. Behind news footage of Soviet tanks rolling down city streets, the criminals help "smuggle" the girl's pursued family past the border's barbed wire to freedom. This was "as it really happened in communist-dominated Hungary shortly before Christmas 1956," the narrator intoned, claiming the tale of underground resistance had been passed on in a letter from a European "social worker" for the supposedly impartial United Nations.

ALL IN THE FAMILY

The "relevance" era of the late 1960s and early 1970s did, however, bring the first real flood of issue-oriented holiday episodes. These were the years of race riots, the Vietnam War, flowering "liberation" movements for women and gays, and the "generation gap" between World War II-bred parents and their suddenly rebellious progeny. Coinciding with all this social upheaval was a natural pendulum swing in the tone of prime time TV programs. The 1960s had been filled with "idiot" sitcoms featuring witches, Martians, and talking horses. Even relatively realistic shows diverted their audience with silly antics and ultimately inconsequential misunderstandings.

Now the tube's new social consciousness would begin to permeate the most playful of programs—even *Bewitched*. Elizabeth Montgomery's ABC sitcom had stuck to gag tomfoolery and Santa storylines in several 1960s Christmas episodes, but when housewife witch Samantha's wardrobe went fluorescent psychedelic in later seasons, her storylines got hip, too. The 1970 holiday episode "Sisters at Heart" was a racial brotherhood pitch actually written by a high school class. And it won the Emmys' Governors Award for its substance. Toddler Tabitha uses her nascent witchcraft skills to paint identical polka dots on the faces of her little black friend and herself, so they can be "sisters" in the face of cross-race disapproval. It's wisdom from the mouths of babes, of course: Their sister act persuades even dad Darrin's racist client at the advertising agency to get with society's new tolerance program. Yes, this was relevant. But still ridiculous. (Polka-dot faces?)

Just a month later, CBS's *All in the Family* would heave a live grenade into prime time television. Most family sitcoms had been sort of lukewarm in their tone of humor—amusing but loving and mild, never truly mocking or cutting—but this creation from writer–producer Norman Lear was downright scalding. His characters went after each other with incendiary rage, and their personal disputes reflected national debates over war, race, religion, and other hot-button issues. The show's raucous approach exploded the genre's polite tidiness, pushing it beyond gentle amusement to side-splitting hilarity. (Tellingly, whereas most sitcoms were shot on fine-grained film, Lear produced his show on harsh-looking videotape, the live-look format of variety hours and news programs. It imparted immediacy. And he shot before a studio audience, although the live-theater filming style pioneered by *I Love Lucy* in the early 1950s had fallen into disuse.) In an era when sitcoms tended to feel distant and controlled, *All in the Family* was in-your-face brashness. It broke not just rules but ratings norms, zooming by the end of its first full season to number one in the Nielsen ratings, attracting a viewership higher than any top-rated sitcom in nearly a decade.

Even Christmas could not bring peace on earth to the contentious working-class Bunker household in the New York City borough of Queens. Never would there be a holiday on disputes among opinionated bigot Archie Bunker (Carroll O'Connor), his gentle wife Edith (Jean Stapleton), their spunky daughter Gloria (Sally Struthers), and her new liberal college-student husband Mike Stivic (Rob Reiner). At their first TV yule in 1971, Archie becomes incensed when first the milkman shows up seeking a Christmas tip and later a nun comes collecting for charity. "Everybody's out on the make, including all your churches," moans indelible Emmy-winner O'Connor. It's the time of year when everybody's giving, "and I'm one of the guys that gets took." Money is a big issue this year, since the annual Christmas bonus at his loading dock won't be coming his way: The oft-ignorant Archie routed a London-bound shipment to England instead of Ontario.

Societal concerns show up in what scriptwriters call the B story and C story: the subplots that flesh out an episode and often contribute more toward shaping the series' tenor and attitudes. Conversation around the Bunker home turns to President Nixon's implementation of price controls and even to the religious origins of Christmas. "There's no proof that Jesus was God's son. That's fairy tales," maintains Archie's atheist nemesis Mike. "Geez, they don't give you a holiday for fairy tales," Archie fumes back, employing his famously twisted logic. "All over the world, they celebrate the birth of that baby, and everybody gets time off from work. Now if that ain't proof that He's the son of God, then nothing is."

Even more to the heart of *All in the Family,* a black neighbor visits dressed as Santa Claus, wearing a black beard, which sets Archie spinning with its implicit challenge to the traditions he holds so dear. "Santa Claus was white," Archie spouts, "and so was his beard." When Santa takes his leave flashing the two-finger V sign used at the time by antiwar marchers to signal "peace," Archie goes absolutely ballistic. "A guy comes into my house dressed up like a famous white person, sits in my chair, then he goes out on Christmas Day making a pinko sign like that!" It's up to simple but sweet wife Edith to set him straight: "I didn't know peace was pinko."

The series' 1973 holiday is a showcase for Jean Stapleton's Edith, who in her "dingbat" way conveys more commonsense wisdom than any of the show's characters. Even more distracted than usual, she seems to provoke a preholiday spat in the kitchen with Gloria. Finally, her anxiety overflowing, Edith blurts to her daughter, "I got a lump in my breast"—news she doesn't want to share with explosive Archie until after she has a biopsy. "I'm afraid if I have this operation," she fears, "Archie won't think of me in the same way." As feminist neighbor Irene Lorenzo (Betty Garrett) later reassures her they'll be okay, Edith insists Irene can't know what she's feeling. "That's just the point, Edith. I do know. I know," Irene pointedly consoles, alluding to her own mastectomy. She doesn't use the word, though. And neither does Archie, after he rushes to the hospital, a supportive husband after all.

All in the Family was only beginning to break down the narrowly defined standards of a reticent society. Its assault would become increasingly full-bore. Both Archie and Edith reexamine their core beliefs in 1977's strong two-part story featuring the return of Edith's female-impersonator friend Beverly LaSalle, gleefully welcomed by Gloria as "you big bogus bimbo!" While Archie gripingly compares the gender-bender to an untelegenic sportscaster—"She looks like Howard Cosell in drag"—Edith's generosity of heart sees only the essence of the kind person played by towering San Francisco drag star Lori Shannon (real name Don McLean, though not the 1970s "American Pie" singer). "To me, you're like a sister," says Edith. "No, I mean brother. Well, both rolled into one." As she assures Archie, "Beverly ain't got no problem. He's a perfectly normal female impersonator."

But others have problems with him/her, and on the way to the subway from the Bunker home, Beverly is jumped and beaten to death. Archie tries to comfort an inconsolable Edith with his own sort of twisted tenderness. "I wish I hadda told Beverly what a nice fella she was. But you don't know how to talk to them people, so you don't say nothin'," he explains, concluding the "lesson there" is "everybody should try hard to be the same as everybody else." As Edith's discontent runs deeper, she refuses to attend her usual Christmas church service, because "I don't think He cares.... I wouldn't know what to pray no more, Archie. I ain't goin'." She won't even say grace over the Christmas turkey, which sends atheist Mike into the kitchen after her.

"I'm mad at God," Edith admits with a then-astonishing frankness. "All I know is Beverly was killed because of what he was, and we're all supposed to be God's children. It don't make sense. I don't understand nothin' no more." Mike tenderly suggests, "Maybe we're not supposed to understand everything at once. Maybe we're just supposed to understand things a little bit at a time." Replies Edith, "The trouble with me is I don't understand nothin'." "Ma," he reassures, "if there is a God, you're one of the most understanding people He ever made. We need you." Such blatantly presented sentiment could resonate because Lear's characters were so deftly developed by his Emmy-winning cast. They were tangible people with personalities, not just standard-bearers for contrasting viewpoints, which ensured the series a long run and an enduring afterlife in repeats.

All in the Family also gave 1970s TV several direct spin-off series that continued to deal seriously with turbulent social trends. *Maude* starred Beatrice Arthur as Edith's cousin, a sort of reverse female Archie, bursting with liberal certitude and indignation. Her show touched on union/management strife in its 1973 holiday outing. Maude's home-hosted Christmas party for the staff of husband Walter's appliance store becomes the occasion for the workers to announce they're unionizing. While bleeding-heart union-booster Maude thinks it'll be "Walter's biggest thrill since the lettuce pickers won that toilet in the fields," it does, of course, set Santa-dressed Walter (Bill Macy) into a tizzy of threatening to fire them all—until he graciously decides before the last commercial break that they'll all get along just fine anyway. It's a cop-out. But hey, it's Christmas: There's a piano in the living room, and they just sing carols till the credits roll.

All ends less tidily on *Good Times,* which centered on the Chicago-projects family of Esther Rolle, who had previously played Maude's acerbic maid Florida Evans. This CBS series' 1974 holiday half-hour hit a tough issue head-on, and crashed right out of the comedy arena. When teen cousin Naomi arrives from Arkansas with her folks to visit Florida's family, she holes up in the bathroom furtively draining most of the family's scant liquor supply. As Florida's daughter, BernNadette Stanis confronts her cousin, only to be told, "Don't be square. I'm only getting into the holiday spirit." Because this show featured three kids and had quickly become a pop catchphrase sensation—string bean teen comic Jimmie Walker was forever wailing "Dyn-o-mite!"—the obvious lesson was bound to be drummed home, hard. Stanis's "dialogue" with her cousin quickly devolves into a litany of statistics and anecdotal disasters caused by the evils of alcohol. But she doesn't have to tattle; Naomi collapses at the Christmas dinner table, where her bottle-toting father starts to get an inkling. "For a while there," he pronounces with a mixture of relief and shame, "I was afraid she was on drugs." The final fade-out doesn't come over laughter or applause. It's an audience gasp to make sure we understand This Is Significant.

Even more so was the 1976 Christmas dinner on *All in the Family,* which symbolically laid to rest the issue of the Vietnam War, whose divisive cultural impact had essentially fueled the creation of the groundbreaking series. American troops had been withdrawn from Vietnam in 1973, and even the embassy was abandoned in 1975, when the Communist North Vietnamese finally took the South Vietnamese capital of Saigon. The battle lines were drawn explicitly one final time as Mike's old Chicago friend David stops by on Christmas Eve just as Archie's pal Pinky is due for dinner. Pinky's son was killed in the war; David is a draft dodger living in Canada as what he calls "your friendly fugitive from justice." Mike asks David to stay for the holiday meal but "steer clear of any subjects that might cause friction—like politics, religion, sex, books, movies, war, peace, guns, grapes, lettuce...." (The last two were being boycotted by some consumers to urge better treatment of farmworkers.)

That doesn't happen, of course. When Pinky reflects upon his loss of "little Stevie" and David gets visibly uncomfortable, the truth comes out, and Archie blows up: "A fugitive from justice! How'd you like the FBI to come and have dinner with you here?" To which Edith leavens the tension with, "Oh, Archie, we ain't got enough turkey for them." But O'Connor's paragon of certainty can't be calmed. "When the hell are you going to admit that the war was wrong?" demands Mike, to Archie's bellowed refusal, "I ain't talking about that war! I don't wanna talk about that rotten damn war no more!" Catching himself, he shifts the focus to defending the draft against the notion of an all-volunteer army (which had in 1973 become a reality): "You couldn't get a decent war off the ground that way! All the young people would say no. Sure, they would. 'Cause they don't wanna get killed. That's why we leave it to the Congress."

But as Pinky, veteran character actor Eugene Roche would have the final word. As had become standard for the clearly liberal-leaning *All in the Family,* Archie is proven ill-informed and stubbornly closed-minded. "My kid hated the war, too," Pinky begins his climactic speech, "but he did what he thought he had to do. And David here did what he thought he had to do. But David's alive to share Christmas dinner with us, and if Steve were here, he'd wanna sit down with him. And that's what I wanna do," he concludes, shaking the draft dodger's hand. The scene plays a bit heavy-handed today, so explicit and maudlin. But this was a style *All in the Family* had long established as its own and for which it had earned our indulgence through its heart-on-its-sleeve passions and its actors' movingly flesh-and-blood characterizations.

FROM M*A*S*H TO HEAVEN

Other socially conscious programs of the 1970s used a bit more creativity, cleverness, and cinematic style to get their equally important points across. *M*A*S*H* struggled to find an audience, too, after its 1972 CBS debut, but this filmed antiwar movie spin-off zoomed into Nielsen's top five after being relocated in its second season to the prime slot following number-one hit *All in the Family*. Many fans likely missed the sitcom's first-season Christmas episode. But this particular mold-breaking half-hour episode scripted by series developer Larry Gelbart would become a perennial favorite among the series' ever-popular repeats.

"Dear Dad" finds Alan Alda's drafted surgeon Hawkeye Pierce writing a Christmas letter to his father after "three straight days of meatball surgery, 70 hours of sewing kids together" just off the Korean War battlefield. His attempt to explain to his father the pressures in a 1950s field war hospital—and the crew with whom he struggles to survive them—encapsulates the show for viewers, too, in both tone and characters. "The tension in the OR is always a foot think, but we do our best to cut through it" is a letter line that sets up visualized anecdotes of the staff's gag attempts at maintaining laughter through the tears. "If jokes seem sacrilegious in an operating room," he writes, "I promise you they're a necessary defense against what we get down here at this end of the draft board."

Resentment at their situation coexists with earnest desire to keep alive as many combatants as possible, both military and civilian. The show's antiwar attitude—emblematic of the then-current Vietnam protest—still respects the efforts of those forced to fight. Over its 11-season run, *M*A*S*H* would become less strident about its politics and more invested in the comedy of its characters. But this early episode (the show's twelfth) exhibits a hard edge to both its (broad) humor and its (incensed) ideology. Even Corporal Klinger (Jamie Farr), later a cross-dressing source of comic relief, is rattled by the war here, so much so that ever-calm chaplain Father Mulcahy (William Christopher) has to disarm him of a grenade heatedly wielded against commanding officers. The letter-writing format was so successful at drawing a nonlinear picture of life in this mobile Army surgical hospital that star Alda borrowed it when he wrote the series' 1978 Christmas episode, "Dear Sis," with Father Mulcahy writing to his nun sister about his frustrations at ministering to people in the heat of war.

Over on ABC, *Barney Miller* tackled present-day urban issues through the unending parade of cops, crooks, victims, ax-grinding citizens, and neighborhood denizens who streamed through the detective squad doors at the sitcom's (fictional) 12th precinct in lower Manhattan from 1975 to 1982. Its first Christmas outing in 1976 has detective Yemana (Jack Soo) interested in a holiday date with a Japanese robbery victim he doesn't realize is also a hooker, while aging staffer Fish (Abe Vigoda) goes undercover as a street-corner Santa to bait a seasonal mugger.

The videotaped sitcom got even more topical by its final season. The 1981 holiday tale of a confrontational shopkeeper, who uses a cattle prod on homeless people sleeping in his store, managed to deftly address both vigilantism in the face of overwhelmed city police and the homeless problem being exacerbated by so-called gentrification of rundown areas after poor residents are evicted. "There's all these marginal people out on the street, trying to survive, sleeping in doorways, trash bins," explains bleeding-heart detective Wojo (Max Gail). He calls in a burned-out city official, who lays it out even more graphically, but amusingly: "What with unemployment, the city clamping down on welfare, psychiatric hospitals all of a sudden going nuts over who's crazy enough to get in, they dump even more of these people out on the street." The message is delivered through vividly comedic characters, and the loud-mouthed vigilante softens enough to take a home-less couple home for Christmas dinner. But not enough to eschew calling the husband "Mr. Potato Head."

By the end of the 1970s, Christmas as an occasion to make a social state-ment had been firmly implanted in prime time. Along with family fun, holi-day heart-warmers, and silly Santa situations, network TV now could also feel comfortable widening its focus to include the broader human issues underlying the meaning of the season—love, faith, charity, spiritual renew-al, and even the more painful discoveries to be made in the midst of all that togetherness and openhearted exchange: the soul-searching among each other and within ourselves. The black/white, good/evil outlook that had dominated the small screen through its first two decades now allowed for shades of gray across a spectrum of personal and cultural issues. Comedies had become more sophisticated.

Dramas were developing their own complexities as well. Single-lead hours with closed-end heroics gave way to ensemble-cast chronicles that wove together varied threads of story, as they continued from week to week, like chapters in a novel. The big breakthrough was NBC's 1981 debut of the police portrait *Hill Street Blues*, reflecting the chaotic law-enforcing lives of urban street cops, detectives, and public defenders intersecting at the inner-city precinct house of an unnamed metropolis. Their 1982 Christmas episode is a typically layered stew of comedy-spiced drama, putting growlingly grubby Belker (Bruce Weitz) into an undercover Santa suit, while the rest of the crew plays reindeer and elves in a children's hospital pageant. ("Oh, Lordy," moans Charles Haid's southern-fried Renko as he's called into action, "it's Christmas Eve and I'm gonna get shot dead in a moose suit.") The drifter dad of Michael Warren's officer Hill shows up, and Belker winds up eating his holiday dinner alone in front of the TV. Crime doesn't stop for Christmas, but the characters' lives are as crucial as their crime fighting.

Even the somewhat more standard dramas of the 1980s were trying to reflect the real world around them, although their deliberations tended to be a bit less dexterous. Michael Landon's do-gooding 1980s NBC hour *Highway to Heaven* cast the beloved star of *Bonanza* and *Little House on the Prairie* as an angel essentially parachuting weekly into the life of someone who might otherwise walk a less godly path. In a nuance-free 1989 installment also written and directed by Landon, he arrives for Christmas on the doorstep of a nuclear plant contractor. "What group are you guys with?" the man asks Landon and companion Victor French. "The human race," asserts Landon, challenging the man's profession. "Are you willing to guarantee your grandson this won't turn into another Three Mile Island?" he asks, following his reference to that nuclear accident with subsequent invocations of Chernobyl and the ill-fated Challenger space shuttle. Then Landon fast-forwards the man to the year 2018 for "a look at the future he guaranteed." The man's grandson stands over the bed of his own son, dying a lingering death as Landon intones, "The plant you built had an accident."

Lest viewers not be hit over the head hard enough, the crusading angel next visits a farmer using "deadly chemicals in your soil and your water," to show him a possible future of dust-bowl land, a dead wife, and his own sickly grandson. Who's left to hound but the President of the United States? As the unnamed commander-in-chief watches *The War of the Worlds* on TV at the White House, Landon takes control of all the stations, to "talk to you, about Earth, about this planet, about its destruction." He preaches that modern society is "polluting our rivers and our oceans, turning them into seas of poison. We're destroying our ozone layers; we're creating millions of tons of nuclear waste." In other words, "we're not going to be destroyed from outer space. Don't you see? We are going to destroy ourselves." The bizarre climax finds a children's choir humming "Silent Night" to the president, representing "the great-grandchildren you would have had, and the great-great-grandchildren." Too bad "the world died, Mr. President. You did nothing to stop it. They were never born." Landon walks off into the sunset alongside costar French with one last burst of absurd audaciousness:

"C'mon. Let's watch the *Miracle on 34th Street*." It's hard to top for bald-faced sermonizing. And unintended nuttiness.

ENSEMBLES AND INTROSPECTION

Topical concerns were a better fit in the new breed of dramas that focused less on plotted stories or contrived incidents, and more on character growth, identity, and shifting moral choices. ABC's *thirtysomething* had led the way in 1987 with its openness of emotion and self-revelation, which fans praised as intimate and detractors considered self-centeredly touchy-feely. Its panoply of questioning, doubting, yet ambitious thirtysomethings were trying to settle into adult life without abandoning the freedom and idealism of their 1960s-bred youth. What they did was less important than how they felt about it. Before 10 episodes were out, the holidays had come in handy for the show's central married couple, who thrashed out the dilemma of whether and how to celebrate the Jewish husband's holiday of Hanukkah and/or the wife's traditional Christmas, yet another look at the cross-cultural currents of their lives.

A different sort of cultural sort-out came in 1987 on *21 Jump Street*, the youthful cop drama that helped launch the new Fox network. Its first Christmas dealt with the fallout of something its teen audience wasn't even likely to remember firsthand—the Vietnam War. Dustin Nguyen's young undercover officer Harry Aoki is discovered to have lied on his police application. His name is actually Vinh Van Tran, and instead of being Japanese-American, he's a Vietnamese refugee. Flashbacks show his life as a 14-year-old fleeing during the 1975 fall of the country to the Viet Cong. His family is killed, and he survives by making friends with American soldiers, we learn, through dialogue often in Vietnamese with English subtitles. His commanding officer fails to endorse his bid to remain a cop because Steven Williams's character served in Vietnam, where his best friend was killed by a grenade thrown by a teen boy about that same age. "We were fighting everybody," Williams maintains bitterly. "The only people on our side were us." But hearing the refugee saga, he finally comes around. "I was somewhere I didn't wanna be," Williams confesses, "and I had no control over it." Replies Nguyen, "I was forced to go somewhere I didn't want to go. I guess I had no control over it, either." They sit down to Christmas dinner with star cop Johnny Depp's family, to his mother's toast, "To all of us, however we got here." "And," adds Williams, "to everyone else we left over there."

Even guest characters got the introspective treatment in TV's next angelic drama, CBS's *Touched by an Angel*. This one became a 1990s hit not by preaching or instilling fear but by instead extolling the healing grace of compassion. Even with Irish-accented angel Roma Downey delivering earnest weekly declarations of God's love to wayward Americans in need of hearing them, this long-running hit's message felt less overt. Under the graceful touch of devout producer Martha Williamson, its weekly soul-searchers were drawn with more depth, giving actors fleshed-out characters to inhabit and thus providing the audience a more involving (and inviting) experience.

If the show's fans tended to be considered the type of conservative believers viewed by those on the other side as being judgmental, the scripts certainly weren't. They stressed, especially in topical tales, that God's love is all-accepting. The 1996 Christmas episode, about a closeted gay son who has returned to his rural home to die, tackled the perception of AIDS as a punishment from God for homosexual behavior. Peter Michael Goetz plays the hard-nosed father, a violin maker who believes "a flaw in the wood is a flaw in the music" and who rejects the son upon learning of his lifestyle. "Your son is not a violin," pleads Millie Perkins as Goetz's wife. "He's not an instrument that you can carve to your specifications. He is the good loving son that we wanted him to be." After Downey reveals herself to the man, she lays it out in God's terms: "I have been sent here to help you see the truth. The truth is that your son is not the person you want him to be. I'm not asking him to change. I'm asking you. God wants you to accept your son for who he is."

Goetz reacts with what some might consider logical skepticism, in more ways than one. "What is an angel from God doing on the side of a queer?" he asks. "Nothing that is made by God is queer," Downey insists. "God loves all of his creations. You don't have to be perfect to receive God's love. In fact, no one ever is. Whatever wood we are made of, the music is always the purest and the most beautiful when we put ourselves in the hands of The Master." His son, she concludes, "is going to die. God will be there. Will you?"

Compassion trips over politics more explicitly in ABC's *Nothing Sacred*, the acclaimed, controversial hour about an activist urban priest played by hunky young Kevin Anderson. Its 1997 Christmas has Salvadoran refugees taking sanctuary in his church, forcing Father Ray to weigh their political persecution against his responsibility to his parishioners. "Ray, we can't do this," argues a fellow priest, to whom Ray responds, "What, shelter the needy? Read your New Testament." If that isn't enough of an issue for one hour, Ann Dowd's Sister Maureen escalates her crusade to expand women's role in the church by asking to give the Christmas homily ("I am tired of second place"). When the parish's three priests are arrested in a tussle with authorities over the refugees, one of them realizes, "Guess who's doing midnight mass?" "This is a prayer service, not a mass," Mo informs the faithful as she retells the virgin birth.

HELPING THE HOMELESS

Helping those without a home becomes a recurrent theme in the 1990s, when the down-and-outers once known as bums were suddenly elevated into "the homeless," an acknowledgment that, just perhaps, their sorry state was not entirely their own fault. "There but for the grace of God go I" was invoked in episode after episode at holiday time. It's even felt by the high school student played by Claire Danes in a classic study of internal struggle that could have been called "teensomething"—ABC's *My So-Called Life*. This raw yet tender 1994 hour immediately set a weighty tone with its first shot: gay teen Wilson Cruz down on his knees spitting blood onto a snowy sidewalk as passersby continue their stride. He tells school friend Danes that he fell, but his true situation becomes clear when another classmate says, "My old man used to knock me around, too." As Danes's parents debate whether they should have taken Cruz in when he showed up at their door, Danes discovers he has crashed in an abandoned warehouse with other homeless kids. "They're like normal," she tells a friend. "They're like us."

The homeless man on NBC's first-season Christmas hour of *The West Wing* isn't quite literally in the shoes of Richard Schiff's presidential adviser, but he is indeed in his coat when he's found dead on a D.C. bench. "I gave that coat to the Goodwill," Schiff says when authorities call him after finding his card inside. Noticing the man's Korean War tattoo, Schiff becomes obsessed with finding out more about him and arranging a veteran's burial with an honor guard. (It dovetails dramatically with the reason Kathryn Joosten as the president's secretary seems down at Christmas: Her twin sons' "lottery number came up at the same time" and they were killed together in Vietnam on Christmas Eve 1970.)

Homelessness turned out to be just the ticket, too, for situation comedies deciding to get serious around Christmastime, presenting what was initially promoted as—and later derisively called—"a very special episode." That phrase let viewers know that that laughs would be joined and perhaps superseded by an "important," if not predictably obvious, social message. A show like NBC's youth-aimed school romp *Saved by the Bell* would suddenly have student Mark-Paul Gosselaar discover in 1991 that a girl he's taken a liking to at the mall is actually homeless. When the four housemate seniors of NBC's *The Golden Girls* serve dinner at a shelter in 1989, they find one's ex-husband among the needy. "You'd be surprised," says the minister running the place, "how many people are only two or three paychecks away from being out on the street." Even Candice Bergen's bristly title character on CBS's *Murphy Brown* would find help in her heart at Christmas 1988 after an indigent mother sends three waifs her way with a note saying "I love them very much, but I can no longer afford to keep them."

HOPING FOR HEALING

Some sitcoms let their regulars be the ones with issue-oriented revelations. For Christmas 2000 on Fox's wildly funny yet emotionally pointed farce *Titus*, comic Christopher Titus opens the episode in the black-and-white "neutral space" where he narrates weekly. "Death is good—if it's someone you don't like," he chats while decorating a Christmas tree. "I myself have loved many psychos." And one, named Noelle, has just killed herself. Back in the show's color "real time," Titus hasn't told current girlfriend Cynthia Watros about Noelle and now must confess at her funeral that "she was the love of my life." It's not true. But the truth is more painful. "Of all the survivors of domestic abuse," he tells us as he reveals scars on his face, "80 percent never tell anyone. Of all the six-foot-two, 200-pound men beaten up by five-foot, 98-pound women, 100 percent never tell anyone."

Between the hard laughs of flashback depictions ("We had one fight where she thought I was watching the Doublemint twins too intently"), *Titus* delivers equally effective insights. Titus thinks he put up with the abuse because the make-up sex was so great. "The bigger the fight, the better the booty." But Watros presents another reason: "Your mother is a violent, manic-depressive schizo," a truth borne out in both Titus's real life (his oft-institutionalized mother finally killed herself) and on the series (which depicted the same). "You couldn't fix your mother, so you tried to fix Noelle. You're here to forgive Noelle because you always forgive your mother." Indeed, the purpose fueling Titus's perceptive stand-up and sitcom humor is that his sick mother and harsh father not only damaged his psyche but indeed made it stronger. And if "death is good, for evil people," he concludes, "who decides who's evil? Hey, Noelle, I never wanted you dead. I only wanted you gone."

Domestic abuse, homelessness, gang warfare, hate crimes, cultural clashes, substance abuse—these social concerns were all part of the season, every season, on NBC's hit medical drama *ER*. Add such obvious hospital matters as managed care restrictions and pharmaceutical research, and there wasn't a week on this top-rated Thursday hour that didn't tackle topical issues, even at Christmas. The series' first holiday in 1994 addressed the desperate need for organ donations. The second year put its arms around a malpractice suit against Anthony Edwards's Dr. Greene, the death of a "gang priest," and a disillusioned Holocaust survivor rediscovering her faith in the ER.

By the third season, the HIV-positive status of Gloria Reuben's physician assistant Jeanie Boulet is the bone of contention. Greene wants her kept away from patients. "I'm just trying to keep us all from being sued," he argues. "Are you frightened here, Mark?" wonders Laura Innes's Dr. Weaver, "is that it?" Weaver contends Jeanie is "too valuable to rubber-stamp admits all day long." As whispers about a staffer having AIDS grow louder, Jeanie finally announces to all that, yes, she's HIV-positive: "Stop calling me Employee X." And after Greene hits his head on a table, he realizes Jeanie's value, too. Overcoming his own skittishness, he asks her to suture it.

Christmas presents are part of the package in 1999, when Noah Wyle's Dr. Carter becomes so exasperated with the volume of gunshot wounds coming through the ER that he offers to exchange inner city residents' guns for toys, the latter coming from the hospital's "secret Santa" exchange. Four years later, Carter spends his Christmas working at a makeshift clinic in the war-torn Congo seeing what "less fortunate" really means. The show's 2004 holiday found Ming-Na's Dr. Chen confronting mercy killing in her own home, when her own ailing father begs to die.

But ER didn't hit viewers over the head with big issues, the way All in the Family once had in bringing them to the forefront of television storytelling. Thirty years later, TV simply presented social concerns as a matter of course, addressing them along the way as everyday life unfolded—every day, even Christmas.

CHAPTER 12

A Christmas Carol:
Adapting a Dickens of a Plot

If you're a real butthead, then neat ghosts will take you to cool places.

—School boy Ben Savage summarizing
A Christmas Carol in *Boy Meets World*, 1993

I wear chains I made in my own life, made of my own free will when I ignored the unpopular and the suffering, and dedicated my every waking moment to being a greedy, hard-ass, self-centered bitch! ... Rest assured, I will haunt your every eight-count and post-lunch purge unless you see the error of your ways!

—Cyia Batten as former cheerleader Marley Jacob, *Popular*, 1999

A Christmas Carol isn't merely the most well-known Christmas tale of the industrial age. This saga of three ghosts appearing on Christmas Eve to make a miserly old man to change his ways is also a literary work out of copyright and in the public domain. That makes it a handy and free-of-charge plot to, uh, adapt, whenever TV writers don't have a great notion.

Lots of kids from the baby boom onward have first discovered this Dickens classic in the form of nearsighted cartoon klutz Mr. Magoo. NBC's 1962 special "Mr. Magoo's Christmas Carol" featured the voice of Jim Backus as the perpetually mixed-up old man who means well but manages to mess up just about everything he blindly touches. (Backus, a veteran of radio and movies including *Rebel without a Cause*, soon brought a similarly snooty sound to millionaire Mr. Howell on CBS's 1960s sitcom *Gilligan's Island.*) Magoo had made his debut in theatrical cartoons from the UPA studio (Gerald McBoing-Boing) in 1949 as a supporting character, quickly becoming a sensation in his own right. As theatrical animation dwindled in the late 1950s, UPA moved the character to television, where his lower-budget adventures looked less inspired.

Except for this musical-framed delight. "Magoo's Christmas Carol" presents Dickens's tale as a stage play with songs, into which Magoo mistakenly stumbles to play the character of Scrooge. Where it could have gone goofy, this *Carol* played things straight. Yes, there was the occasional punch line: A ghost tells Magoo, "You have never seen the like of me before," and Magoo replies "I'm not sure I see the like of you now." But Barbara Chain's script is more often a fairly ruthless interpretation, in which Magoo's more-than-usually-competent Scrooge really does quake at the sight of the ghosts who appear on Christmas Eve in his bedroom to set him straight. Backus's emotional vocal work emphasizes the pathos of Scrooge's life, and it's embellished by surprisingly clever little touches in the animation. The half-dozen songs from the Broadway composing team of Jule Styne and Bob Merrill (*Funny Girl*) also aim for the heart, striking a warm note.

Fear was more the tone of a 1964 cautionary tale from acclaimed TV writer Rod Serling. Best known now for his long-running CBS *Twilight Zone* anthology, Serling had made his name in live TV drama with *Patterns* and *Requiem for a Heavyweight*. Asked to pen a United Nations special, the brooding writer adapted Dickens into ABC's "Carol for Another Christmas," a Cold-War morality play in which a go-it-alone mogul named Grudge (Sterling Hayden) is persuaded by three ghosts (Steve Lawrence, Pat Hingle, and Robert Shaw) that the future lies in international teamwork. His visits to World War I, Hiroshima, and an apocalyptic post-nuke world (run by Peter Sellers!) make rather blatant warnings for him to change his ways.

SITCOM CAROLS

But *A Christmas Carol* isn't always presented so gravely. It's a frequent font for sitcoms, too. CBS's fondly remembered *WKRP in Cincinnati* moved the story to a contemporary office context in 1980. The mean-boss part of Scrooge is what's crucial here, as embodied by Gordon Jump's radio station manager Arthur Carlson. The staff figures he's "gonna stiff us all again this year" on holiday bonus money. As he does. Just after delivering a lecture on "hard and frugal times," Carlson's nap at his desk provides an opening for Dickens's three ghosts. Christmas Past is a sterner version of bosomy blonde secretary Loni Anderson, showing Carlson how he started down his penny-pinching road as an eager-beaver young station exec. Christmas Present lets Tim Reid's flashy black DJ Venus Flytrap cut loose as a glittery, throne-sitting god, playing off the racial humor then being groundbreakingly sprinkled through sitcoms. That leaves Christmas Future to be none other than Howard Hesseman's drugged-out DJ Johnny Fever, who clues Carlson in to the automated radio station his penury will necessitate. Upon realizing the resentment he engenders, the waking Carlson can't hand out bonuses fast enough to his bewildered staff.

If the episode sounds a bit too sentimentally indulgent for this rock-and-roll series, the ever-witty *WKRP* sneaks in a sort of yeah-we-know awareness to excuse its indulgence. First confronted by a ghost, Carlton disdainfully wonders, "This isn't gonna be another one of those Charles Dickens's *A Christmas Carol* things, is it?" He's hip to the trick. Just can't do anything about it. And why should he? *Christmas Carol* flashbacks let other cast members strut their stuff, not only as ghosts but as younger flashback versions of themselves, always a favorite tube technique. At the end, *WKRP* writers get in another 1970s counterculture dig at the mainstream: Carlson attributes his mind-bending experience to having eaten one of Fever's "special" brownies.

The Scrooge story moved into the greed-decade 1980s with NBC's *Family Ties*, where it dovetailed perfectly with Michael J. Fox's capitalistic yuppie teen Alex Keaton. "They can put a man on the moon," he moans at 1983's Christmas Eve snowfall, "but they can't stop this white slop from falling out of the sky?" After heckling carolers, this modern-day cynic falls asleep to visits from two ghosts (they've only got 22 minutes)—youngest sister Tina Yothers, taking him back 10 years to see his tiny self scorning Christmas cheer to work on the family's taxes, and teen sister Justine Bateman, showing his family's future, living in rags as wealthy miser Alex squeezes them for debt payments. And what of the present time? Once he's spiritually renewed, Alex races out Christmas morning to splurge on gifts at 7-Eleven. *TV Guide* and beef jerky are his inadequate but well-intentioned symbols of affection for his oft-neglected family.

Alex's final realization echoes many TV characters in *Carols* over the years: "You're the most important people in the world to me, and I know I don't show it sometimes, but I love you all very much." It's the kind of sweetly sentimental, lesson-learned, "very special episode" type of denouement on which crowd-pleasing TV sitcoms thrive. Scrooge-y characters scoff at the seasonal spirit, then come around to a warm heart, thanks to the intervention of Dickens's set-it-right spirits. All they're really doing is forcing the cynic to stop and take a look at his life—what he most appreciated from his childhood, how he has wandered away from that loving warmth in pursuit of cold hard cash, whom he has hurt along the way, and how he might put those wrongs right.

When Christmas-scorning Detroit disc jockey Martin Lawrence goes "back in the day" during his 1996 nap on the Fox sitcom *Martin*, he revisits the time he lost his Christmas spirit as a child whose longed-for gift of Chuck Taylor sneakers turned out to be a "Chuck Tyler" knockoff. The black cast hits other ethnic touchstones. The ghosts who escort Martin into the past are his homeboys, dressed up not as rappers Run-DMC but "Dumb-DMC," handily morphing Scrooge's *Christmas Carol* chains into the gold jewelry paraded by hip-hop acts. The future visit shows that only Martin's nemesis Pam (Tichina Arnold) is still around his sorry self 40 years on, dropping by to steal his Social Security check while he watches TV alone—precisely what he's doing before his nap, before he sees the light, before he finally shows up at his friends' holiday party bearing gifts truly "from the heart."

Cranky characters like Martin are naturals for the Scrooge treatment, both expert at the orneriness and in need of humanizing to excuse their crabbiness week after week. Oscar the grouch of Neil Simon's hit play and ABC's hit sitcom *The Odd Couple* turns mean in a 1970 episode when Tony Randall's fussy Felix wants Jack Klugman's sloppy Oscar to play the Dickens character in a charity staging for the local orphanage. "Don't talk to me about Christmas, will ya?" gripes Oscar, who continues to owe alimony now that his ex-wife's remarriage failed to take place. "All that sticky phony good will. I'd like to get a giant candy cane and beat the wings off a sugar plum fairy!" Cop friend Murray (Al Molinaro) pleads, "Please, Oscar. The kids need a Scrooge they can hate."

Cue the Dickensian dream. Oscar dozes before the TV, where his beloved roller derby has been preempted by *A Christmas Carol*. His sleeping self is guided by a Felix-in-chains through the past, present, and yet-to-come of his nastiness. As a "child" in short pants and knee socks, Oscar writes a spiteful letter to Santa when he doesn't get the toys he wants. In the present, he's cruel to the Bob Crachit-like Felix and to the Tiny Tim-ish Murray. ("Tiny," chastises the neatnik dream Felix, "don't bang the furniture with the crutch.") After seeing his future tombstone with clothes sloppily strewn atop it, Oscar comes around, agreeing to play Scrooge after all and even buying ultra-tidy Felix an "air germ humidifier" as a holiday gift.

Scrooge-like behavior was a daily attitude for another 1970s favorite. Gravelly voiced Redd Foxx, the legendary "blue" comedian of 1950s party albums and black-audience nightclubs on the "chitlin' circuit," finally made it to TV in typically cantankerous style in NBC's hit *Sanford & Son*, another adaptation of a British sitcom from *All in the Family* makers Norman Lear and Bud Yorkin. As a prickly elderly junkman making life miserable for Demond Wilson as his adult son and roommate, Foxx also delights in tormenting his late wife's stern-minded sister. "You don't upset me, Fred Sanford," roars back LaWanda Page's Bible-thumping dowager. "I have the feeling of Christmas!" "And the face of Halloween," snaps Foxx.

Fred takes advantage of a neighborhood kid trying to make $10 to buy gifts at holiday time 1975, overworking the boy while he falls asleep—and into his own *Christmas Carol* dream. As Lamont plays three different ghosts (the last so gaudily attired that Fred quips, "Who are you, the spirit of Liberace?"), Foxx's character sees himself as a tyke lying to his mother, as a thoughtless current-day friend, and alone in a chilling future. It's enough to make him pay the kid double and then give the kid's parents gifts suspiciously bearing the same LS monogram that would otherwise go to his own son. He tells them it means to "love somebody."

CARTOON CAROLS

Such overt sentiment is less necessary in cartoon form. When *The Jetsons* casts greedy boss Mr. Spacely as its Scrooge in 1985, he learns his lesson not by revisiting the past, where he exploits young Georgie Jetson running a childhood lemonade stand, but by glimpsing the future, where the Jetsons have taken his money. "You had to sue Mr. Spacely for all those millions," wife Jane tells George. "He made the sprocket that Astro swallowed." Yes, the Jetsons' dog is this tale's sickly Tiny Tim.

That *The Simpsons* would also turn to this classic tale seems inevitable, considering how long Fox's animated hit has been running. But it wasn't till its fifteenth season in 2003 that Matt Groening's writers decided to get Dickensian. After Homer is told by a coworker, "You're the most selfish man I know," he zones out at home on the couch with *A Christmas Carol* playing on TV. "Oh my God!" he gasps. "It's like looking at a cartoon version of myself!" Realizing "I have time to reform my ways," Homer promises "I'll be the nicest man in town." (He's made that promise before, of course. "But this time I'm sober.") That puts him directly into competition with ultra-nice neighbor Ned Flanders. Soon, each is doing so much good around town that a news anchor says they're "holding families at nice-point." The episode also indulges in spoofing other TV holiday staples—"How the Grinch Stole Christmas" (Homer takes away presents, to the strains of a "mean" song, so people won't get unhappily greedy); "A Charlie Brown Christmas" (Flanders reads from the Bible); and even "Christmas with the California Prunes" (which the tube-tied Simpsons are seen watching on TV).

Lizzie McGuire also mixes her TV metaphors, in a 2002 Disney Channel episode of Hillary Duff's live-action 'tween comedy. She's so obsessed with building a winning float for the Christmas parade that she loses sight of the holiday's warm and generous spirit. Helping her find it again after she dozes off are her Christmas-past mom ("the pepperoni pizza that I ate for dinner"), her little brother (who does a "Charlie Brown Christmas" reading), and an elf who wants to be a dentist (à la TV's "Rudolph the Red Nosed Reindeer"). Topping off both the episode and her float, in a burst of final outlandishness, is Aerosmith's Steven Tyler screaming "Santa Claus Is Coming to Town" in a St. Nick suit.

ACROSS THE ATLANTIC

It's less obvious for some other series to adapt Dickens. And *The Avengers* doesn't quite. The 1965 holiday airing of this literate and sophisticated secret agent lark on England's ITV (imported to America by ABC) finds Patrick Macnee's dapper John Steed and Diana Rigg's sexy sidekick Emma Peel at an estate party held by a publisher proclaimed "a great authority on Dickens." The guests are delivered costumes to attend as the author's characters—Steed as *A Tale of Two Cities*' guillotine-bound Sydney Carton, Mrs. Peel as young Oliver Twist. Meanwhile, Steed is tormented by "a Christmas nightmare" featuring an old friend who died of "a brain storm" ("It, metaphorically speaking, exploded"), just as he was suspected of passing national secrets. The traitorous evil is actually being executed by a troupe of villains playing a dastardly party game of mind control, "poking around in one's innermost thoughts," as Steed puts it. The expressionist nightmares he's been psychically sent—a blank room with a forest of white tree cut-outs, a maniacally masked Santa Claus, Steed's own head on the guillotine—suddenly come to life at the party castle. And this quite tangible Father Christmas totes a very real gun.

Another English import adapts Dickens's enduring yule tale more directly, while turning it on its redemptionist head. Rowan Atkinson's several BBC *Blackadder* series of period-set shenanigans (aired Stateside on PBS) spent the 1980s visiting dire historical eras, linking the various time frames with abiding scoundrel Edmund Blackadder's attempts to take personal advantage of crises afflicting the British nation. Their plotlines cleverly came together for the 1988 special "Blackadder's Christmas Carol" in the person of Dickens-era shopkeeper Ebenezer Blackadder, whom narration describes as "the kindest and loveliest man in all England." Not, however, for long. Soon after Ebenezer falls for sob stories from London's every poor urchin to give away nearly everything he has, he gets "a wee bit of haunting" from ghostly comic Robbie Coltrane on Christmas Eve. The imposing Coltrane's task is "getting misers to change their evil ways—but you're obviously such a good chap, there'll be no need for any of that nonsense, so I'll just say cheery-bye."

Detained by Ebenezer's curiosity as to just how ghosts get baddies to go good, Coltrane confides "we just show them how rotten their ancestors were." Seems the Dickensian Blackadder doesn't realize his were "stinkers to a man. Ooh," says Coltrane, "perhaps you'd like to see." And so he shows Ebenezer his forebears on the make with Queen Elizabeth I and King George III, and even a futuristic disco/*Star Wars*/computerized queen-in-space. That last exhibit takes things unfortunately too far. "So let's get this straight," Ebenezer summarizes. "If I was bad, my descendants would rule the entire universe? ... You don't think it points the very clear lesson that bad guys have all the fun?" Soon Atkinson is back in dastardly Blackadder form, having "changed from the nicest man in England into," as one neighbor declares, "the horridest man in the world!"

DRAMA DOES DICKENS

Dickens-inspired time trips can go even further into history than *Blackadder's* British royal ramblings. American syndication's 1990s fantasy adventure *Xena—The Warrior Princess* takes place in the mythological time of the syndicated *Hercules* series from which this cult favorite was spun off. The Scrooge figure in *Xena's* 1996 holiday hour is a king so evil, he imprisons subjects for "singing carols and decorating a tree" to celebrate their big holiday of the winter solstice. (This is, remember, the polytheistic era before Christ.) But *Hercules* and *Xena* always did play fast with the action and loose with cultural anachronisms. So Lucy Lawless's wandering warrior and Renee O'Connor's teen sidekick Gabrielle corral the king's men by using Xena's flying chakram disc to swiftly bind them in red ribbons. Quips Gabrielle, "I didn't know you did gift wrapping."

They also do Dickens. After Gabrielle tells local orphans the bedtime story of a miserly man to whom the gods "sent the fates to separate the strings of his life so that he might see himself more clearly," our dynamic duo is inspired to help the king reconsider his own existence. Xena appears in his bedchamber as the "fate" who shows him the wife who left him, played through pratfalls by Gabrielle. He views the present by following Xena out among his subjects in disguise, to learn he's considered "the meanest, most tightfisted ruler," the type who would evict orphans on Christmas Eve. He's knocked out and awakes in a darkened room believing it's his future tomb: "Can it change if I change my life? … I'll prove to you I'm not the man I was." Since the wife who left him has become the matron of the orphanage, she's on hand to see his change of heart. He pleads, "Can you ever forgive me for closing my heart to you and to our people, for wasting 30 precious years in bitterness and greed?"

Of course—if *Xena* fans can forgive a script that casts the king's reluctant subordinate as a frustrated toy maker, who tumbles down the orphanage chimney in a red suit and white beard, bearing a sack of kiddie gifts. "By Zeus," he chuckles, "I'm gonna do that every solstice eve!" Lest this tale leave a Christmas tradition untouched, Xena and Gabrielle meet a couple on the road as they leave town, giving the pair their donkey so the woman and the baby she's carrying won't have to walk westward. "May God smile on you always for your kindness," the beatific woman beams.

A fanciful show can sometimes get away with laying it on thick, and that's a trick used more than once, too, by NBC's *Quantum Leap*. Playing a scientist able to "leap" into others' bodies in various eras spanning his own lifetime, Scott Bakula could know then what he knows now, thus aiding victims of previous prejudices, crimes, and tragedies, and even coming to his own empathetic understanding of such afflictions. In 1990's Christmas tale, Bakula leaps back to 1962 to change Charles Rocket's scheming developer, who plans to tear down an urban mission desperately needed by the city's poor. "He's alone, he's miserable," observes Bakula to his unseen-by-others holographic supervisor, Dean Stockwell. "It's like Charles, uh, Dickens," Bakula formulates as his scheme takes shape. "So, we Scrooge him, we take him back to his beginnings. We try and remind him that there's more important things in life."

Bakula has "leaped" into being the tycoon's valet, so he can drive Rocket down to skid row to visualize himself as the poor kid he once was. A visit to the mission demonstrates why the place is now so crucial to the neighborhood. But Bakula and the mission's fetching young female leader lay it on a bit too thick, sending a pleading young boy into the mix, and Rocket realizes he's being played: "You were trying to make a mark out of me, but it's not going to work. This building comes down in one week!" Bakula tells Stockwell, "I think we should just keep at it, and give him the ghost of Christmas Future." Stockwell's hologram wears chains to the tycoon's bedside, then shows him a "future" TV newscast from the 1970s explaining how his wealth was "undone by his unbridled greed and uncontrollable lust for power." Before long, the chastened mogul is back at the mission in "real"

1962 time: "Do you have room for one more lost soul?" The wit and sense of wonder infusing *Quantum Leap* on a weekly basis buy it enough viewer goodwill that we forgive its bleeding-heart blatancy and accept its earnest evocation of the Christmas spirit.

The WB's youth-aimed *Popular* proves yet more powerfully that even the hippest, savviest, and most irreverent among us can take Dickens's age-old lessons to heart. In fact, the series' cheeky 1999 Christmas hour offers one of series TV's best versions of the classic narrative, from the pen (computer keyboard?) of one of the industry's youngest and most cynical writers. Ryan Murphy was 31 when his acerbic creation tackled the tale as part of its dry-wit depiction of high school's social-status sadism. Murphy's "Fall on Your Knees" script finds cold-blooded in-crowd arbiter Nicole (Tammy Lynn Michaels) sniffily disdaining all that "spirit of the season crap." She steals money from the street-corner charity kettle to buy designer duds and haughtily rejects fellow cheerleaders' pleas that talented dancer Carmen (Sara Rue) join their ranks despite being "fat." (Only in Hollywood. Rue is barely large enough to wear so-called full-figured clothes.)

Christmas, as Nicole speedily scoffs in Murphy's hyperverbal discourse, is "the time of year when the suicide rate is highest, when lonely deluded people pretend to feel comfort and joy and then crash two weeks later because all they're left with is credit card debt. Christmas is just a silly holiday kept alive to bolster the national economic index and relieve a little guilt." Which means her own guilt must now come into play. Home alone at night, Nicole is first visited by the see-through ghost of her late, bulimic friend Marley Jacob. ("I always knew you had no bowels, but now I can see it so clearly," moans Nic. "You're so lucky.") After the homage-named Marley (Cyia Batten) promises to "haunt your every eight-count and post-lunch purge unless you see the error of your ways," the three spirits appear. Drill-sergeant school teacher (Diane Delano) recalls Nicole's unloved childhood: "Although you've turned into a spiteful bilious hag, you weren't born that way." Goody-goody pal Mary Cherry (Leslie Grossman) suggests present-day psychological help, to which Nic contends, "I'm always smarter than the therapists they send me to." And a figure hooded in black arrives to reveal a possibly toxic future. Murphy's script even manages to maneuver would-be cheerleader Carmen onto crutches to set up a Tiny Tim reference.

Such faithfulness to Dickens actually allows Murphy quite a bit of latitude in reframing the story's well-known elements in his own twisted tone, displaying the scalpel-like precision that would mark his later FX adult hit *Nip/Tuck*. That acclaimed drama of disturbed plastic surgeons and their identity-chasing patients would gradually flesh out (pun partly intended) many of the questions of character he first approached in *Popular*. How do we become who we are? What do we allow to define us? Can we deliberately transform ourselves? And at what cost? Perhaps only a show so seemingly obsessed with the superficiality of modern image-making can so effectively plumb beneath the surface to the soul-searching that Dickens rendered so enduringly—and that Christmas nearly two centuries later still seems designed to stir up.

Daytime Dickens

Daytime drama also taps into the Dickens well—and why not? Soap operas sometimes service the same characters for decades. New plots are hard to come by. Tony Geary's rascally Luke Spencer character had been a leading light on ABC's *General Hospital* over a 25-year span by the time of 2003's holiday hour, in which a Scrooge-y Luke was so despondent over disturbed wife Laura's institutionalization that he wouldn't even make a yuletide visit to his kindergarten-age daughter. Helping show him the error of his sulking, self-pitying ways are ghosts appearing in the form of his hated rivals from the nasty Cassadine clan. After visiting some alternative possibilities during this "tour through my life's regrets," the dispirited Luke comes to realize he needs to stay engaged in life, despite his legendary true love being relegated to some Swiss asylum. (Well, it *is* a soap. And Laura-playing actress Genie Francis had a falling-out with the producers.) His ghostly encounters transform Luke into a bouncy backslapper who makes the rounds of Port Charles making merry—right into his little daughter's holiday dinner, brightening her heart. At least for one day, daytime's ever-disastrous predicaments give way to a (temporary) happy ending.

A TV-Movie Carol

Among the made-for-TV movie adaptations:

- *An American Christmas Carol* (1979, ABC)—Henry Winkler in a Depression-era setting
- *Skinflint: A Country Christmas Carol* (1979, NBC)—Hoyt Axton, Barbara Mandrell, and other country singers in modern-day Tennessee
- *A Christmas Carol* (1984, CBS)—George C. Scott in a faithful adaptation
- *Ebbie* (1995, Lifetime)—Susan Lucci as a modern store executive
- *Ms. Scrooge* (1997, USA)—Cicely Tyson as a modern bank owner
- *A Christmas Carol* (1999, TNT)—Patrick Stewart in a full production of his popular one-man stage show
- *A Diva's Christmas Carol* (2000, VH1)—Vanessa Williams as a pop superstar
- *A Carol Christmas* (2003, Hallmark)—Tori Spelling as a talk show host, with William Shatner as a nutty ghost
- *Karroll's Christmas* (2004, A&E)—Tom Everett Scott in a spoof where he's mistakenly taken through somebody else's life
- *A Christmas Carol* (2004, NBC)—Kelsey Grammer in a location-shot musical based on Madison Square Garden's extravaganza

CHAPTER 13

It's a Wonderful Life: Wishing They'd Never Been Born

Popular paid homage to a more modern Christmas classic in its second season, again giving a familiar tale a more youthful spin in a surprisingly mature manner. The 2000 WB episode "The Consequences of Falling" used Frank Capra's 1946 movie perennial *It's a Wonderful Life* as a jumping-off point—literally. Christopher Gorham's teen cancer patient Harrison John decides his painful life isn't worth living and considers leaping off the hospital roof, much as James Stewart's original movie character despondently threw himself off a bridge.

But, of course, there's a guardian angel nearby this time, too, also named Clarence (Mike Damus), the hospital roommate that Harrison has just seen die. "I'm an angel in training, and I don't get my wings unless I save you," the late teen warns Harrison. "So for God's sake, don't do anything stupid and ruin my career." That dash of contemporary attitude is the key as this new-age Clarence shows Harrison what his friends' lives would have been like if he had never been born: A liberal free-spirit friend would instead be a fur-wearing Republican. Two of the high school's "popular" fashionistas would "turn into toothless penny-ante whores with mullets." Another pal dies of anorexia. An innocent girl becomes corrupt without the "moral guideposts" Harrison provided. "You were the only thing they all had in common," Clarence tells Harrison as they view this alternate life from the stalls of the school's girls' bathroom. "Without you, they drifted."

Harrison's "wonderful life" experience may resound even more deeply because of the impressionable time in his life it takes place. "Who we are as adults is determined by who we are as teenagers," Clarence notes. And we pass that on to yet another generation, as Harrison understands when he's shown a vision of the son he might have if he continues to live. "The love you have for your child," says Clarence, "erases the hurt you inherited from your father." Harrison resolves to fight for his life as friends gather in his hospital room for a Christmas celebration—and it turns out that nasty Nicole is the bone-marrow match that might make him better: "What are the odds, huh? Talk about karmic payback." Murphy's script is all the more emotionally effective for delivering its bald-faced seasonal sentiment through *Popular*'s satiric sting and outrageous characters.

IT'S A MISERABLE LIFE

Sometimes, however, outrageous characters should simply remain that way. Nobody wants to see a mushy Al Bundy. The suburban Chicago shoe salesman had a horrible life, and that was precisely the comedic point of *Married...with Children*. Fox's gleefully trashy 1987–97 sitcom never hit its points so hard as in its seriously unsentimental Christmas episodes. After their first holiday half-hour had Santa splattered in the Bundys' backyard, the devilish writing duo of Ron Leavitt and Michael Moye turned to the schmaltz of Capra's ubiquitous yuletide yarn for their 1989 script.

Ed O'Neill's Al has a horrible day at the mall, fighting with "a 300-pound alcoholic in a red suit"—that would be Santa, who never got a break here—but coming home is no improvement. "I know what would make you feel better," quips Katey Sagal's tawdry, sarcastic wife, Peg. "But I'll never leave you, not in a million years." After making Bundy-styled snow cones of yard precipitation slathered in "lime" mouthwash and "cherry" cough syrup, the family leaves for Christmas dinner at Denny's, while Al goes out to put up Christmas lights—and gets the literal shock of his life. He revives to find crude screamer comic Sam Kinison as his guardian angel. ("I thought I was here to save a human soul," barks the flask-lifting Kinison.) Life inside his tacky-turned-stylish house is what it would have been without Al around: sleazy daughter Kelly now a straitlaced college student, boorish son Bud a preppie, and indolent sleaze Peg all prim and cooking, blissfully married to a model-handsome executive. "She doesn't know you're there, Bundy," barks Kinison. "Just like when you're having sex." Accomplished griper O'Neill whines back, "What do we do next? Go back in time to the day I should have been conceived and watch my father invent the condom?"

"I'm sorry, Bundy, I've failed you," Kinison admits. "I was supposed to show you why you should live, but I can't think of one darn reason." But

Al can: "Look at them; they're happy, not a care in the world. You think I'm gonna let that happen after all the grief they put me through? I want to live!" A positive negative lesson—just the kind of subversive satire, craftily delivered, that kept *Married...with Children* on the air through critical disdain and conservative boycotts, thriving into a wonderful afterlife in perpetual syndication.

LOVE LIVES ON

Robert Guillaume's title character on ABC's much sweeter *Benson* has a less strident guide through his what-if trip. Veteran actress Beah Richards plays dearly departed mother to his governor's aide, only slightly annoyed that an accident during her son's holiday shopping trip has left him in the emergency room at death's door, knocking at her abode in the clouds. She shows him how needed he is back on earth with a glimpse seven years into the future. ("I saw this movie once with Jimmy Stewart," Benson exclaims.) It isn't good for the dimwit governor, who's been framed by enemies and impeached. It isn't good for the governor's teen daughter, now divorced from a defensive lineman named Lunkhead. It isn't even good for Benson's verbal sparring partner in the governor's mansion, cranky cook Kraus (Inga Swenson), homelessly selling fruitcake door to door. The comedy is broad, and Guillaume, a musical theater veteran (*Purlie*), gets to sing "O Little Town of Bethlehem." This 1984 episode is a virtual template for sitcom Christmas traditions with its paint-by-numbers employment of corny situations, exaggerated play-acting, seasonal singing, and blatant sentimentality. "Our bodies can't live forever," pronounces Richards, "but our love can."

So, of course, can teen nerd Steve Urkel's infatuation with neighbor Laura on ABC's *Family Matters*. The 1992 holiday finds Kellie Shanygne Williams's exasperated object of affection lashing out, after Jaleel White's obsessed klutz breaks a crystal vase she bought for her mother: "I have had it with you, Steve!...I don't want to think about you, don't want to talk about you, and I don't want to hear about you. From now on, you don't exist. Now go!" But after the audience's sympathetic "awww," she adds the clincher: "You know what? I wish you knew what it was like to be me."

A sentimental familycom like this loves to make a wish come true. Laura walks past a store window where rows of TV sets are playing *It's a Wonderful Life* as James Stewart meets his guardian angel Clarence. And into Laura's life pops her own aspirant angel, Tyrone P. Jackson, with a similar winged goal ("You know if you go to a restaurant in heaven and you don't have your wings, they sit you right next to the kitchen"). Tyrone shows her Urkel in her shoes, suddenly "charming, handsome, popular—Steve is the perfect son," enthuses Reginald VelJohnson as Laura's, now Steve's, father. Then the angel warns, "Now you're about to find out what it's like to be Steve Urkel." That would be a nerdy Laura in glasses and pigtails, wiggling weirdly and zealously eyeing Steve as her "sweetums," until he lashes out, "From this moment on, you don't exist. Now go!" She realizes nerds "have feelings just like anybody else" and wishes she'd been nicer to Steve. "That's the wish I'm really here to grant," reveals her angel. "I'm going to send you back in time, give you a second chance." In his world, "every time a star lights up, an angel gets his wings." Urkel comes over for Christmas, and the shorted-out star atop the family tree suddenly lights up. "Either your feelings for me have changed," Urkel says, "or you've suffered a nervous breakdown."

FROM JOKES TO THE JUGULAR

Could be one or the other, too, on ABC's 1980s push-pull romantic comedy hour *Moonlighting*. Though Cybill Shepherd's ex-model Maddie had intended to sell the Blue Moon detective agency that her shady advisers had bought, she ended up investigating alongside Bruce Willis's fast-talking rascal. If she had sold the agency? Well, we'd never have had the ripe repartee that made the previously unknown Willis a bankable movie star (*Die Hard*). But more to the plot's point, Richard Libertini's angel reveals their office would have been taken over by the wealthy sleuths played by Robert Wagner and Stefanie Powers in *Hart to Hart*—a previous occupant of *Moonlighting*'s Tuesday ABC time slot. The in-joke irony of this 1986 episode exuberantly illustrated the entire series' winking appreciation of its own artifice, while letting the human warmth between Maddie and colleague David shine through.

Even more heartfelt was the TV-tinged 2003 celebration on ABC's *Life with Bonnie*, the distinctive semi-improvised comedy series written, directed, and starred in by offbeat wit (and frequent David Letterman banterer) Bonnie Hunt. Her Chicago talk-show host is not happy about a live Christmas show that takes her away from her family. "I swear to God, sometimes I wish I never had this job," she says, which, of course, conjures the dream of a guardian angel—in this case, *Eight Is Enough* dad Dick Van Patten, whom Bonnie had seen on TV the night before.

"You never left your job as researcher for the local news, and you were never on *Morning Chicago*," Van Patten says, guiding her through a now impersonal TV studio, where her once-friendly staff members drink and sulk as Phyllis Diller hosts the show. Upon waking from her "dream," Bonnie brings her family to the studio to appear on her Christmas show, where they sing "Auld Lang Syne" and she opens her "secret Santa" present—an autographed picture of Dick Van Patten. The episode's ending gets the personal touch of the camera's pan across the faces of her Chicago TV studio "crew," also the actual Hollywood crew members who produced *Life with Bonnie* each week.

But it's family, of course, that's at the heart of Christmas, and at the heart of a delicately straightforward adaptation that may be TV's best. NBC's *Providence* already had a built-in guardian angel in the character of Conchita Ferrell's control-freak mother, whose death brings Melina Kanakaredes's sleek California doctor Syd back to her Rhode Island homestead. In the series' first episode, Syd has already faced the monumental choice of staying there or returning to her glam beachside life. The choice to stay is one she regrets when that family seems less than eager to jointly celebrate the 1999 yule, even as Syd enthuses, "I want Christmas to be special again this year, like mom used to put together." Syd finds herself alone watching *It's a Wonderful Life* and wondering "why I moved back here in the first place." Hearing her, of course, is the mother whose perfectly coiffed, cigarette-smoking spirit weekly accompanies Syd through her life's choices: "You really believe things would be better for everyone if you'd stayed in California?"

And so Syd sees that alternative in action. The homestead has been sold. Her father is mopily married to the manipulative woman Syd has recently seen trying to lure him to that year's Christmas party. Syd's sister is pregnant (again) by a married man, while her brother is jailed for selling the counterfeit toy-of-the-year he has just left the house to peddle. Even her clinic is taken over by a managed-care conglomerate. Back in California, Syd finds herself married to an old boyfriend given to lines like "Are we a power couple or what?" Amid caustic commentary on the proceedings, Mom counsels that "Every family needs a leader, Syd, and whether you want it or not, for our family that person is you." In that spirit, the real Syd manages to corral everyone for a traditional celebration, to warmly watch home movies of Farrell long ago telling them, "Just being here spending the day with all of you is the real gift of Christmas."

It's a Wonderful Life doesn't always inspire such ponder-the-purpose introspection. Sometimes it inspires acting out. Especially among cynics who feel they've been force-fed its seemingly ubiquitous inspiration once too many times. NBC's *Saturday Night Live* let it rip in 1986 with guest host William Shatner introducing a "lost ending" of Capra's classic. Footage from the black-and-white original is woven into a monochrome sketch with Dana

Carvey in the Stewart role and Phil Hartman as his Uncle Billy. After the latter realizes the plot's missing money landed in the hands of town villain Old Man Potter, Carvey leads an angry mob in revenge. Bleating "I want a piece of you, Potter!" he kicks Jon Lovitz's Potter from his wheelchair, to the dark strains of Bernard Herrmann-ish soundtrack music. The movie still ends with "Auld Lang Syne"—but it's sung as the townspeople beat Potter with sticks. It's a wonderful anti-tribute.

WONDERFUL WATCHING

TV show writers seem to love referencing *It's a Wonderful Life* even when they don't echo its wish-I-was-never-born storyline. Maybe that's because viewers could so easily relate to stumbling over the film's incessant TV airings in the 1970s and 1980s. Broadcasters, believing the film had fallen into the public domain, took the opportunity to air this "free" seasonal programming seemingly every other hour on every other station. (The film's owners later firmly established copyright protection through the movie's registered musical score.)

Roseanne Barr's title character in ABC's *Roseanne* tries to gather her family to watch the seasonal perennial in 1992, but Sara Gilbert's daughter Darlene prefers to spend the evening at her boyfriend's. Anyway, she says, "It's on again at 9, and 9:30, and 11, and at midnight in Spanish—'Una Vida Wonderfulmente.'" In 1994, Brett Butler's lead in ABC's *Grace under Fire* bemoans getting dragged to a movie theater by an excited friend to see the 1946 classic. "Nadine, were you born on Tuesday?" Butler drawls. "That movie's showing [on TV] like 30 times this week. I think it's on in my medicine cabinet at eight o'clock." As Woody Harrelson puts it on NBC's 1987 *Cheers*, "From now until New Year's on Channel 13, it's a wonderful month."

Married...with Children didn't just rip off—uh, pay homage to—the film's plot. This subversive Fox hit also built an episode around its tube inescapability. Since Ed O'Neill's sad-sack Al Bundy character only wants to be left alone by his dreaded family to watch TV, it's perfect for him to be flipping channels in 1993 in search of something else. "And now, for your Christmas viewing pleasure," says the TV announcer, "Channel 2 presents..." "Anything but *It's a Wonderful Life*," moans Al, as the TV proclaims, "...*It's a Wonderful Life!*" A click of the remote finds: "*It's a Wonderful Life!*" And another click: "*It's a Wonderful Life!*" And another: "It's *The Good, the Bad and the Ugly!*" "Great," rejoices Al, only to hear "...right after *It's a Wonderful Life!*"

There's even "the TV movie version of *It's a Wonderful Life*," notes wife Peg. "It's from a female perspective, starring Suzanne Pleshette." (Al's retort: "Who plays the female?") "I hate this movie!" grouses Bundy. "Because it's a horrible life. You know the reason they never made a sequel? Because when the guy came back, he killed himself. And this time, he took that angel with him."

The annual viewing ritual can conversely be an anticipated event. Group viewing of *It's a Wonderful Life* is a tradition in 2000's Christmas episode of ABC's one-season sitcom *The Geena Davis Show*. The star's newly married character may miss watching the movie with her friends, who down a shot in a drinking game every time James Stewart coos his wife's name, Mary. "How does *Wonderful Life* end?" costar Mimi Rogers wonders. How would they know? The pals actually make it through by the episode's end-credits kicker, when Rogers leads group weeping over the movie's maudlin conclusion. The TV broadcast proceeds to announce live coverage from Bethlehem, where Jesus was born to—"Maaaarrrrry!" they toast, one more time, in their best Jimmy Stewart drawl. Even Fred Flintstone is a fan, watching "It's a Wonderful Stone-Age Life" in 1993's "The Flintstones Family Christmas": "Oh, this is my all-time favorite Christmas movie!...Gets me every time."

Despite the venerable film's one-time ubiquity, some folks nevertheless have completely missed connecting with it. "You know I've never seen that," millionaire/superhero Bruce "Batman" Wayne tells his ward Dick "Robin" Grayson on The WB's dark and delirious *Batman: The Animated Series* in 1992. "It's about how much of a difference one man can make to a city," replies Robin. "Sound familiar?" Batman won't know for a while. Their screening is interrupted by the villainous Joker's holiday escape from Gotham City prison to seize control of local broadcasting and present his own "Christmas with the Joker" TV special.

Viewing the film isn't always an excuse for humor. It's often an evocation of irony. As the lead character's parents in ABC's acclaimed high school portrait *My So-Called Life* watch *It's a Wonderful Life* in 1994, they feel guilty for not having taken in their daughter's gay classmate after his family kicked him out. Other times, it's an important experience shared. On the Fox youth soap *Beverly Hills 90210* in 1992, teen friends Brandon (Jason Priestley) and Andrea (Gabrielle Carteris) are inspired to kiss as the film unreels.

Jimmy Stewart's fable provokes all kinds of reflections and realizations. The 2002 Christmas episode of ABC's *8 Simple Rules* finds John Ritter's family decorating their tree. "This is going to be the best Christmas of all time," enthuses dad Ritter. "It's like that James Stewart movie," he says, snapping his fingers to try to recall the title. "You know, where he gets hit on the head, and he wakes up in Potterville, in a bar with drunks and hookers, and he realizes that he has more friends than anybody." Wife Katey Sagal remembers, "*It's a Wonderful Life,*" to which pubescent son Martin Spanjers lustily concurs, "Sounds like it." Not exactly the way Stewart would have seen things. But a hearty sentiment nonetheless.

CHAPTER 14

Hark the Herald Angels Sing: Variety Shows and Holiday Songs

Suzanne Somers (as Chrissy Snow): You know I was named after today?

John Ritter: Chrissy is short for Christmas Snow?

Suzanne Somers: My father was a big fan of Bing Crosby.

—*Three's Company*, 1977

Vanessa Williams (shooting a holiday music video): I'm stuck in this cheeseball, fake-fur, Bigfoot get-up surrounded by smelly brats!

—*A Diva's Christmas Carol*, 2000

What simpler way to celebrate Christmas on a new and low-budget medium than a seasonal song or two in a stripped-down setting? Early television used musical interludes to fill broadcast time cheaply, before expanding as the medium advanced to larger variety shows and performer showcases. With music such a TV standard, giving the sounds a holiday angle was a natural.

Many of the nation's most popular performers were already well attached to seasonal sentiment. Bing Crosby, who'd been doing radio Christmas shows since 1936, introduced Irving Berlin's song "White Christmas" in the 1942 theatrical film *Holiday Inn*, turning it into the best-selling recording for decades. Bob Hope was a king of holiday radio, too, reigning as the self-proclaimed Bob "Christmas Tree" Hope since 1938. He'd especially endeared himself to Americans by entertaining the troops during World War II, starting his tradition of an annual USO Christmas show in Germany in 1948. And if Hope is better remembered for comedy than music, he introduced the now-classic carol "Silver Bells" in the 1951 film *The Lemon Drop Kid*. Another holiday favorite, Perry Como had hit big with his album of "Merry Christmas Music" in 1946.

Two years later, Como actually premiered his NBC series—a weekly 15-minute affair—on Christmas Eve 1948, spotlighting a boys' choir that included his own son Ronnie. By 1955, the laid-back crooner rated a weekly hour for NBC, which presented such holiday treats as a 1960 appearance by the now elderly woman who had written the "Yes, Virginia" letter to *The New York Sun* as a little girl in 1897. Como's touching and reverent Christmas productions grew into an American institution, enduring even after the series ceased in 1963. In specials for 30 years thereafter, Como and guests would begin to traverse the world, to celebrate in Austria (1976), the Holy Land (1980) and, in his final stop, Ireland (1994). Something about Como's relaxed singing style seemed to suit the yuletide season with its underlying message of peace and warmth.

Christmas quickly found its way onto other music and variety shows of TV's early years through the 1950s. NBC's weekly *Your Hit Parade* performance of popular songs was a natural. (Its 1955 Christmas Eve show featured footage shot at Manhattan's Rockefeller Center skating rink.) Ed Sullivan's weekly *Talk of the Town* showcase, which CBS later named after the newspaper gossip columnist who hosted it, made a point of presenting Christmas performances ranging from the latest hit-makers to highbrow classical stars. Other mixed-bag programs like NBC's *The Colgate Comedy Hour* did the same. That conveniently associated their sponsors (who then exercised extensive control over the shows they backed) with the season's spirit of generosity, otherwise known as shopping and gifting.

Even more inclined to celebrate were shows built around a specific performer. Flamboyant pianist Liberace's self-titled syndicated half-hour of the early 1950s mounted a memorable Christmas celebration in 1954, and Dinah Shore (a Jewish girl from Nashville) sang of the season as part of her NBC series from 1951 to 1963. As musical variety flourished, holiday sounds were hosted by the likes of Arthur Godfrey, Kate Smith, Rosemary Clooney, Eddie Fisher, Tennessee Ernie Ford, comic Red Skelton, and bandleaders Mitch Miller and Lawrence Welk.

BOB HOPE

But three stars besides Como cemented reputations in the 1950s and 1960s as Christmas archetypes for decades to come—Crosby, Hope, and the kid in the bunch, Andy Williams.

Hope came first, despite Crosby's subsequent status as a holiday fix- ture who seemed to have been on television forever. While Crosby con- tinued on CBS radio through 1962, the comedian made the leap to video early. In his 1950 NBC Christmas special, "Ol' Ski Nose" followed his well-established radio pattern of a seasonal/topical monologue, followed by songs and sketches. Hope and actor Bob Cummings played Santas on the subway, and opera's Lily Pons led a parade of musical guests. Soon Hope was an annual holiday presenter, either doing studio shtick with celebrity guests or, by 1954, filming his renowned yuletide tours to military bases around the world with an entertainment troupe heavily populated by bombshells such as Jayne Mansfield and Miss Universe. (Because these holiday visits were filmed overseas, they sometimes did not air until mid-January.)

The military shows became a national sensation in the 1960s as America's troop deployment in the Vietnam War escalated, and audiences appreciated Hope's efforts to brighten the lives of young soldiers and sailors risking all in the controversial conflict. NBC's 1965 Christmas broadcast with Joey Heatherton and Anita Bryant won an Emmy as outstanding variety special, and the 1970 and 1971 specials continue to rank three decades later among Nielsen's 30 highest-rated programs of all time. More than 60 percent of all TV-equipped homes in America tuned in to see Connie Stevens and Lola Falana getting physical in scantily clad musical numbers before cheering service members, while Hope chatted with male heroes such as astronaut Neil Armstrong and baseball's Johnny Bench. The comedian's nine Vietnam Christmas broadcasts made such an impression on American culture that they are literally used as the setting for the 1999 Christmas episode of CBS's contemporary military drama *JAG*, with a flashback to its lead character's father as he served on an aircraft carrier visited by the Hope troupe. Actors impersonating entertainers Phyllis Diller and Diana Ross are intercut with vintage footage of Hope joking with carrier troops.

When American combat in Vietnam ended, Hope returned to annual stu- dio fare that remained highly rated but seemed increasingly old-fashioned to younger viewers raised on rock music and cultural tumult. The Christmas shows' format stayed the same—Hope would joke about Santa using valet parking in Beverly Hills—though younger guests such as Brooke Shields, Olivia Newton-John, and Reba McEntire were included alongside Lucille Ball, Red Skelton, or John Wayne. Hope would sing "Silver Bells" each sea- son with that year's young songstress, and introduce the latest Associated Press all-America college football team members. By 1994, when Hope was 91, his four-decade reign as NBC's Christmas show stalwart had come to an end. A 1993 clip compilation from those previous celebrations would continue to play on TV and on DVD, keeping alive the name of an entertainer beloved to three generations of GIs and their nation.

BING CROSBY

Another kind of appeal entirely lies behind the Christmas legacy of Hope's *Road* pictures partner, Bing Crosby (from 1940's *The Road to Singapore* and five later global comedy pairings). "Der Bingle" arrived on TV much later, preferring to stay on CBS radio through 1962 with his annual "A Christmas Sing with Bing," featuring singing stars and seasonal choirs. Crosby was still a big-screen star in movies like 1954's *White Christmas,* nonseasonal musicals like *High Society,* and even the dramatic film *A Country Girl.* The crooner with the big ears finally made his small-screen Christmas splash as a guest—in 1957's "Happy Holidays with Frank and Bing," a special installment of Sinatra's half-hour ABC series. Sinatra, who owned the show, filmed it in color, though the great majority of American TV sets were still black-and-white. That lends an even more festive mood today to its swingin' bachelor merriment (though both men were married with families). Bing arrives at Frank's ultramodern multilevel home, complete with aluminum Christmas tree, Polynesian house-boy, and freestanding fireplace. While sharing "a little toddy for the body," the two stars trade lines on "Jingle Bells," before doing some dream-sequence caroling on a snowy nineteenth-century village set.

Crosby's own Christmas show tradition finally began in 1961, when the 58-year-old vocalist welcomed *Road* buddy Hope for comedy antics along-side gap-toothed English comic Terry-Thomas and British chanteuse Shirley Bassey. ABC specials would continue yearly. But the family format that most fans remember so nostalgically wouldn't take hold until the mid-1960s.

That's when Bing, appearing under the banner of ABC's Saturday variety hour *The Hollywood Palace,* brought his family onto the stage—his glamor-ous second wife, former starlet Kathryn Grant (whom he'd met on the set of *White Christmas),* and their three young children. Though Bing's four adult sons by his first wife were leading troubled lives (Gary Crosby wrote a con-fessional book about paternal abuse, and two others committed suicide), this new family was widely accepted as all-American holiday happiness personified. The Christmas Eve 1966 show featured seven-year-old Mary Frances in a gown and swept-up hairdo matching mommy's, with eight-year-old Harry (Bing's birth name) and five-year-old Nathaniel wearing maroon jackets and bow ties (and shorts?).

For a dozen years, America would watch the Crosby kids grow and mature, December to December, from shy (if not frightened) kids to more

seasoned performers. Whereas 1966's *Palace* appearance had the kids awk-
wardly singing one segment of "yuletide roundelays" on stage with mom
and dad (amid routines by trained dog acts and tightrope walkers), later
years would take the family into TV studios for more elaborately staged holiday segments—intricate bell-ringing acts and costumed song-and-dance
numbers with the family dressed as hobos. Harry played guitar for dad's
rendition of "The Christmas Song." The whole family bounced through town
to "We Need a Little Christmas" in 1973's Sun Valley resort special, complete with actual sleigh rides in the snow.

Although the specials' musical guests even in this rock era tended toward
easy listening—the Lennon Sisters, Robert Goulet, Fred Astaire, Jackie
Gleason—Crosby did take note of changing times every so often. By 1970,
when the TV studio setting allowed for taped comedy sketches with changes
of scenery, Afro-topped *Hair* musical veteran Melba Moore introduced diversity, trading song lines with Bing as rival street-corner charity collectors.

The most modern twist of all was uncorked by Crosby's final taped
special, broadcast at Thanksgiving 1977 just weeks after its star had died
of a heart attack. "Bing Crosby's Merrie Olde Christmas" paired America's
quintessential 1920s crooner with British glam-pop's most avant-garde personality, David Bowie. Their duet of "The Little Drummer Boy"/"Peace on
Earth" would go down in music history. Bowie's androgynous performances
in the space-alien persona of Ziggy Stardust were light years from Crosby's
low-key crooning. But Bowie came underdressed (for him) to the London
taping, wearing a suit jacket and just a smidge of eye makeup, and the
men's voices melded beautifully despite the gap of generations and cultures.
Two decades later, *TV Guide* saluted the unlikely duet as one of television's
top 25 musical moments.

Yet the most lasting impression of the Crosby Christmas era would be
left by the depiction of the crooner's family in a "home" location interest-
ingly like the one Crosby and Sinatra had shared back in 1957—but with
wife and kids ensconced to make it more familial. Fire in the fireplace,
Kathryn and kids trimming the tree and wrapping presents, Bing in leisure
suit watching fondly and intoning "Christmas is a time for coming home,
for gathering with those you love to share the joy of the season"—the iconography seemed to represent what sophisticated critics might call "laying
on the schmaltz." These carefully perfected "casual" celebrations, in a pur-
ported home setting, were often viewed as the epitome of what Christmas
was supposed to be. Especially with father-figure Bing declaiming a virtual
definition of the holiday. For children of the era, in particular, such annual
gather-the-family-round-the-TV specials provided powerful cultural sym-

bolism that begged comparison with their own household's celebrations. Thanks to TV's uber-perfection, idealistic viewers could only find their first-hand festivity to be lacking.

ANDY WILLIAMS

Even more intimidating in their display of white-tooth smiles, crackling-fireplace warmth, and homespun harmonies were the Christmas shows of Andy Williams and his exceedingly extended family. The clean-cut singer had broken into show business in the 1940s as part of the four-sibling Williams Brothers act, which would be resurrected for the holidays when Andy established his TV presence with various variety series from 1958 to 1971, mostly on NBC. Andy, Bob, Dick, and Don provided not only classic quartet style each December on favorites like "Winter Wonderland," but also a new holiday archetype with their matched white turtlenecks under bright red or green sweaters. (NBC, which owned RCA, promoted its color television sets by using vibrant visuals.)

Also featured in Williams's holiday shows would be the brothers' parents, various wives and children, including Andy's singer–wife Claudine Longet and their three progeny, all gathered in home and lodge settings for the season and song. In 1962, the next-generation family group the Osmond Brothers came on board as series regulars with their own Utah white-bread charm and vocal talents. Here in Williams's studio staging, the holiday iconography grew stronger. Singers performed bundled up in heavy jackets with "snow" falling. Outdoor sets recreated snow-covered trees, bridges, and ponds, with Williams skating on the latter as he vocalized. Andy might dance with his blue-haired mother to the strains of "White Christmas." Or stand before a steeple and stained-glass window to sing the religiously observant lyrics of an "Ave Maria" or "Silent Night."

Perhaps because NBC had a weekly, year-round investment in Williams's success, his holiday outings generally boasted superior production values over the Hope and Crosby specials. The sets and lighting are more evocative of a winter mood. The music sounds richer. The direction seems more creative.

That was certainly true in Williams's 1970 Christmas show, when his second NBC series was aiming for younger viewers with rock guests, quirky humor, and almost psychedelic touches. Though Andy still introduced his parents, brothers, wife and kids, gathered in a ski lodge setting, the middle of the hour was more *Yellow Submarine* than *White Christmas*. A storybook being read to the kids by Longet came to life: Andy and guests John Astin and Bob (Captain Kangaroo) Keeshan cavorted through the fancifully hand-drawn backgrounds of Christmasland trying to replace a stolen tree for Rockland, whose inhabitants had only, well, rocks with which to celebrate. Its abstractions played like a live-action cartoon that, in this era, might well have seemed drug-inspired. Yet its mind-expanding splashes of color and energy soon gave way to Andy as traditional balladeer, cooing "The Christmas Song" to a babe in arms.

It's that tradition that would continue into Williams's subsequent TV specials, right up to 1993's "Andy Williams Christmas Show Live from Branson" for PBS. By then, Williams had set up his own theater in the Missouri town filled with venues for performers no longer topping the charts. He still does his Christmas show there for live audiences each fall. Williams even sent a live feed of the production in 1997 to Comedy Central's current events satire *The Daily Show*, which paid semi-tongue-in-cheek homage with host Craig Kilborn appearing in his own green sweater over white turtleneck. Thirty years later, those TV Christmas symbols resound still.

Other vintage Christmas specials have lived on over the years, even if no other performer has managed to carve out such a lasting place in the holiday heart. "The Judy Garland Christmas Show" from the musical movie star's CBS variety series of 1963–1964 retains its power thanks to both the edgy performer's legendary magnetism and her loving inclusion of teen daughter Liza Minnelli, pre-stardom, alongside younger kids Lorna and Joey Luft. Taped on a soundstage built to resemble what might be a Hollywood star's family home, the atmosphere was nevertheless relaxed; even her nonprofessional kids seemed at ease singing and dancing with mom. The early appearance by a gangly Liza delights, Garland's obvious affection in watching her kids sing is touching, and riotous dancing Santas who keep invading the house add a nutty touch. It also doesn't hurt that Garland's backstage wranglings on the CBS series have been well-documented, down to the way she "accidentally" mangled the lyrics to musical director and accompanist Mel Torme's "The Christmas Song" on camera as a riposte in their off-camera feud. That adds an ironic touch for modern viewers. Even the conceit of Garland and family speaking directly to us, beckoning us into their "home," seems to work in the magical context of this sleekly directed black-and-white production.

But Garland's series didn't last long, and the variety format itself had not much longer to live. The very conceits that had made it popular—its artificial neatness and cheer, so perfect for the squeaky-clean 1950s—were giving way to the wilder, more assertive attitude of the tumultuous rock/Vietnam era. Naively merry performance shows that had begun in the 1950s, like

Red Skelton's or Jackie Gleason's, were by the late 1960s being replaced by the comedy-centered bite of *The Smothers Brothers* and the zip-cut zingers of *Rowan & Martin's Laugh-In*.

VARIETY GETS HIP

The contrast was stark. Gleason's 1967 CBS holiday show was "A Christmasland Fairy Tale," with his Poor Soul character being ushered through wordless dance sketches enacting the fables of Goldilocks, Alice in Wonderland, and The Nutcracker. *Laugh-In* premiered on NBC a month later, and its first holiday hour joked about the eternal Christmas spirit in the hippie enclave of San Francisco's Haight-Ashbury neighborhood: "Every day of the week," deadpanned regular Dave Madden in the show's "party" segment, "you can see jolly bearded guys on the street, holding a little pot and going ho-ho-ho." Of course, this "pot" wasn't a Salvation Army kettle. "What a pity," said Henry Gibson's proper minister character in another party remark, "most of the Christmas spirit one finds these days is 90-proof." Even guest Douglas Fairbanks, Jr., got in a social lampoon one-liner: "Only 34,239 commercials until Christmas, folks." Topical musical comedy numbers took aim, too, with trumpet-voiced JoAnne Worley singing about charge accounts: "We're hoping next year you'll start to buy/On the Fourth of July."

Some grown-ups nostalgic for that vaunted "simpler time" took refuge in the continuing seasonal specials of Hope and Crosby. But other traditionalists were trying to get hip. Andy Williams's psychedelic romp was echoed a decade later with the disco excess of ABC's 1979 special "Pat Boone & Family." The white-buck-shoes vocalist who'd had a 1950s variety series in his clean-cut youth returned here with wife Shirley and their four adult daughters, including Debby (of the hit single "You Light Up My Life"). But the uber-cheery musical routines by the Boone girls and the three merry Hudson Brothers, not to mention dancers in Yogi Bear and other cartoons costumes, felt more like a last gasp than a fresh start.

Younger viewers were finding their own generational representatives. *The Smothers Brothers Comedy Hour* arrived on CBS in 1967 with its heady brew of political and cultural comedy (which the skittish network canned in 1970 despite strong ratings). *The Flip Wilson Show*, TV's first variety hit built around a black star, was a brief sensation after the comic's 1970 NBC debut. Rarely did these new successes go the traditional parents-and-kids route, even at holiday time. But CBS's *Sonny & Cher* managed to straddle sensibilities. The married singers of "The Beat Goes On" and other Top 40 hits turned "Jingle Bells" into a laid-back rhythm-and-blues tune in 1972, and adopted Stevie Wonder's hit "Higher Ground" as a peace-on-earth anthem in 1973. Toddler daughter Chastity joined them on stage, held by her parents as they sang and humorously sniped at each other. Even their cornier moments—Cher and Sonny in a skit as Raggedy Ann and Andy—boasted a winking awareness of themselves. And when Cher sang Mason Williams's new folk ballad "A Gift of Song" in a nineteenth-century town setting with a backing chorus, the raven-haired fashion plate managed to convey a hip reverence.

The duo's next-generation appeal even tried to bridge a chasm the older generation would have found unthinkable—divorce. When Cher divorced Sonny, and their subsequent solo shows failed to catch on, they reunited for a season that included the 1976 Christmas hour for which Cher brought along her baby son with new husband Gregg Allman. She opened the show in "a cleaned-up version of the infamous dress" in which she'd appeared seemingly see-through nude on a Time magazine cover ("lots more sequins," she promised), and jokes ran along the lines of a bar patron (played in fact by Cher) wondering what she'd give her ex for Christmas: "Last year, she gave him the shaft!" Still, the couple drew laughs in a sweet Gift of the Magi turn with their gawky dating characters Laverne and Alvin, and delivered a touching dramatic skit in which a maître'd played by guest Bob (Captain Kangaroo) Keeshan explores the stories of several lonely single diners in order to seat them together for Christmas dinner.

If Sonny and Cher's production seemed to have the touch for Christmas, few other casts or crews made much of a lasting mark. Osmond siblings *Donny & Marie* took the Christmas episode of their 1976 ABC variety hour outdoors in their home state of Utah. The networks kept trying traditional holiday specials in the 1970s and 1980s, with performers including Johnny Mathis, John Davidson, Johnny Cash, Anne Murray, Mac Davis, John Denver, and George Burns. Denver added puppet help in ABC's 1979 special "John Denver and the Muppets: A Christmas Together." Dolly Parton and Kenny Rogers did a period piece for their 1984 CBS music special "Kenny & Dolly: A Christmas to Remember," playing 1940s characters meeting in a service can-teen during World War II. Parton went homespun in ABC's 1990 "Christmas at Home," shooting at her Tennessee theme park Dollywood, showing clips from her July recording sessions for a holiday album, and gathering with her 11 sisters and brothers, their kids, and her parents at the family's Pigeon Forge homestead to bake Christmas cookies and sing carols.

TRADITION FIGHTS BACK

At least Dolly's bubbly outing with her guitar-strumming siblings came across as unaffected, whether it actually was or not. Kathie Lee Gifford's vigorous CBS attempts at "warm" and "homey" Christmas specials in the traditional manner only further exercised pop-culture cynics of the 1990s. The lightning-rod cohost of the syndicated morning show *Live with Regis & Kathie Lee* was viewed as an outspoken beacon of morality by her (often older and rural) fans and a judgmental prig by her many and vocal (often youthful and urban) detractors. The CBS network, which relied heavily on viewers of more mature age and less urban locale, offered a proper home for her 1995 special "Kathie Lee: Home for Christmas." This overtly earnest throwback to perfect-family outings was shot at a resort home (in Colorado's Vail) with so-called celebrity friends (Aaron Neville, Kathy Mattea, and Andy Williams) who sing holiday tunes when the clan isn't cooking, decorating, showing off its too-cute kids (and their child-choir friends), or sharing "a favorite Christmas memory." There's even "unscripted" banter with ex-football hero husband Frank Gifford and their guests, earlier introduced at their home locations while opening written "invitations" to Vail.

Although the chats did offer a more personal glimpse of celebrities in nonperformance mode, many critics ironically found themselves yearning for the more polished and less indulgent holiday productions of yesteryear, ones that relied not on an assumption of the star's inherent interest as a human being but on his or her entertainment value. At least those openly acknowledged their own artificiality, with no intent to reflect reality. And their Christmas aphorisms tended to be delivered as conventional wisdom, not as personal social insight along the lines of Gifford expounding, "The child that grows up knowing they're loved by their parents and loved by God is not the kind of child that will grow up into an adult that will do harm to anyone."

No less intimately homey was CBS's 1995 hour "Martha Stewart: Home for the Holidays," which dispensed with music to concentrate on the craftiness of the season: "My father taught me to make my first wreath when I was five." The white-bread media queen of do-it-yourself perfection made plum pudding with her mother, and, for the celebrity touch, welcomed Muppet puppet diva Miss Piggy to build a gingerbread house. In a location jaunt to Washington, Stewart visited First Lady Hillary Clinton to hang a wreath on the White House and hear that "Everything about Christmas in the White House is a real reflection of America." Martha had to nod and murmur, "As it should be."

Less serious, though earnest enough in their own way, were family throwbacks like NBC's "A Clay Aiken Christmas" and ABC's "Nick and Jessica's Family Christmas," both in 2004. The former showcased the clean-cut *American Idol* finalist. The latter paired the pretty young marrieds of MTV's *Newlyweds* reality show, who'd gained fame in song (Nick Lachey as a member of the boy band 98 Degrees and Jessica Simpson with her own solo hits). Together, they seemed determined to become their generation's Sonny and Cher, minus actual wit and, some would argue, personality. Their self-aware yule hour strived to revive the Crosby family's homey style ("Nick, you've gotta try this eggnog, I just made it"), bringing in relatives, sharing holiday memories, and staging comedy skits, in a studio made up to look like "a snowy ski lodge." Not that Hollywood knew how to pull that off anymore. It was painful enough that supreme ironist David Letterman took note in his CBS *Late Show* monologue: "Apparently the [George W.] Bush administration knew all about it but did nothing to stop it."

RUPAUL VERSUS BARRY MANILOW

Yes, the oft-proclaimed Age of Irony struck back against that super-slick showbiz so-called sincerity. The mid-1990s saw the rise of twisted takes on holiday hoopla, often on cable channels targeting a narrower and less conventional audience. (Not exclusively, however. Throughout the 1990s, Nashville-based TNN presented holiday music from country favorites including Barbara Mandrell, Randy Travis, and Sawyer Brown.)

You couldn't get much wilder than VH1's 1997 special "Ho-Ho-Ho! A RuPaul Christmas," casting the towering drag queen as a grinch-y diva reluctantly hosting a holiday talk show to pay the mortgage on his/her Malibu beach house. It did make sense, however, for its begowned star to warble "I'll Be Home with Bells On" and "All I Want for Christmas Is My Liposuction." Also natural were guests like cranky comedian Sandra Bernhard, explaining Hanukkah, and porn star Chaisy Lane, demonstrating a fine strip-club pole dance. By show's end, Ru's attitude is handily explained away—"Oh my God, I had a terrible dream that I was like this awful Scrooge woman!"—because nobody wants to actually disrespect the season.

The stringy-haired redneck belter of 2003's VH1 special "A Kid Rock Christmas" certainly didn't. But the wild man celebrated back home in a Detroit concert featuring bosomy, bouncing snow bunnies dancing in scanty red-and-white outfits that made them look like Santa's strippers. Kid did take time to visit his mom to help make holiday dinner. And he wished his fans "love, compassion, all that good [bleep]."

More often, these new holiday specials were playful enough to avoid incurring the wrath of the Christmas gods. A good example was Comedy Central's *Viva Variety*, a weekly send-up of luridly exaggerated foreign variety shows (seen through American eyes on cable, big-city stations, or

Spanish-language extravaganzas like *Sábado Gigante)*, which got even more festive in 1997. The Euro-trash host's ex-wife cohost sported a bouffant Christmas-tree hairdo, and the too-personal pair showed old holiday home movies ("We were high a lot"). In the inevitable novelty act, Japanese hibachi chefs chopped food on xylophones while playing "Jingle Bells." Featured player Johnny Blue Jeans promoted his own disco Christmas special.

This didn't mean nobody was taking the Christmas season seriously anymore. You could have argued that it was finally being done right on the musical side, with specials showcasing song performances without all that counterfeit family "togetherness." In the 1980s, cable's TNT started an annual "Christmas in Washington" charity concert attended by the President and featuring a spectrum of entertainment from pop (Tony Bennett, Neil Diamond) to country (Vince Gill, Alison Krauss) to Latin (Gloria Estefan, Marc Anthony) to blues (B.B. King) to rock (Brian Setzer) and soul (Luther Vandross, Ashanti). NBC gathered a similar musical mix to spice up its annual "Christmas in Rockefeller Center" New York City tree-lighting special. These harked back to all those 1950s and 1960s presentations of Christmas cornucopias on CBS's long-running *Ed Sullivan Show*, where Bing Crosby singing "White Christmas" could give way to a Stiller and Meara comedy interview of Mrs. Claus, before a routine with badminton champ Hugh Forgie playing a Santa speedily knocking the cock over the net to himself. (You had to be there.)

Some music specials took a narrower focus, like CBS's 1996 country hour "Christmas at Opryland" or NBC's 1993 "David Foster's Christmas Album," named after the record producer whose new CD of the same name showcased big-name talent including Celine Dion, Tom Jones, and holiday standby Johnny Mathis. Fox got more mileage out of its *American Idol* talent competition with specials of holiday numbers sung by competitors (2003) and winners (2004).

The star special hadn't completely gone away, though it tended less toward personal celebration and more toward the tunes. The music had become so much the focus that even nice Jewish boys from Brooklyn were getting into the act. While making "Neil Diamond's Christmas Special" for HBO in 1992, Diamond told the Los Angeles Times that "Christmas music is so gorgeous that as a singer you really want to sing it, beyond anything to do with religion. And don't forget Jesus was a nice Jewish boy once, too." Diamond was hot on the heels of Barry Manilow, whose 1990 album *Because It's Christmas* had been critically acclaimed for its lush arrangements and seamless continuity. After releasing the follow-up CD "A Christmas Gift of Love," Manilow did a special two-hour version of A&E cable's "Live by

Request" in 2003 with a big band backing him in a TV studio. The call-in concert format suited his off-the-cuff charm as he bantered with guests José Feliciano, Cyndi Lauper, and Bette Midler (a nice Jewish girl from Hawaii), and with callers who dropped comments like "I don't light a tree, but I light a menorah." "That's what I love about this season," Manilow gushed, "that it brings everybody together." The show even closed with an audience sing-along of "Deck the Halls" and other carols. Grinned Manilow, "It's tacky, and it's cheesy, and I lovvvve it!"

AND MUSIC VIDEO, TOO

By the late 1980s, loving, or at least wallowing in, the tacky traditions of the season was also big in TV's newest dominant music format. Music video had taken over from the fading variety show, as artists forsook the stagy format in favor of expensively produced song-long mini-movies they could control, while more directly promoting their own products and images. Though many of music video's techniques had soon calcified into their own clichés through overexposure on cable's music-heavy MTV, this was the way young viewers would come to know the performers of their era, in concert gigs, pantomime playlets and surreal odysseys neatly packed into five-minute entireties.

Christmas provided a chance for acts to get festive or, conversely, serious with holiday sentiment. A charity conglomeration of British acts called Band Aid released 1984's "Do They Know It's Christmas?" as a fundraiser to help alleviate African famine; the song's video was merely footage of the recording session featuring Sting, Bono, George Michael, Boy George, and other stars. The rockers of No Doubt make playlet peace among clashing cultures of punks and skinheads in 1997's "Oy to the World." But goofy getups and seasonal silliness were also pervasive. Daryl Hall & John Oates play 1950s super-straight in 1983's campy "Jingle Bell Rock." Mariah Carey romps nostalgically in her 1994 video "All I Want for Christmas Is You," trimming the tree and playing in the snow with Santa.

Many artists simply abridged traditional hour variety formulas to a few minutes. Christmas videos from Elton John and John Cougar Mellencamp are merely filmed concert performances. Paul McCartney bounces around the pub with family and friends in 1979's "Wonderful Christmastime." As Leon Redbone and Dr. John sing in a studio, their "Frosty the Snowman" intercuts old black-and-white home movies, a trick repeated in Natalie Cole's 1991 video of her father's hit "The Christmas Song." Producer Quincy Jones leads a 1992 all-star soul chorus in "Handel's Messiah." Vince Gill croons to family around the fireplace in 1993's "Have Yourself a Merry Little Christmas." Aaron Neville performs among pageant-costumed kids in 1993's "Please Come Home for Christmas." And vocal group Boyz II Men harmonizes a cappella in church on "Silent Night." The more things change... .

R-RATED SINGING SATIRE

Music video's anything-goes approach is taken to the extreme in Comedy Central's bitingly adult (and wildly scatological) cartoon satire *South Park*. Using four foul-mouthed third-grade boys who constantly misinterpret all the adult doings in their Colorado mountain town, creators Trey Parker and Matt Stone skewer politics, social relations, and pop culture in purposely primitive cardboard-cutout animation. They turned their attention to Christmas in the smash series' very first season with 1997's introduction of Mr. Hankey, a talking piece of excrement appearing annually for the holidays. By the 1999 season, the festive feces was hosting "Mr. Hankey's Christmas Classics," a collection of music videos attached to a holiday music CD send-up written and performed by the show's creators.

It's impossible to effectively lampoon something without a clear understanding of, and indeed some level of appreciation for, the subject's distinctiveness. Parker and Stone's keen observance of yuletide iconography is clear from the beginning of "Christmas Classics," as Mr. Hankey speaks to the audience from his wing-back chair in front of a raging fireplace next to a Christmas tree. The songs themselves, mostly by Parker and Broadway arranger Marc Shaiman, are musically dead-on variations of holiday ballads and up-tempo jingles, even traditional carols like "O Holy Night" as sweetly cooed and lyrically mangled by egocentric fat kid Eric Cartman ("Jesus was born, and so I get presents/Thank you, Jesus, for being born").

But these numbers are merrily ruthless in their subversion of expectations and evisceration of sacred cows, not to mention boundaries of taste. The original song "Merry F**king Christmas" wickedly lampoons American cultural egotism, with ignorant teacher Mr. Garrison roaming the world to berate foreign citizens for slighting the yule—but with a jolly lilt to his voice ("Hey there, Mr. Shinto-ist/Merry f***ing Christmas!/God is gonna kick your ass/You infidelic pagan scum"). "Christmastime in Hell" finds Adolf Hitler moping in the underworld while Satan tries to cheer him up by wickedly name-checking some Hades comrades, from sex killer Jeffrey Dahmer to John F. Kennedy (and his son) to TV's beloved Michael Landon.

Sick as it sounds, the juxtaposition of crassly outrageous imagery with jaunty holiday melodies and their syrupy sentiment is, shall we say, devilishly hilarious. Where the send-ups could have been laced with disdain, they're imbued with vigilant wit, informed perspective, and even good humor. The creators' (twisted) affection for both the holiday and its traditions is everywhere evident.

Crosby and Como may have existed light-years away from *South Park*. But their seasonal enthusiasm lingered on in this diametrically opposed program. Instead of finding common ground in familiar and overt sentiment, viewers and show now shared a more jaded sensibility—a pop culture been-there-done-that—which couldn't quite bring itself to indulge seasonal clichés after 50 years of repetition without spinning them a new twist.

Pee-wee's Corny/Cool Christmas

It *would* take a childish, postmodern, fictional kiddie-show host to salute sentimental old-time variety holidays with precisely the right mix of admiration and attitude. Paul Reubens pulled off this neat trick in his 1988 CBS hour send-up *Pee-wee's Playhouse Christmas Special*, with help from a cast of seemingly thousands, from lesbian cowboy singer k.d. lang to 1950s sweetheart Dinah Shore.

Reubens's comic brat-boy character Pee-wee Herman, who'd emerged in a snickering stand-up act beloved by college hipsters, was hosting an award-winning Saturday morning show that appealed to both innocent little kids and their kinkier older cousins. His snooty, suited, uber-nerd Pee-wee rode herd on a magical playhouse built on slightly twisted ground. He loaded it with sassy puppets, in the 1950s mode; drop-in human friends, peculiarized from *Mister Rogers's Neighborhood*; a wish-granting genie and talking furniture, for surreality; and seemingly random interjections of vintage cartoons, musical numbers, and colorful stop-motion animation. This riot of wild design and even wilder humor was at its zenith in the prime-time Christmas hour.

The conceit of the special is Pee-wee doing a special. The snickering host fields video calls from celebrities who want to be involved (Whoopi Goldberg, Joan Rivers, Oprah Winfrey), then welcomes cameo visits from a crazy quilt of culture icons. Superstar Cher screams to Pee-wee's secret word of the day. Nightclub diva Grace Jones sashays to a minimalist "Little Drummer Boy." Campy Charo makes it multicultural with "Feliz Navidad." Rock and roll legend Little Richard pratfalls on ice skates. Adding zest are Zsa Zsa Gabor, just because, and basketballer Magic Johnson, who turns out to be cousins with Pee-wee's animated Magic Screen. Meanwhile, our bossy host keeps Frankie Avalon and Annette Funicello working sweatshop-style on hundreds of Christmas cards for him to send out. He turns up his nose at a succession of gift fruitcakes. And he greedily implores Santa for all the presents in the world, then generously helps St. Nick deliver them to other kids.

Reubens resonates as a silly boy, a sarcastic wit, a preserver of tradition, and a jaded master of irony. His tongue-in-cheek holiday special nonetheless relishes the myriad Christmas customs we've come to cherish, both on TV and in our lives. When Pee-wee uses all those fruitcakes to build a new wing onto the playhouse—and employs two half-naked musclemen to do it—he's operating on so many levels of humor and culture that we can hardly begin to identify them all. Almost anyone can watch *Pee-wee's Playhouse Christmas Special* and glean from its jam-packed cornucopia whatever picture of Christmas they want to see. Now *that's* variety.

CHAPTER 15

Run, Rudolph, Run: Christmas Cartoons and Animation

If TV has taught me anything, it's that miracles always happen to poor kids at Christmas. It happened to Tiny Tim, it happened to Charlie Brown, it happened to The Smurfs, and it's gonna happen to us.

—Bart Simpson, *The Simpsons*, 1989

When people use the term "Christmas specials," this is usually what they're talking about—the sentimental animated adventures that have become perennial touchstones of the American holiday season for both kids and adult kids at heart. The shows that draw big audiences every year, decade after decade. The shows we know by heart.

"A Charlie Brown Christmas."
"Rudolph the Red-Nosed Reindeer."
"How the Grinch Stole Christmas."

Although it seems as if these shows have been around forever, TV didn't actually start making prime time animation until the 1960s. "Mr. Magoo's Christmas Carol" led the holiday way on NBC in 1962, and it set a high standard. With original songs by Broadway's Jule Styne and Bob Merrill (*Funny Girl*), and a faithful adaptation of Dickens through the prism of the goofy nearsighted codger voiced by Jim Backus, this cartoon hour was actually a delightful musical made with enough sophistication to appeal to everybody.

"RUDOLPH THE RED-NOSED REINDEER"

The next big offering reached high itself. "Rudolph the Red-Nosed Reindeer" was state-of-the-art stop-motion animation on NBC in 1964, bringing to (herky-jerky) life the story of Johnny Marks' classic 1949 song about the North Pole misfit whose "nose so bright" makes him the hero of the hour on a foggy Christmas Eve. (Marks actually wrote only the music. The words had been penned by his brother-in-law, Robert L. May, for a coloring book used in a 1939 Montgomery Ward store promotion.) Rankin/Bass animation studio partner Arthur Rankin Jr. was living next door to Marks in Greenwich Village in the 1960s, and suggested the song's story could make a good special. Its several minutes were fleshed out into an hour by writer Romeo Muller, with seven original songs and a host of new characters. Bringing it to "life" were 6- to 12-inch miniature characters built on armature with joints so they could be moved, frame by frame, to approximate human and animal activity. The rich tapestry was narrated by a friendly snowman voiced by folk singer–actor Burl Ives, the only "name" draw in the entire hour.

In this family-aimed Sunday night offering, not only was Rudolph treated like a pariah because of his red-light nose, but the boyish elf Hermie was also a poor fit in Santa's toy workshop because he really wanted to be a dentist. "The two of them overcome their handicaps and become heroes," Rankin noted in his introduction to the show's DVD release. "Kids are like that. They're hoping for that one thing in their life that will bring them up and make them a hero"—if not a hero, perhaps, at least accepted, despite being, as Hermie puts it, "independent."

Describing themselves in song as "A Couple of Misfits," the fast-friend pair gets help from other loners—the blustery prospector Yukon Cornelius and, eventually, the abominable snowman Bumble, who initially seems villainous but turns out simply to have a terrible toothache. Hermie saves the day there, and Rudolph's lit-up nose bails out Santa when the weather turns nasty. A quintessential story of underdogs triumphant while staying true to their nonconformist selves, "Rudolph" instantly proved itself a Christmas perennial. Songs like Ives's "A Holly Jolly Christmas" became new additions to the ranks of Christmas music. And Rankin/Bass turned into a holiday animation powerhouse, delivering stop-motion tales based on "The Little Drummer Boy" (1968) and "Santa Claus Is Coming to Town" (1970).

Their cartoon "Frosty the Snowman" from 1969 probably ranks right behind "Rudolph" in public affection, celebrating the friendly title character from the 1951 song who comes "alive" when children place a magic hat on his head. If he doesn't get to the North Pole, he'll eventually melt, and the nasty magician whose hat enlivened him is hot on Frosty's trail to get it back. Rankin/Bass again employs a folksy narrator in veteran comedian Jimmy Durante, while this time including a child, a little girl named Karen who tries to keep Frosty cool. Her momentary failure becomes a sort of *Bambi* moment of trauma to younger viewers when Frosty climactically melts (at least until the next snowfall). Add Santa Claus, the thrill of the chase, and deadpan comic Jackie Vernon as Frosty's voice, and it's a half-hour almost as beloved as the more nuanced "Rudolph."

"The Little Drummer Boy" never quite reached that status, despite its same-creators pedigree and their stop-motion animation reminiscent of "Rudolph." Some viewers consider it richer, more complex, and certainly the most plugged-in to the spirituality behind Christmas. But built around human characters and a dramatic storyline, it's also less enticing to children entranced by the bright colors and endearing cartoonishness of a Rudolph or Frosty. Expanding on the 1958 song, the "Drummer" half-hour follows the emotional odyssey of an embittered orphan boy whose faith in humanity is restored by the birth of the Christ child. The depiction's darker undertones—the drummer boy's parents have been killed, and he gets kidnapped—are most effective for adults, though film veteran Greer Garson narrates with overt poignancy, lacking the distinctive flavor of Ives or Durante. Certainly the open faith behind this Bible-based tale might also make broadcasters nervous about re-airing "Drummer Boy," which has for years been relegated to cable, whereas "Frosty" and "Rudolph" repeat on the networks annually.

"A CHARLIE BROWN CHRISTMAS"

Charlie Brown from the Peanuts comic strip probably should have beaten "Rudolph" to the air as a holiday special. There had long been some interest in bringing the sad-sack little boy to the airwaves. Ford used Peanuts characters in ads for its Falcon cars in 1961, the first time they were animated. The gang reappeared in 1963 as part of a documentary on cartoonist Charles Schulz, made by producer Lee Mendelson and animator Bill Melendez, who provided two minutes of antics in action. But the TV networks still weren't interested—until *Time* magazine ran a spring 1965 cover story describing how the characters tapped into the American psyche. That spurred the interest of the advertising agency representing Coca-Cola, which was looking for a holiday special to sponsor. And almost immediately. It needed to air in just six months—a fast turnaround for any hand-drawn animation but especially one that was essentially animating its characters from scratch.

Schulz had firm ideas about what he wanted. Winter scenes, echoing his own Minnesota childhood. A children's play. And the "true meaning" of Christmas. Both Mendelson and Melendez were concerned about that last one. "I told Sparky [Schulz's nickname] at the time, and I think Lee did, too," animator Bill Melendez remembered in 2001's "The Making of 'A Charlie Brown Christmas'" special on ABC, " 'It's very dangerous for us to start talking about religion now.' And I remember he turned to me with his strange blue eyes, and he said, 'Bill, if we don't do it, who will?' So I said, you know, I'll go with that."

And so they did. "A Charlie Brown Christmas" would become an instant classic with its eloquently plain depiction of kids celebrating the season. Skating on the pond. Hoping for cards to come. Writing letters to Santa. Charlie, feeling "sort of let down" about the holiday, turning to crabby Lucy's "psychiatric help." She drafts him to direct their holiday play and sends him out to find a tree, "a great big shiny aluminum Christmas tree." But Charlie is drawn to "this little green one," a short and scrawny pine that "seems to need a home." When the other kids mock Charlie Brown's selection, and him as being "completely hopeless," he screams, "Isn't there anyone who knows what Christmas is all about?"

"Sure, Charlie Brown," answers Lucy's blanket-dragging little brother Linus. "I can tell you what Christmas is all about." And he steps into the spotlight to straightforwardly recite the King James Bible verses Luke 2: 8–14, of shepherds told by an angel that "unto you is born this day in the city of David a savior, which is Christ the Lord." Concludes Linus, "That's what Christmas is all about, Charlie Brown." The kids are inspired to trim the sad little tree for Charlie Brown until it's a sparkling example of Christmas cheer. As Linus had said, "Maybe it just needs a little love." The second true meaning of the season.

Yet the half-hour's directness and simplicity scared even its creators. Against standard practice, they had used real kids' voices, rather than trained adult actors, and backed them with flowing jazz from "Cast Your Fate to the Wind" pianist Vince Guaraldi. The show didn't seem to sparkle somehow. "I had very little confidence when I took it back to the network in New York," Mendelson remembered in the making-of retrospective. "And the two network executives who looked at it really didn't like the show. They thought it was too slow, they thought the music didn't work, they thought the animation was too simple. And I really believe if it hadn't been scheduled for the following week, there's no way they were going to broadcast that show."

Well, nearly half the TV-watching population disagreed, tuning in that next Thursday night, December 9, 1965, making "A Charlie Brown

Christmas" the week's second most viewed program. It won an Emmy the following year—"Charlie Brown is not used to winning," Schulz would say in accepting the award, "but we thank you"—and it would be shown every Christmastime from then on, via network TV, videocassette, and DVD. Like "Rudolph" with its "couple of misfits," the story of "A Charlie Brown Christmas" was that of "a loser" finding a way to win. In every sense of the word.

THE GRINCH

The golden age of animated Christmas specials continued the following December, with another adaptation of drawn characters who had become childhood classics. *The Cat in the Hat* author Theodor Geisel had published *Dr. Seuss' How the Grinch Stole Christmas!* in 1957 as another of his simple rhyme tales with line illustrations that could be enjoyed by small children just learning to read. Its story centered on the Scrooge-y sort of title creature who feels compelled to stomp all over the holiday joy of the kids of Who-ville, not out of any ingrained meanness but simply because "his heart was two sizes too small."

Geisel's Dr. Seuss books, which also included *Green Eggs and Ham* and *Horton Hears a Who*, always had a freewheeling sense of whimsy about their invented worlds. Television animation now added edge. That came from director Chuck Jones, the master of Warner Bros. cartoons who had created the nearly surreal duels of the Road Runner and Wile E. Coyote. Jones was inspired to make Geisel's black-and-white-sketched Grinch a creepy color of pea green—with envy?—and he hired fright film legend Boris Karloff to read the tale in his oh-so-precise British accent.

It almost didn't happen. Geisel was protective of his work and reluctant to see it animated. Because he had known Jones since the two worked together during World War II on Private Snafu cartoons made for the Army, Geisel finally agreed to let him give *The Grinch* a go. Like "Rudolph" and "Mr. Magoo," the story was extended to its half-hour length by adding songs like the wittily classic "You're a Mean One, Mr. Grinch" ("You're a bad banana/ with a greasy black peel!"), its Dr. Seuss lyrics growlingly crooned by deep-voiced Thurl Ravenscroft. Jones picked up on the smallest allusions in the book's illustrations to amplify Seuss's droll humor and visual vibrancy with movement. A jack-in-the-box pops up yards high to place the star atop the Whos' tree. Their holiday toy contraptions and feast foods are so lovingly detailed as to swamp the screen. Even the description of the Grinch's too-small heart gets animated Jones-style with a size diagram.

That zest makes moving what could have become too maudlin. The Grinch impersonates Santa to steal all of Who-ville's presents—only to discover that Christmas "doesn't come from a store. Maybe Christmas, perhaps, means a little bit more." That realization of the holiday spirit causes the Grinch's heart to grow three sizes, redeeming yet another Christmas special villain before the show comes to its happy end. The moral? It's not to vanquish evil or triumph over it. It's to transform it to good.

MODERN ANIMATION

After a golden era in the 1960s, television animation slipped into a kind of dark ages, as cost-cutting measures degraded the quality of cartoons so sharply that most adults were turned off. Christmas classics repeated year after year, but few new gems joined their ranks for the next two decades.

Rankin/Bass continued to pump out stop-motion specials—"Rudolph's Shiny New Year" (1976), "Nestor the Long-Eared Christmas Donkey" (1977), "The Leprechaun's Christmas Gold" (1981)—reaching further and further afield from the familiar stories and carols that had established their reputation. Alvin and the Chipmunks, whose speeded-up voices had hit the record charts in 1958 with "The Christmas Song" ("Hurry, Christmas, don't be late"), made it to cartoon form with 1981's "A Chipmunk Christmas." Video games got seasonal with 1982's "Christmas Comes to Pac-Land." Comic strip characters were common adaptations, as in 1979's "A Family Circus Christmas" and 1987's "A Garfield Christmas." Even the stop-motion TV commercial pitchmen The California Raisins celebrated in 1987's "A Claymation Christmas Celebration."

But TV was no longer a three-network world where Americans watched the same shows by the tens of millions. As cable lured more viewers through the 1980s, the viewing audience fragmented into ever smaller slivers, spread over dozens of channels. It was harder to establish "a classic" when fewer viewers were likely to catch any single telecast. Not that the networks didn't keep trying. Animator Phil Roman, who'd worked 30 years earlier on the great "Grinch," directed 2000's "Grandma Got Run Over by a Reindeer," based on the novelty song and lengthened to an hour with the plot of Grandma's store being poached by an evil tycoon. "Santa, Baby!" offered an ethnic twist in 2001 with its black cast (Gregory Hines, Eartha Kitt, Patti LaBelle) and jazzy songs in the tale of a tapped-out songwriter.

Only two of the later network specials seemed to click, one each from opposite sides of the Atlantic. Matt Groening, creator of *The Simpsons*, used a sort of 3-D storybook cartoon style and a sardonic sense of humor in

Fox's 1999 arrival "Olive the Other Reindeer." Based on the 1997 children's book by J. Otto Seibold and Vivian Walsh, it followed the quest of an inno-cent little misfit dog named Olive to "un-cancel" Christmas after Santa's reindeer Blitzen is injured during a practice flight. Olive's hard-of-hearing flea friend misinterprets a quote from Santa on the radio—"Maybe some-how we'll make do with all of the other reindeer"—as "make do with Olive the other reindeer." He enthuses, "That's why you're not interested in chas-ing cars and barking like an idiot—you're a reindeer, not a dog."

Olive, voiced by Drew Barrymore, is helped on her bus journey to the North Pole by a fast-talking zoo-fleeing penguin named Martini (the wry Joe Pantoliano), while being chased by "a very mean postman who wants to wreck Christmas" because he hates the extra workload (Dan Castellaneta, who voices Homer Simpson). Olive saves Christmas twice, first by taking unlikely flight, and later by using her dog's sniffing skills to track the post-man when he steals Santa's bag of gifts. It's an hour with a thoroughly mod-ern attitude—scamming penguin Martini sets off to "do a little loan-shark-ing, sell a little Amway"—and four rocking songs from Christopher Tyng and scriptwriter Steve Young, featuring R.E.M. front man Michael Stipe and Big Bad Voodoo Daddy. In league with Barrymore's plucky voice work, "Olive" radiates a smart and sassy tone that's sweet without being saccharine.

Christmas classics seem to come in waves. At the same time over in England, "Robbie the Reindeer" was also finding inspiration in the Rudolph legend and twisting it into sharper wit. In the BBC's 1999 stop-motion "Robbie the Reindeer in Hooves of Fire," Rudolph's "easily distracted" son arrives at the North Pole (also by bus, a nice red British one) to join "the sleigh team." This is not appreciated by head reindeer Blitzen, still hold-ing a grudge over all that attention paid Rudolph ("Do I endorse carpet cleaner? No!"). The villain packs Rudolph with burgers and fries, now that all of Santa's reindeer work out till they're buff, and he persuades Santa to install an automatic navigation system on his sleek new Sleighmark II. Robbie's only chance to join the crew is to triumph in the steeplechase at the Reindeer Games, à la Britain's 1981 Oscar-winner *Chariots of Fire*.

"Robbie" is directed more at older kids and adults, much like the Wallace and Gromit stop-motion shorts of the same British animation era. Robbie has the hots for reindeer babe Vixen, while "support crew" female Donner pines quietly. The games are covered by sportscasters ("Fears about Prancer's form have been realized"), sponsored by hay ("the official snack food"), and opened by an aria from The Three Ten-Tonners. Its verbal and visual lampoonery is echoed in 2002's "Robbie the Reindeer in Legend of the Lost Tribe," when the team is running a tour guide business beset by Vikings (and the return of Blitzen). Both half-hour shows were "Americanized" when CBS debuted them in 2002 with newly dubbed comic voices including Ben Stiller, Jim Belushi, and Brad Garrett (with Brit Hugh Grant as bad old Blitzen). BBC Video's American DVD release included both audio tracks, so the user could choose between Yank accents and the more puckishly ironic British originals carrying forward the spirit of Monty Python.

Cable was otherwise the home of the most creative Christmas animation of the millennial era. HBO's 2001 half-hour special "'Twas the Night" used various cartoon styles to elegantly render multicultural carols from the likes of Nat King Cole ("The Christmas Song"), Macy Gray ("Winter Wonderland") and Los Lobos ("Feliz Navidad"), while also honoring Kwanzaa and Hanukkah (Bette Midler's "Chanukah, Oh Chanukah"). Cult animator Bill Plympton delivered 2001's Cartoon Network delight "12 Tiny Christmas Tales," a twisted collection of line-drawn holiday anecdotes for grown-ups. And 1960s kiddie favorites Davey and Goliath, who starred for the Evangelical Lutheran Church of America in humble anecdotes illustrating basic human virtues, reappeared in 2004's Hallmark Channel presentation "Davey and Goliath's Snowboard Christmas," a gentle tale of a boy and his dog again animated by the Clokey studio known for its Gumby classics. (Art Clokey had pioneered yuletide TV animation with 1957's clay-motion *Gumby Show* quickies "Santa Witch," where horse Pokey visits Santa, and "Scrooge Loose," in which Gumby and Pokey tail Scrooge when he escapes from their *Christmas Carol* volume to wreak havoc on the holiday.)

ANIMATED SERIES

Back in the 1960s, prime time's first animated series was already going strong by the time "Mr. Magoo" and "Rudolph" made their mark on holiday TV. But that series groundbreaker only got around to Christmas after the specials had made their mark. In its fifth ABC season, *The Flintstones* aired a seasonal musical episode on Christmas night 1964: Stone-age dad Fred Flintstone, who needs some extra money for Christmas presents, takes a Macyrock department store job that turns into a real-life Santa gig when a nasty cold keeps the actual St. Nick from making his holiday deliveries.

But Fred was out there alone in yule-land. The era's other network nighttime cartoons, *The Jetsons* and *Jonny Quest*, didn't go in for Christmas tales. *The Jetsons* wouldn't get around to its "Jetsons Christmas Carol" for nasty boss Mr. Spacely until its 1980s revival. The problem was that most cartoons were intended to repeat two or three or four times a year, while holiday episodes were best suited to air just once annually. Saturday morning kids' cartoons were even more limited, most of them producing just 13 episodes a year to rerun over and over.

And Saturday morning was where animation was relegated after the flurry of 1960s nighttime hits abated. Kids still flocked to network creations like 1969's *Scooby-Doo, Where Are You?* series of comic mysteries from the Hanna-Barbera factory that had made *The Flintstones* and *The Jetsons*. But their latest series didn't produce a holiday episode until 1984's "The Nutcracker Scoob." In the meantime, cartoons stretching back to 1950s vintage had finally gotten festive. "Casper's First Christmas" arrived in 1979, and "Yogi's First Christmas" in 1980, though neither was something to write home about in terms of either storytelling or animation. The simplistic blue troll-like clan called *The Smurfs* made their way to the holiday a little more quickly, in 1982 after their 1981 NBC debut.

But animation was about to come roaring back to TV in a big way with the explosion of cable networks. Nickelodeon and The Disney Channel launched for child viewers in the 1980s, followed by Cartoon Network and its Boomerang spin-off. In addition to acquiring existing cartoons, the channels produced new series. As a sister network to MTV—and sharing its cool sensibilities—Nick became a leading force in the 1990s. Its more pointed animation was led by toddler mega-smash *Rugrats*, whose crawl-level view of life appealed to everyone up to adults. Other long runs included the everykid hit *Doug* and animator John Kricfalusi's incredibly warped prime-time gross-fest *Ren & Stimpy*, with its teen/adult following.

All of them cooked up Christmas offerings, even *Ren & Stimpy* with its whacked-out 1992 "Son of Stimpy" pseudo-tearjerker. Blubbery, chubby, dumb cat Stimpy unleashes some gas that he names Stinky. It soon leaves home, to Stimpy's flood-weeping despair, but returns for the holidays with its " fiancée"—a dead fish head. The two are married as Stimpy throws kitty litter over the happy couple.

Meanwhile, MTV was trying out its own cartoon animation, and hitting a teen bull's-eye. Introduced on MTV's *Liquid Television* showcase and given their own show in 1993, *Beavis and Butt-head* were two dim-brained high school metalheads forever chortling over their own stunted humor. Creator Mike Judge's 1995 special "A Beavis and Butt-head Christmas" rips apart both *A Christmas Carol* and *It's a Wonderful Life* in typically snickering slacker fashion. Beavis is the focus of "Huh Huh Humbug," where spirits played by his neighbor Anderson, his teacher Van Driessen and coach Buzzcut materialize from the porno tape he's watching, to scare him into making "some changes in your life." Closest to effective is the gravestone reading: "Here lies Beavis. He never scored" (the boys' greatest unrequited desire: "Let's go out and find some chicks"). Butt-head gets his chance in "It's a Miserable Life," when a guardian angel shows him "how much better the world would be if you were never born." His neighbor's house is lovely, Burger World actually has customers ("You weren't there to drive them away"), and Beavis has half a brain enough to help out at a homeless shelter. But neither could-be depiction can impress our puerile pair. "It's like even though the world sucks," concludes Butt-head, "it would probably suck even worse without us."

The networks, too, were playing adult animation catch-up after the stunning 1990s success of *The Simpsons*. Fox gave *Beavis* creator Judge a more mainstream platform with his just-folks Texas family tale *King of the Hill*. The WB also got aggressive with animation after its 1995 sign-on. The warped world-domination schemes of *Pinky and the Brain* have the scheming scientist mouse The Brain trying to trick Santa into getting his Noodlenoggin doll "into every home on the planet" in 1995 to broadcast the hypnotic suggestion that Brain rules the world. Eddie Murphy's life-in-the-projects project *The PJs* casts his building superintendent character as 1999's Grinch of the ghetto. To earn money to buy his wife a computer for Christmas, Murphy's Thurgood plays repo-Claus throughout his building, which makes him "feel like shi-at-su" when his tenants buy him a massage chair. "Look, even the porno theater's in the holiday spirit," he says, pointing at the marquee reading "Merry XXXmas."

Family Guy was a ratings disaster in its intermittent 1999–2002 Fox run, but hit big in Cartoon Network repeats and sold millions of copies on DVD—and that prompted a 2005 network revival of its satirically sad-sack suburban household. The 2001 Christmas episode is creator–voice artist Seth MacFarlane at his most lightning-speed ruthless. The skewerings are especially scattershot. Drunken dad Peter drives his car into a manger scene. He also gets a "lemon" snow cone (remember, don't eat the yellow snow). Mom goes on a holiday icon–bashing rampage in which she shoves the angel Clarence from *It's a Wonderful Life* off that bridge and punches off the head of Frosty the Snowman. There's talk of "a three-way with the Olsen twins," those now-teen *Full House* girls. Thrown in are parodies on the family's television set of Bob Hope's Christmas with the troops (this time it's Union soldiers) and the so-called action movie "KISS Saves Santa" ("Everyone knows pterodactyls can't stand the screech of a guitar").

Adult animation had also been discovered by Cartoon Network, which launched its late-night franchise Adult Swim in 2001. *Family Guy* repeated there after 11 p.m., alongside such tongue-in-cheek originals as the courtroom superheroics of *Harvey Birdman, Attorney at Law*, the disembodied talk show *Space Ghost Coast to Coast*, and the surreally demented fast-food slackers of the 'hood, *Aqua Teen Hunger Force*. In the latter's 2002 "Cybernetic

Ghost of Christmas Past from the Future," a robot ghost informs the guys' fat, hairy, gold-wearing human neighbor Carl that his house is built on the graveyard of "a warlike race of elves from the red planet" once enslaved by a prehistoric apelike Sir Santa of Claws. When his above-ground pool fills with blood, Carl sells the house for $1 million to morbid metal punk rocker Glenn Danzig (voicing himself), who asks only one question: "Is there a way to get the blood to flow *up* the walls?" Definitely not for the toddlers.

But kids were the initial targets of other prime-time Cartoon concoctions that attracted plenty of adult viewers with their holiday tomfoolery—*Johnny Bravo; The Powerpuff Girls; Ed, Edd N Eddy*. Nickelodeon played its originals into later hours, too, including the reliable *Rugrats* and *All Grown Up, Jimmy Neutron, CatDog, My Life as a Teenage Robot*, and the broad-appeal under-sea idiocy of *Spongebob Squarepants*. Adults took particular pleasure in the insanely dark adventures of bug-eyed green space alien *Invader ZIM*, who promised "The Most Horrible X-mas Ever" to the humans among whom he dwelled disguised as a schoolboy—except in this 2002 episode. Here, the inept ZIM disguises himself in a huge Santa suit to "reclaim my rightful place as ruler of this world." But the suit "takes over, filling me with hideous, jolly feelings." He's finally vanquished by kid alien-hunter Dib with his scientist father's "anti-Santa arsenal I made when I was a child." In dad's immortal words, "Good luck destroying Santa. And merry Christmas."

The Nanny Gets Animated

"I'm traveling via marshmallow down a hot chocolate river with a dog that's talking my ear off." Obviously, this is not your average episode of CBS's live-action sitcom *The Nanny*. It's a Queens-accented cartoon called "Oy to the World," written by series star/creator Fran Drescher and (then-) husband Peter Marc Jacobson, animated to look like the series' weekly cartoon credits, and aired as the sitcom's 1995 Christmas episode. During a holiday blizzard, Drescher's caretaker character is magically whisked out of Manhattan, along with child charge Brighton and dog Chester, to the North Pole. In Santa's cartoon candy land, Fran lusts after a "banana split level" house—and St. Nick himself, here a dashing dude suspiciously similar to Fran's boss Charles Shaughnessy. ("If I knew he looked like this," squawks the nasal Jewish diva, "I might have converted.") They join forces to save Christmas by battling The Abominable Babcock, based on the chilly Shaughnessy assistant who's Fran's ongoing nemesis. Fran melts the "ice princess" by finding her a date, and then hops aboard Santa's sleigh to help deliver presents, all the while teaching young Brighton that Christmas is more than "two weeks off" from school. This change-of-pace half-hour is a breezy romp, packed with zippy visual touches and spiced with gay winks and Jewish jokes (the reindeer Blitzen is now named Blintzes). Sitcomedy's Jewish princess turns out to be a Christmas queen.

CHAPTER 16

Other Kinds of Christmas TV

CHRISTMAS OUT WEST

Did Americans really celebrate Christmas with quite as much whoop-de-do in nineteenth century frontier days? In TV's vision of the West, they certainly do. Back in 1959, when more than 30 Western series were running on the three networks, prime time almost had to depict festivity of the frontier to get any on the air at all. Many shoot-'em-up westerns did shy away from holiday sentiment, but the genre was then so ubiquitous that it eventually touched on all aspects of American life. From half-hour series like *Johnny Ringo* and *Tales of Wells Fargo* to hour-long dramas like *Wagon Train* and *Rawhide*, viewers who'd just been through 1950s Communist allegations and quiz-show scandals seemed happy to relate to a bygone (and largely idealized) era. Heroes were brave and noble, morals were black and white, and good vanquished evil.

Richard Boone in CBS's 1957 arrival *Have Gun, Will Travel* was the rare exception to that rule of simplicity—an elegant, educated, and sardonic San Francisco do-gooder, dressed in black, motivated by hefty payments, more likely to spout Shakespeare than cowboy slang, so attuned to moral complexity that he might switch sides mid-episode. That's sort of what happens in the first-season Christmas episode "The Hanging Cross," in which Paladin has been hired by a hard-hearted rancher to find his son stolen by Indians years earlier. By the time the gunslinger arrives, they've already found the boy—at least, some boy—and plan to celebrate the holiday with him, until the Pawnee snatch him back. The rancher prepares to hang the Indian chief. But his gallows is turned into a celebratory cross after the unflappable Paladin mediates between the ranch residents and the Pawnee, whose culture gets more respect here than in most 1950s westerns. It's no wonder; the episode's writer is Gene Roddenberry, who'd go on to advance notions of multicultural brotherhood in his legendary *Star Trek* series.

Sticking closer to the traditional Western formula were long-running sagas like NBC's *Bonanza*, about Cartwright ranch patriarch Ben Cartwright and his three adult sons, and CBS's *Gunsmoke*, in which Marshal Matt Dillon rode herd on the roughnecks of Dodge City. These were adult tales, sometimes violent but more often focused on the charged emotion of swindling, vendettas, romantic rivalries, and other flashpoints of frontier life. Though children were rarely seen at all, both shows turned to orphan tykes to spur sentiment in their Christmas scripts.

In *Bonanza*'s 1961 outing, a blind girl hoping to live with her hard-bitten hermit grandfather is told by Lorne Greene's Ben Cartwright, "You can't make someone love you if they don't want to." But after Ben and his three sons form a barbershop quartet to sing "Joy to the World" at Christmas dinner, the geezer's heart softens and the girl gets her wish.

Gunsmoke plumbs the same theme in 1971, when classic character actor Jack Elam decides to arrange that vaunted "real Christmas" for seven too-cute orphans who flee to Dodge City from their mean housemistress. (The kids included future movie star Jodie Foster, plus Erin Moran of *Happy Days* and Willie Aames of *Eight Is Enough*.) By episode's end, the woman has softened enough to attend the kids' Christmas party (at the Long Branch Saloon!), where Santa-suited Elam gives her a kiss. That inspires the rarest of *Gunsmoke* happenings—overt affection between James Arness's Marshal Dillon and Amanda Blake's saloon-keeping Miss Kitty, a reputed couple who'd spent 20 TV years being vague about the extent of their "friendship." It's only a peck on the cheek (and "Merry Christmas, cowboy"). But it's all that our inquiring minds would ever get.

Kids got their own Western action throughout the 1950s in syndicated daytime half-hour shows wrapping simple stories in mild action often involving youngsters. Produced from 1953 to 1956, *Annie Oakley* was one of the most popular, involving both the legendary female sharpshooter (Gail Davis) and her kid brother Tagg (Jimmy Hawkins). In "Santa Claus Wears a Gun," the carnival sharpshooter Snowy Kringle hits town with his flintlock Old Betsy and is promptly suspected of hijacking Army payrolls. Of course the white-haired gent isn't the culprit; it's the railway agent tracking him. The episode actually doesn't have much to do with Christmas except a character's name, a beard, and a line of dialogue every now and then—the railway agent threatens Snowy at gunpoint, "You got a date to slide down a chimney tonight—right into a cell at the Diablo jail."

Westerns were washed up by the 1980s, despite occasional TV attempts to revive them—and wishful dabblings in the genre by contemporary shows. CBS's old-fashioned morality hour *Walker, Texas Ranger* cast Chuck Norris as a present-day state lawman, but one who envisioned himself in the 1996 episode as a nineteenth-century ranger determined to retrieve a kidnapped baby before Christmas. By then, it was the best West TV could come up with.

SCIENCE FICTION/FANTASY

If there could be Christmas way back when, why not way out there, too? The holiday worked its way into science fiction, fantasy, time-travel, and ghost stories, even taking a bite out of vampires. On The WB's smarter-than-the-title-sounds hit *Buffy the Vampire Slayer* in 1998, Sarah Michelle Geller's contemporary crusader sees her reforming blood-sucker boyfriend David Boreanaz suffer a mental remembrance of his past kills. It's a *Christmas Carol* mind-bender revisiting Angel's nineteenth-century holidays. *The X-Files* takes a kind of time trip in 1998, too. FBI agents David Duchovny and Gillian Anderson investigate a mysterious house whose inhabitants always seem to meet their maker at holiday time. Turns out two of them are still there—Ed Asner and Lily Tomlin, as apparitions who take the phrase "hole in the head" quite literally. And they wouldn't mind if our heroes stuck around awhile.

The intrepid young quartet of Fox's *Sliders* rarely stayed anywhere long as they hopped among parallel universes. Christmas 1996 lands them in an acquisitive world where consumers are enslaved by an evil mall city. Subliminal commercials help drive citizens into debt they'll have to work off forever. "They hook you with the ads," observes young scientist Jerry O'Connell, "then they loan you money to support your habit. It's like a drug addiction." Rotund "slider" John Rhys Davies makes a perfect Santa Claus, converting the mall's spendthrift kids with warm tales of holidays offering "nothing machine made or store bought."

Even superheroes get into the spirit. Dean Cain's hunky young Superman defeats holiday-hating Sherman Hemsley's mood-poisoning toys in 1994 on ABC's *Lois & Clark,* then terminates a 1996 Christmas time loop created by Howie Mandel's dastardly dimension-tripper Mxyzpltlk. Lynda Carter's modern-day *Wonder Woman* sees its own toy trauma on CBS in 1977, when shopkeeper Frank Gorshin uses toy soldiers to help him kidnap secret-weapon scientists by putting androids in their place.

But the most affecting fantasies involve everyday human beings in extraordinary circumstances. *The Twilight Zone* has a down-and-out department store Santa find a magical bag "that gives everybody exactly what they want for Christmas." Series creator–presenter Rod Serling wrote the script for CBS's 1960 original starring Art Carney as its skid-row bum, later adapted on the network's 1985 revival with Richard Mulligan. Both dissolute Santas get "intoxicated with the magic and wonder that is Christmas Eve," delighting their poverty-stricken city neighbors by plucking from the sack whatever each person most desires. But when the store manager tracks down his "stealing" Santa, the sack suddenly holds only trash. "This bag doesn't know whether to give out gifts or garbage," marvels Carney. While Serling's original "Night of the Meek" has a sweetly naïve magic to its mood, the remake's more central confrontation between Mulligan and store manager William Atherton shines a brighter light on the plight of the poor in a callous commercial society. "This isn't merchandise," Mulligan corrects his boss. "These are *Christmas presents*." And his gift turns out to be the best of all—serving as a sublime St. Nick in that timeless twilight zone.

TV MOVIES

When broadcast networks ABC, CBS, and NBC began making their own feature-length TV films in the late 1960s, Christmas was part of the package. NBC's 1969 *Silent Night, Lonely Night* paired Lloyd Bridges and Shirley Jones as two strangers and frustrated spouses who connect over a holiday weekend. That same year, CBS's family film *J.T.* depicted a lonely Harlem boy caring for an ailing stray cat at Christmastime.

Other network films followed: *Sunshine Christmas* (1977), a seasonal sequel to an earlier tearjerker, about a young widower and his daughter; *It Happened One Christmas* (1977), with Marlo Thomas in James Stewart's *It's a Wonderful Life* role (and Orson Welles as evil Mr. Potter!); *An American Christmas Carol* (1979), for *Happy Days* star Henry Winkler; *Christmas Lilies of the Field* (1979), another sequel, with Billy Dee Williams in the handyman-to-nuns role that won Sidney Poitier an Oscar; Fred Astaire in the whimsical *The Man in the Santa Claus Suit* (1979); Loretta Young reemerging after 20 years, in the family drama *Christmas Eve* (1986); and Katharine Hepburn's final performance in *One Christmas* (1984). Real life was reflected in the dramatization of a nineteenth-century girl's letter sent to *The New York Sun* in *Yes, Virginia, There Is a Santa Claus* (1991). Actor Jason Robards seemed to have his own cottage industry, starring in *The House without a Christmas Tree* (1972), *The Holiday Treasure* (1973), *A Christmas to Remember* (1978), and *The Christmas Wife* (1988).

Christmas TV movies proved a handy genre for networks to sell series reunions and satisfy performers wanting to "stretch" themselves. Robert Young's entire 1950s TV clan returned in 1977's *Father Knows Best: Home for Christmas,* as did almost everyone from *The Brady Bunch* in 1988's *A Very Brady Christmas.* Even a franchise could be revived: 1988's *Roots: The Gift* had nineteenth-century southern slaves escaping over the holidays. CBS brought back its *Dukes of Hazzard* stars, John Schneider and Tom Wopat, in the unrelated tale *Christmas Comes to Willow Creek* (1987). Acting vehicles were given to recording artists who could also sing Christmas songs amid the often syrupy melodrama. Dolly Parton had *A Smoky Mountain Christmas* (1986), John Denver found *The Christmas Gift* (1986), and Olivia Newton-John became *A Mom for Christmas* (1990).

Christmas TV movies mushroomed with the advance of cable in the 1990s, when more channels had established themselves firmly enough to have the budgets for star-powered originals. USA, Lifetime, The Family Channel, TBS, TNT, A&E, and others would get into the game. By the time of digital cable in the 2000s, viewers could turn on the TV any night between Thanksgiving and Christmas to find some sort of sentimental, romantic, or whimsical holiday movie. Serving as Santa was a particularly common plot, in TNT's *Call Me Claus* (2001) with Whoopi Goldberg, Hallmark's *Santa Jr.* (2002) with Judd Nelson, USA's *Stealing Christmas* (2003) with Tony Danza, and ABC Family's *Snow* (2004) with *Ed* star Tom Cavanagh. (The networks liked that idea, too. CBS starred Angela Lansbury as a musical *Mrs. Santa Claus* in 1996, and ABC cast Kelsey Grammer as *Mr. St. Nick* in 2002.) Every now and then, a daring cable channel would try a different approach, as in Showtime's 2000 drama *Holiday Heart,* casting big-guy Ving Rhames against type as a drag queen helping a drug addict (Alfre Woodard) and her daughter get through the yule.

Cable's Hallmark Channel especially got busy, which made sense. The greeting card company that owned it had long sponsored network "Hallmark Hall of Fame" movies around the holidays that brought it so much revenue. By 2004, its growing cable operation was premiering nearly a movie a week in the holiday season: *Single Santa Seeks Mrs. Claus*, *A Boyfriend for Christmas*, *Love's Enduring Promise*, and *Angel in the Family*.

Back on the network side, CBS had already made holiday tales a mini-specialty in its time-honored Sunday night TV movie slot. The network that continued to make more holiday variety specials, too, seemed to present a couple of Christmas films every year, even after the other networks essentially abandoned TV movies in the new millennium. CBS's biggest hits included 1995's bestseller adaptation *The Christmas Box* with Richard Thomas and Maureen O'Hara, and its 1996 prequel *Timepiece* with James Earl Jones. Jones also brought to life a Dutch Christmas legend in 1999's *Santa & Pete*. Peter Falk played an angel in *A Town without Christmas* (2001), *Finding John Christmas* (2003), and *When Angels Come to Town* (2004). ABC and NBC occasionally pitched in, too, often to showcase their existing talent. In 2004, *Frasier* star Kelsey Grammer headlined NBC's big-budget musical *A Christmas Carol*, and the title comic of ABC's *George Lopez* played a reforming radio shock-jock in the comedy *Naughty or Nice*.

SATIRE/PARODIES

Spoofing the Christmas season was a TV tradition going all the way back to radio. Comedy/variety stars like Bob Hope and Jack Benny brought their humorous takes on the holiday over to video, and this gentle joshing continued through Carol Burnett's variety valediction. But the seasonal send-ups were evolving from warm to wicked as the 1960s counterculture encouraged a sharper, more pointed brand of wit, introduced on NBC's joke-fest *Rowan & Martin's Laugh-In* and CBS's hip *The Smothers Brothers Comedy Hour*.

This new-generation sensibility exploded into prominence when NBC debuted the no-holds-barred late-night revue *Saturday Night Live* in 1975. Its troupe of young comic writers and actors schooled by Second City and *National Lampoon* had a more subversive sensibility and delighted in satirizing sacred cows—entire herds when possible. Christmas, TV, and marketing all got hit by its commercial parody for Santy Wrap, a sort of toilet-seat cover to lay on the lap of a department store Santa Claus before sitting. "He's so jolly, he's smart, he knows if you've been sleeping," intoned announcer Dan Aykroyd, "but do you know where *he's* been sleeping? Use Santy Wrap, and I promise you won't get one tick from jolly St. Nick."

Over the next 30 years, *SNL*'s ever-changing crew of wild wits would get around to giving us Steve Martin's $30 million "wish for Christmas," Jon Lovitz's Hanukkah Harry, Adam Sandler's "Hanukkah Song," and Eddie Murphy's ghetto Christmas as Mr. Robinson. The last adapted Fred Rogers's kindly kids' show host into a street schemer trying to avoid his landlord. "That's why Mr. Robinson has to wear this Santa Claus suit to sneak in and out of his building," he merrily informs his 1984 audience. "But this isn't just a disguise, boys and girls. Because when I add this little kettle here, and when I add this little bell, it becomes a small business. Yes, Christmas is a season for giving, and for taking. And with this little operation, I figure I'll be taking in about three or four hundred dollars a day."

SCTV, a Canadian import run by NBC late-night on Fridays, had a similarly warped spirit. The 1981 holiday outing has its small-town Melonville TV station celebrating with a Liberace-meets-Elton John music special, beer nog from the "Canadian content" know-nothings Bob and Doug McKenzie, and a Christmas commercial for Frank-Incense, an aroma-spewing Sinatra doll.

Fox finally offered Saturday late-night competition in 1995 with *MADtv,* which uncorked an instant classic that same season. Animated in clay stop-motion by Corky Quakenbush, "Raging Rudolph" merged family favorite "Rudolph the Red-Nosed Reindeer" with graphic director Martin Scorsese's adult predilection for gangland violence (à la his boxing saga *Raging Bull).* Drenched in audio bleeps and spurting blood, this short spoof traced Rudolph's climb to being "one of Santa's 'made' reindeer" with help from Yukon Cornelione, amid jolly song lyrics like "We'll get even/We'll make Santa pay." The moral of the story is read as "Keep your (bleeping) mouth shut," before one final festive musical chorus: "Have a merry freakin' Christmas, and you'll hear what we have said/Don't you squeal or rat us out, or you will end up dead."

The *MAD* people and Quakenbush would soon top themselves. After 1996's sequel "The Reinfather" (Rudolph's in charge now), they went to war in 1997 with "A Pack of Gifts Now." This shot-by-shot invocation of *Apocalypse Now,* from its ceiling-fan start to its slice-and-dice conclusion, proved their most wickedly inspired mix of sweet Christmas TV traditions and merciless movie brutality—a bracing brew for a generation immersed in irony. Like their spiritual cousin *South Park,* these parodies truly appreciated both ends of the sensibility spectrum, and could show it no better than by throwing them together in the cocktail shaker of satire. (It should also be noted that Saturday night competitor *SNL* had previously broken sadistic-satire ground with clay creature Mr. Bill's regular poundings in 1970s bits. He got his own Christmas special in 1996.) *MADtv* also excelled in live-action movie collisions: In its 1996 bit "The Greatest Action Story Ever Told," The Terminator travels back in time to save Jesus (who says no thanks).

Non-skit shows were also finding ways to lampoon TV's Christmas traditions. Sitcom characters became Grinches with their own green faces and/or "mean" songs in fanciful parodies in both live-action (NBC's *Scrubs* and *Just Shoot Me)* and animation (Fox's *The Simpsons* and The WB's *The PJs).* The variety format returned in spoof style in 2003's "The Nick at Nite Holiday

Special." This hour assimilated many of the old-time attributes—cheery host Martin Mull, snowy ski-lodge setting, "spontaneous" production numbers—as well as some newer ones (token Hanukkah segment, weatherman Al Roker's Santa progress reports). It had good guests, too. Ted Danson read a children's story. Natalie Cole, Clay Aiken, Michael McDonald, and Sarah McLachlan came by to sing. But recapturing the old magic while winking at its clichés was a tough balancing act the hour couldn't quite achieve.

Even kids were into sending up the season by the 1990s. Cable's Nickelodeon channel gave them their own skit-fests in *Roundhouse* and *Kenan and Kel*, which presented goofy Christmas bits with youthful performers. Though children's TV was the target of mockery in Comedy Central's *TV Funhouse*, this ferocious satire was hardly kid stuff. Crafted by Robert Smigel, the comic mind behind Triumph the Insult Comic Dog on Conan O'Brien's NBC *Late Night* show, the 2000 holiday stop at the funhouse incorporated seemingly every kids-TV touchstone—an idiot human host, cursing Anipals puppets (thankfully bleeped), "classic" animated sentiment (black-and-white cartoon "Christmas with Tingles," a character who "sprinkles tension dust" to provoke drinking and abuse), educational films ("Places to Look for Your Christmas Presents") and more. The Anipals did a spinal tap on host Doug Dale to imbibe his "Christmas cheer," which they promptly powdered, snorted, and free-based, setting themselves on fire. Could excrement and animal-sex gags be far behind? Nope. TV lampoonery wasn't in nice clean Kansas anymore.

KIDS' TV

If Christmas is for the kids, TV has always been happy to keep the tykes entertained—and, we should add, watching advertisements suggesting what they might add to their Christmas "gimme" lists. From its explosive growth as a commercial medium in the late 1940s and early 1950s, television was designing shows for its youngest   viewers/consumers, most legendarily *Howdy Doody.* Many local stations also produced their own daytime kid-fests in those low-tech years. Christmas games and gags became another attraction for shows summoning children to the studio audience of shows like New York's *Wonderama*, Chicago's *Bozo's Circus*, and the franchised *Romper Room*. CBS's long-running morning show *Captain Kangaroo* (1955–84), with Bob Keeshan in the title host role, tried to add a touch of edification to its shenanigans involving puppets Mr. Moose and Talking Rabbit (and costumed Dancing Bear). Keeshan read children's books aloud and explained various aspects and traditions of the world kids encountered.

Public TV was developing as a national force when the 1969 arrival of *Sesame Street* really put it on the map. Designed to give preschoolers a jump on learning, the daily hour from Children's Television Workshop used quick-cut commercial TV techniques to present simple concepts in letters and numbers, as well as to reflect daily life on the title avenue of its urban neighborhood. With most kids encountering at least the commercial celebration of Christmas—along with Hanukkah in some homes —the series used its Muppet puppets and other familiar characters in specials such as 1978's *Christmas Eve on Sesame Street* and 1986's *Elmo Saves Christmas*.

As the broadcast networks essentially abandoned children's programming in the next decades, cable jumped in. Nickelodeon became a multimedia force by programming strictly for kids, presenting live-action play-alongs (*Blue's Clues*), cartoons (*Doug*) and comedy series (*The Secret World of Alex Mack*). Ditto for Disney Channel (*The Wiggles, Kim Possible, That's So Raven*). And all those shows found ways to portray the holidays. As both channels grew to produce dozens of original series, characters from top hits like Nickelodeon's *Rugrats* cartoon and Disney's teen comedy *Lizzie McGuire* became so ingrained in kids' lives that their Christmas stories became perennial favorites.

TV movies were increasingly made for younger viewers. And not just obvious kiddie series spin-offs like Cartoon Network's Powerpuff Girls adventure *'Twas the Fight before Christmas*. The broadcast networks that mostly ignored kids the rest of the year seemed able to find them at Christmas (consumer) time, when they aired established-brand movie titles like ABC's 2003 *Eloise at Christmastime* and The WB's 2004 *Samantha: An American Girl Holiday*.

SOAPS

Home has always been at the heart of daytime drama, those five-day-a-week "soap operas" centered on romance, family conflict, paternity doubts, and the fallout of secrets and lies. That makes it easy for shows producing 250 original episodes a year to cook up lots of holiday hoopla to fill time and provoke fresh fireworks.

Decorating the tree with the family has always been big, along with holiday dinners and the attendant coming together of relatives with both affection to share and grudges to nurse. NBC's venerable *Days of Our Lives* celebrated its 35 years of Christmases past in a 2001 special episode, aired in the wake of that year's September 11 terrorist attacks on the World Trade Center and the Pentagon. The hour intercut clips from the show's very first Christmas in 1965, introduced by original cast members Frances Reid and

John Clarke, who said, "Today, with everything going on in our country, there's comfort in remembering the past." The cast gathered on set but out of character to set up clips featuring their characters: Bo and Hope's first Christmas, Jack and Jennifer's Christmas reunion, Julie and Doug years earlier with baby Hope.

But this soap was particularly sentimental. Late leading man Macdonald Carey was seen reading the Bible nativity to kids at the show's central hospital, a tradition carried on after his death by Reid. Carey even quoted from St. Paul about being on earth to serve God and our fellow man. And *DOOL*'s traditional hanging of ornaments on the Horton family tree was adapted in the 2001 special to a solemn 10 minutes of hanging ornaments representing the fire fighters, police, and other public servants who lost their lives in the line of duty on September 11.

Most soaps indulged in some sentiment for the holidays—hardly a proper time for enormous tragedies to rock their worlds. Although rivalries played out, the tone was more often conciliatory and even miraculous. ABC's *All My Children* devoted its 2003 holiday to Eden Riegel's beloved young Bianca, daughter of series diva Erica Kane (Susan Lucci), then pregnant after a vicious rape. Bianca found a baby in a country church, though it later seemed never to have existed, when a manger scene doll was the only figure found there. The magical incident helped Bianca come to the realization she could love her own child no matter how she was conceived.

GAME SHOWS

From the days when quiz and game shows were riding high in 1950s prime time, the holidays have been a convenient source of Christmas-themed categories and seasonal questions. Not to mention seasonal set decorations. And even guests. Santa Claus was the "mystery guest" on CBS's weekly job-guessing game *What's My Line?* on Christmas Eve 1950, the first yule of that celebrity panel's 17-year CBS prime-time run. Future seasons would feature reindeer wranglers, Santa Claus instructors, Christmas tree farmers, and "Rudolph the Red-Nosed Reindeer" songwriter Johnny Marks. CBS's *I've Got a Secret* offered broader unknowns. Carol Burnett joined the guessers in 1960 to deduce that three generations of a family all got married on Christmas Eve.

Holidays were even more fun when the games became giddier, after they faded from the prime time spotlight. Joke-filled shows with goofy celebrity guests would come to dominate weekday daytime, led by NBC's 1960s tic-tac-toe bluff-fest *Hollywood Squares* and then CBS's bawdy 1970s revival of *Match Game* (where resident wit Charles Nelson Reilly played as Santa Claus). Since these games aired every weekday, they often aired on Christmas. Costumed kiddie-show character H.R. Pufnstuf showed up on a 1972 Christmas edition of ABC's *The Dating Game,* and Lucille Ball and Richard Simmons played a sort of charades with holiday terms on CBS's 1984 *Body Language.* As late as 1990, a syndicated revival of CBS's venerable *To Tell the Truth* was asking Hollywood panelists to choose the real Santa trainer among three claimers.

But game shows were a fringe genre by then, relegated largely to cable, where Game Show Network showcased repeats of vintage diversions. They had a momentary prime time revival at the turn of the century, when Regis Philbin's *Who Wants to Be a Millionaire* topped the 2000 ratings for ABC. Holiday editions were presented by Comedy Central's droll showdown *Win Ben Stein's Money* in 2000 and NBC's arch elimination game *The Weakest Link* in 2001.

REALITY SHOWS

The suddenly hot reality genre was dominated by competition series like the one that started it all in summer 2000. CBS's *Survivor* took a dozen or more "castaways" to a remote location and had them scrounge for food, compete in games, and deviously backbite until "the ultimate survivor" walked away with $1 million. Fox's *Joe Millionaire,* NBC's *Average Joe,* and ABC's *The Mole, The Bachelor,* and *I'm a Celebrity, Get Me Out of Here!* usually had closed-end runs of 8 to 13 weeks that didn't lend themselves to holiday outings. Only NBC's weekly *Fear Factor,* which challenged participants to scary stunts like eating bugs, took the opportunity to get seasonal, asking them in 2003 to ride standing on a sled a hundred feet above the ground plucking candy canes from overhead wires.

But Christmas was widely celebrated on other unscripted series that played more like documentary eavesdropping on people's lives. Fox's seminal (and seemingly eternal) *Cops,* which had been following around real-life police since 1989, presented two "Ho Ho Ho" special edition episodes of holiday crime. Christmas calamities were an annual laugh riot on ABC's long-lived send-in-your-tapes showcase *America's Funniest Home Videos.* Celebrities could be seen celebrating in such "candid" day-to-day chronicles as MTV's *The Osbournes,* E!'s *The Anna Nicole Show,* A&E's *Growing Up Gotti,* and MTV's *Newlyweds* about singers Jessica Simpson and Nick Lachey. (How real were these "reality" shows? Anna Nicole Smith admitted in commentary for her show's DVD release that many holiday happenings had been staged for the cameras.)

Discovery Channel appealed to male viewers by melding holiday drama into hit toolbox watch-alongs. *Monster Garage* in 2003 had engine-head host Jesse James build a skeleton-Santa parade float that shot candy out of its cannon arms. *Monster House* in 2004 revisited a house redecorated the previous year to evoke Christmas in an English town; its ex-Briton owner had wept (and not for joy) over the finished product. On the family-dynamics saga *American Chopper,* the battling Teutul dad and sons of New York's Orange County Choppers tried to get along long enough to craft 2003's antler-handled Santa bike and 2004's cycle sleigh.

Bravo's 2003 sensation *Queer Eye for the Straight Guy* had its five gay style gurus throw a Christmas dinner for the subjects of previous makeovers. Over holiday dishes, the Fab Five dished over how the made-overs were or weren't following advice. And then there was MTV's destructo-show *Viva La Bam,* in which skateboard hero Bam Margera weekly "punked" the parents with whom he lived in suburban Philadelphia, crushing his dad's beloved van or painting everything in the house blue. For Christmas 2003, Bam and his buds filled the house with floor ice to skate from room to room, then brought in snowmaking equipment to smother the yard in white stuff. After that, American parents must have been relieved to see those nice young singers from Fox's hit talent search *American Idol* merely crooning Christmas songs in their 2003 and 2004 holiday specials.

DOCUMENTARY/LEARNING

The explosion of cable networks in the 1980s and 1990s fueled an equal flood in programming focused on real-world history, explanatory how-tos and real-life situations. Christmas was included as channels like Animal Planet and National Geographic captured the natural world, Discovery and History explored past and present events, and do-it-yourselfers glimpsed what might be in Food Network's cooking shows ("12 Days of Cookies") and HGTV's home and garden tips ("Christmas Tree Ornaments").

These often quickly and cheaply produced programs mushroomed, and they found far-reaching ways to embrace the holidays as hundreds of channels teemed in digital cable and satellite post-2000 new millennium. History's *Mail Call* series on military life and tactics remembered times of soldiers "praying for peace on earth at the same time they're doing battle." Its 2003 hour detailed George Washington's Christmas at Valley Forge, World War II's Battle of the Bulge, and twentieth-century Christmas truces. The Weather Channel documented the 1912 sinking of a Chicago Christmas tree ship on Lake Michigan (with underwater footage of the wreck), along with a 2004 *Storm Stories* study of a Christmastime mud slide in California's San Bernardino Mountains. Food Network traveled for "Hawaiian Holidays" and Christmas-themed cooking competitions in the Japanese import cult favorite *Iron Chef*.

Christmas itself was the subject of many December documentaries. "The Science of Christmas" on Discovery in 1999 explored "miraculous physical forces" that may explain when the star of Bethlehem appeared, why Rudolph's nose is red, and how reindeer might fly. Food's 2001 "Holidays Unwrapped" peeked inside the making of such treats as candy canes and fruitcakes. HGTV's "Hey Remember Christmas" in 2004 nostalgically used old home movies to look back at "bubble" lights, downtown department store shopping, and caroling door to door. Its 2003 "Extreme Christmas: Bigger and Brighter" celebrated "over the top" outdoor decorating—1 million lights, laser shows—while "Holiday Windows" traced the creation of elaborate store displays around the world. Local stations weren't to be left behind: NYC's WNBC/4 spent a 2004 hour detailing "New York Holiday Windows" at Lord & Taylor, Bloomingdale's, Bergdorf Goodman, and other stores.

COMMERCIALS

Viewers say they hate commercials. But they sure seem to relish their favorites. And some of the most beloved are holiday-themed. A few have become so classic that they're mentioned within the shows themselves. "I look for those special Kraft [food] commercials where they make those holiday desserts out of cheese food, marshmallows, pineapple chunks, and macaroni," says John Femia's high school nerd on CBS's 1982 satire *Square Pegs*. Annie Potts is more emotional in CBS's 1987 *Designing Women,* when her character's kids are with their dad instead of her. "I saw that Anheuser-Busch commercial last night," moans Potts. "Just about killed me." "You mean the one with the horse-drawn sleigh speeding through snowy woods to the tune of 'I'll Be Home for Christmas'?" sympathizes soft touch Jean Smart. "Every time I see that, I lay face down on my carpet and cry my guts out."

An entire party full of people on NBC's 1990 *Fresh Prince of Bel-Air* knows what Will Smith means when he gushes "This is what Christmas is all about." He calls them round the TV to "sit and watch for this certain commercial. You know the one where it's all snowy and the little jolly Santa is riding around on the Norelco shaver." When the ad comes on, the whole gang says, "Awwwww."

Norelco's electric shaver spot seems to have touched some sort of sweet spot in the American psyche in its various incarnations since debuting in

1961. Its stop-motion animation appeared at about the same time as NBC's similar-looking "Rudolph the Red-Nosed Reindeer," and its "floating heads, floating heads" jingle to the tune of "Jingle Bells" wormed its way into viewers' heads as all classic commercial jingles find a way to do. Add to that the timing: Electric shavers are a gift-for-dad perennial, barely advertised at other times of the year. Speaking of gift-only items, consider the Chia Pets, the variously shaped ceramic animals that grow grassy instead of hairy after being slathered with an included seed-paste. (Chia Heads would later also simulate such peculiar characters as Homer Simpson and Mr. T.) And of course, there's The Clapper, that clap-on-clap-off contraption designed to turn power to lamps on and off with the clapping of hands rather than actual physical contact (sort of a low-rent remote control).

But those two couldn't quite rise to Christmas classic status. They don't incorporate holiday imagery. Santa is the most familiar pitchman, going back to his debut in Coke ads in 1931—some credit these print pitches for solidifying our visual conception of the red-suited gift-giver—and arriving on TV two decades later. He has recently been seen doing his shopping at Toys 'R' Us and using his Sprint cell phone to call for help when he gets stuck in a chimney. Comcast cable coyly used his visit in competitor-knocking spots: "You better watch out. It's tough to land on your roof if there's a satellite dish on it." UPS saved Santa's behind by arriving to help him deliver after his sleigh crashes. Santa's family gets equal time. In a series of 2004 ads with Kris Kringle's everyman brother Kevin, he explained how the store's gift certificates eased his holiday shopping: "When you're a Kringle, you're born into a family that's more diverse than most," he said, sitting next to a reindeer. Santa's costumed elves are in on it, too. Their oddest appearance may be as wiggling, cramping gastrointestinal victims on those strange Pepto-Bismol ads when they dance to chants of "nausea...upset stomach...diarrhea..."

And now for something completely different: Family togetherness is another holiday theme. Folgers coffee hit big with its 1985 "Home for the Holidays" commercial, still airing 20 years later, in which a grown son sneaks into his parents' house; they literally wake up and smell the coffee as he surprises them with his Christmas visit. Even advertising characters can get gushy: An animated Mr. Peanut nostalgically watches home movies of his tinier-peanut self in recent Planters holiday spots. Friends and perhaps family share good times in recurrent Martini & Rossi Asti Spumante ads in which imbibers clink glasses to the ringing tune of "Carol of the Bells."

Christmas isn't the only holiday helping advertisers sell things these days. A Hallmark spot for Hanukkah cards portrays an elderly Jewish man telling his grandkids about his boyhood boat trip to America, just as he emotionally opens a card from the best friend he made there. McDonald's shows black families lighting candles for Kwanzaa. Virgin Mobile covered all bases in 2004 with its irreverently festive Chrismahanukwanzaa spot, throwing together every holiday's imagery, adding Indians and pagans, to a song that boasts "An all-inclusive celebration, no contractual obligation."

But there's one thing every tradition can agree on: food. Everybody eats. One of the most enduring holiday spots over the past decade has been the American Dairy Association's "Behold the power of cheese": A little girl implores her parents on Christmas morning to come see what Santa has left her: floor to ceiling goodies including a convertible, a motorcycle, several bikes, a snowmobile, a life-size stuffed bear, model trains, glittery gowns, and dozens of beautifully wrapped boxes. "Whoa," marvels dad, "those must've been some cookies you left Santa." But the little girl grins, "I didn't leave him cookies. I left him cheeeeese." It's not only memorable, it's effective. There's no way to forget what the product being pitched is.

THE YULE LOG

"For some, the yule log is an easy, pleasantly cheesy backdrop to tree trimming and gift-wrapping. But it is also a Dadaist joke: television as the hearth, not just metaphorically but literally," wrote Alessandra Stanley on Christmas 2004 in *The New York Times*.

Deep thoughts for a shallow reality. The Yule Log—devotees of Christmas kitsch accord it the status of capital letters—began airing on New York's WPIX in 1966 as a simple loop of film showing a fire burning in the fireplace of Gracie Mansion, the city mayor's residence. Later updated to the immediacy of videotape, the loop played for hours each Christmas morning for more than two decades, filling unsellable time for the station and establishing itself as a silly tradition to city-dwellers (and suburbanites) who were not fireplace-equipped. Christmas carols played in the background, creating a campy coziness as "real" as anything else on television.

The Yule Log disappeared for 12 years and reappeared in 2001, in the aftermath of the city's shattering September 11 experience, representing the revival of reassuring tradition, a sort of "comfort TV." After winning its time-slot ratings for three years, the original log went national in 2004 over Chicago's cable-distributed "super station" WGN (owned by Tribune, which also owns WPIX). Other stations around the country have offered their own variations.

GLOBAL TV

Christmas isn't a TV obsession only in the United States. Or only, for that matter, for American English-speakers. U.S. Spanish-language networks Univision and Telemundo also take note of a holiday perhaps more religiously oriented for their largely Catholic audience. Christmas even makes the *telenovela* scene in such productions as 1999's two-week *Cuento de Navidad*, a modern adaptation of Dickens's classic "A Christmas Carol" made by Mexico's Televisa and regularly rebroadcast north of the border by Univision.

The British, too, have been doing it up for decades. The "Christmas special" edition for scripted dramas and comedies is a widespread tradition. Many British programs run in seasons of as little as six weeks at a time, as opposed to the United States' current standard of 22 episodes (at one time as many as 39 originals per year). And they don't incessantly repeat the same way. Some shows simply aren't airing at holiday time.

Thus, the Christmas special, produced for holiday airing. The "Carry On" movies mutated to TV in 1969's "Carry On Christmas" retelling of the Scrooge story, 1970's "Carry On Again Christmas" and several subsequent farces. As American audiences began to see such Britcoms on public television in the 1970s, they took to holiday outings of *Last of the Summer Wine, Keeping up Appearances, Are You Being Served?* and *Chef!* among many imported favorites. The outrageous and irreverent trend-chaser send-up *Absolutely Fabulous* celebrated with Jennifer Saunders's tacky Edina and Joanna Lumley's drunkenly vain Patsy, while Ricky Gervais's "seedy boss" character returned to the scene of his personnel crimes in the "reality" satire *The Office*. His three-years-on tale gave the series a surprisingly sweet ending.

Canadian TV could be almost as willingly wicked, operating under much less political correctness pressure than American television. Being "PC" became the point of a mocking 1999 episode of the CBC's inside-TV spoof *The Industry* (so titled on America's Bravo cable and on public TV; Canadians know it as *Made in Canada*). Everyone down to witchy Wiccans is "complaining about the Christmas message" running on the air. "You can't say 'Christmas' on TV," the staff is told. "You have to say 'season's greetings' or 'happy holidays.' Christmas is exclusionary."

Not in Japan. Kurisumasu is no religious holiday there, but another chance to engage in the excessive consumer spending on which the Japanese economy thrives. Traditions like decorations, trees, and gift-giving are catching on, along with representations of Santa. And Christmas carols. The 1984 Wham! pop song "Last Christmas" is especially popular, and it provided the basis of a fall 2004 Fuji TV drama by the same name, involving lovelorn neighbors/colleagues and the woman's life-threatening illness. Christmas is also considered a time for lovers to connect. Some Japan observers attribute the younger generations' fascination with Christmas to—you guessed it—the impact of American pop culture, including all those gushy TV movie Christmases from the 1970s and 1980s.

The impact of the American TV Christmas reaches further than many realize.

III

Wrapping It Up

We (Don't) Need a Little Christmas: Alternative Holidays, from Hanukkah to Festivus

You know this Christmas/Hanukkah thing? I think you ought to let [baby] Janey decide. Give her a knish, give her a candy cane, see what she goes for.

—Melanie Mayron, *thirtysomething*, 1987

It's just like Hanukkah at my house—food, friends, gifts, a rededication to what's important in our lives, a moment to reflect on the future, a celebration of our children, our heritage.

—Ron Rifkin (hearing about Christmas), *The Trials of Rosie O'Neill*, 1990

"Have a joyous holiday of your choosing, if indeed you choose to celebrate a holiday at all." In 1997, Alan Rachins's hippie dad of Jenna Elfman's free-spirited wife was covering all the bases when he offered seasonal good wishes to Mitchell Ryan as the uptight wealthy father of more conservative son-in-law Thomas Gibson on ABC's *Dharma & Greg.*

But Rachins wasn't alone. By that point, multicultural awareness of American diversity had crept into the culture in a multitude of ways, never so overtly as at Christmastime. Or Hanukkah time. Or Kwanzaa season. Or that "holiday of your choosing."

Christmas had become such a central focus of American festivity, of the winter calendar, of capitalistic free enterprise at its utmost and 1980s style greed-is-good consumerism. TV had long since gone into overdrive with both celebratory entertainment and blizzards of seasonal salesmanship during all those commercial breaks. And for those who didn't or wouldn't celebrate Christmas in its traditional religious sense? Well, advertiser-driven TV wasn't about to let them evade its marketing clutches. (Or maybe they were just feeling warmheartedly inclusive. Right.)

HANUKKAH

Hanukkah was the first alternative holiday to make its appearance, perhaps because so much of the show business community had been raised Jewish. Not that Hanukkah ranked among that religion's holidays anywhere near the "high holy days" of early fall's Yom Kippur and Rosh Hashanah. But its commemoration of the Jews' 165 b.c. victory over oppressive Greek armies—when one day's sacramental oil lasted miraculously for eight in rededicating the Temple Mount—falls conveniently in December amid the flurry of the Christmas (shopping) season.

The intersection of the two was how Hanukkah most often made its appearance when it broke arguably into the mainstream in the 1980s, inching into the awareness even of Christians in Bible-belt middle America, where Jewish neighbors, never mind Jewish culture, were rarely encountered. Intermarriage between religions set things off on ABC's touchy-feely drama *thirtysomething*, in which striving young couples of that age weekly bared their feelings, to impress some viewers with their apparent introspection and alienate others with their perceived self-absorbed whining.

The first season's 1987 holiday hour found Ken Olin's Jewish husband Michael and Mel Harris's Christian wife Hope disagreeing how to celebrate baby Janey's first Christmas/Hanukkah. Hope's desire to do up the yule irritates Michael, who maintains, "You haven't set foot in a church since I've known you." Hope argues, "I want Janey to have what I had—the lights and the reindeer and a window to watch for Santa. For all I care, Santa could be a nice Jewish boy." But Michael's stand isn't religious, either. It's equally personal. The new father now sees himself in Janey: "What are we going to tell her about who I am?" After moody flashbacks to Michael's childhood and strains from Joni Mitchell's plaintive holiday-tinged ballad "River," each spouse comes around. Michael comes home ready to enjoy Christmas trappings—and finds Hope lighting the candles of the Jewish menorah.

Other shows reflected deeper conflicts in young Jews strongly drawn to all that colorfully pervasive secular Christmas hoopla—trees with ornaments, seasonal songs, Santa Claus, gift giving, the sense of peace and togetherness, even TV traditions from sitcom yules to the annual "Rudolph the Red-Nosed Reindeer" special. Often yearning to share in the festivity, they could also feel alienated by the holiday's roots in the birth of a savior their culture could not comfortably endorse.

Northern Exposure was the perfect show to express that dilemma in 1991. The CBS hour about a Jewish doctor from New York establishing a practice in a small Alaska town could utilize its quirky sense of humor and its warm eye for assorted citizens bonding despite disparities in age, race, and attitude. Newly arrived in timber country, Rob Morrow's Joel Fleischman debates decorating a tree for the first time. "A Christmas tree is a Christian symbol," he frets to friends. "Next to the cross itself, you can't get anything that's more Christian than that." With even the town animist decorating a tree, though, Joel quickly persuades himself.

"Not that I haven't fantasized about having a Christmas tree—so warm, so inviting," he rationalizes. "Actually, you know, I've always liked Christmas. It's a great holiday for a Jewish kid—two weeks off from school and nothing expected of you. And it's true that I've enjoyed and even embraced other trappings of the holiday season—the music, the gift giving. You don't have to be Republican to celebrate Lincoln's birthday. So when you think about it, I'm probably splitting hairs in denying myself a tree."

He doesn't know how to do it "right," though—placing ornaments on the branches before the lights (a theme repeated on CBS in 1993 when the Jewish title character of *The Nanny* exuberantly layers tinsel before anything else). As friends help him learn the process, he's still talking it through, and not only to himself. "Okay, let me get something straight," Joel tells his first-ever tree. "The fact that I have you in my living room is meaningless. I'm not betraying anything. You're a tree. Flora, a plant, a non-sentient being, that's all. I know, there are people who like to endow you with religious significance, but even at that, you're really more of a cultural symbol, like the Easter bunny, Uncle Sam, Tony the Tiger" of cereal-commercial fame.

After much ado, however, Joel must finally concede that the effort just doesn't feel right to him. "Scratch the plum pudding, there's a matzo ball underneath. I'm a Jew, that's all there is to it." But he understands the season well enough to take his tree, with all its trimmings, to the house of Christian friend and bush pilot Janine Turner, who's been feeling grinch-y without her family around. Joel knocks on the door and says, "I have something that I think belongs to you," before plugging in the decorated tree he just placed on her lawn.

The holiday is an easier immersion for Fran Drescher's oh-so-Jewish title character in *The Nanny*, a shopaholic New York clothes horse whose fashion-conscious eyes are dazzled by the holiday's more glittery material aspects. She's thrilled to finally partake in Christmas festivity, something she's wished for since childhood, as we learn in a 1998 flashback to Fran as a hippie-ish kid decades earlier. "It's so boring compared to Christmas," she moans. "Why don't we have a Hanukkah parade?" "Oy," replies her mother, "after all that walking we did in the desert, we like to sit on the holiday. Preferably by a pool in Miami Beach."

But this episode late in the series also salutes her own traditions. Having married her widowed employer (Charles Shaughnessy) and become permanent caretaker to his three children, she says, "I want to start a Hanukkah tradition with my new family." Like most Jewish characters in a largely Christian culture, Fran finds herself having to explain the meaning of Hanukkah to more mainstream characters (and, of course, TV's mainstream audience). She does the usual one-night's-oil-lasting-eight-nights spiel. Then the story illustrates it, when her husband's car is stranded in a Northeast snowstorm. "I thought we had enough gas to keep the engine going and the heater on for, I don't know, about an hour," he later reports. "But, well, it lasted for eight." "It's like Hanukkah!" she exclaims.

A similar miracle helps a Jewish basketball team triumph in Disney Channel's 2003 family movie *Full Court Miracle*. Jason Blicker's Philadelphia Hebrew school student dreams of court fame like city hero Julius Erving. He begs a black former college star from their playground to coach him and his hapless pals after he notices the guy's car has the license plate JM165—like Judah Maccabee in the year 165! ("You wouldn't happen to be a Jewish military hero who started Hanukkah and has been dead for over two thousand years?") Blicker chases his dream through two hours of practices and pratfalls, till his team amazingly reaches the finals of the holiday tourney, where a storm knocks out the power midgame. Using the school's emergency generator, they agree to keep playing the big, bad other team until the fuel runs out: "Eighteen points [down] and hardly any fuel—we need a miracle." Is anyone surprised that, with five minutes on the game clock and one minute of fuel left, they get one, leading to a last-second triumph? Even the boy's career-minded, sports-scorning mom is persuaded: "I still see a doctor in your future. Ah, maybe it's a Doctor J."

Such a miracle is not fated to arrive, however, for David Schwimmer's Ross in the 2000 Christmas/Hanukkah episode of NBC's *Friends*, "The One with the Holiday Armadillo." To perpetuate his Jewish heritage, Ross explains the festival of lights to his kindergarten son Ben (the child he'd fathered for his lesbian ex-wife). But all the boy wants to do is sing Christmas carols and wait for Santa. A desperate Ross rents the only costume-store outfit left at Christmastime—a huge armadillo with a chubby tail. When Ross arrives to tell Ben the story of Hanukkah, he's followed in swift succession by Matthew Perry's Chandler in a Santa suit and Matt LeBlanc's Joey dressed as Superman. Together, the three somehow convey the significance of Hanukkah to a newly excited Ben. "My favorite part," Santa Chandler bellows at Joey, "was when Superman flew all the Jews out of Egypt!" (OK, so Joey didn't help much.)

KWANZAA AND QUILTS

The 1990s movement toward multicultural inclusiveness made it seem every race, creed, and culture deserved a December holiday on equal footing. This approach was most invested in programs intended for children, as if no child of whatever cultural tradition should feel excluded from the holiday merriment and all kids should value each others' traditions. Nickelodeon's blockbuster family cartoon *Rugrats* explained Hanukkah in 1996 with the toddlers being read stories of Jewish history, then imagining themselves heading into religious battle, crying "a maccababy's gotta do what a maccababy's gotta do." The same animated characters actually get to age into Nickelodeon's follow-up series *All Grown Up*, where in 2004 they're struggling to create Hanukkah traditions equal to Christmas's. "Nothing rhymes with 'dreidel.' Maybe that's why Hanukkah has only one song," says Susie as Dil struggles to write one. Eventually the 'tweens come up with a latke song: "Hanukkah is coming, so shred those taters fast/Be thankful it's a holiday where you don't have to fast."

The durable *Rugrats* franchise also saluted the nascent African-American celebration of Kwanzaa. The 2001 holiday episode sees black preschooler Susie's Aunt T arriving with hopes of "an extra special Kwanzaa this year." "What's Kwanzo?" asks Susie. "Kwan-zaa," stresses brother Edwin, "is a cultural holiday established in 1966, commemorating the first harvest celebrations of Africa." As if that weren't overt enough, the animated tale proceeds through a who's-who and what's-what of African and black American culture. When T isn't teaching the kids Swahili words, she's cooking African peanut butter stew and giving gifts like a tribal mask or drum. The title clan in Disney Channel's cartoon *The Proud Family* gets its own Kwanzaa lesson in 2001, when a magical, mysterious homeless family keeps arriving at the Proud house to light candles, venerate ancestors, and lead celebrations of such "African principles" as self-determination, cooperative economics, and "*umoja*" unity.

Other shows tried to cover all the holiday bases at once. Even the preschool learning show *Blue's Clues* on Nickelodeon does that in its 1999 episode, when animated dog Blue and her live-action human owner Steve debate which memory patch should be the annual addition to their "holiday quilt." The two visit country star Wynonna (and Green Puppy) decorating a Christmas tree, friend Sam (and Orange Kitten) lighting candles on the Hanukkah menorah, and singer Tyrese (and Purple Kangaroo) at their table with a cup and corn for Kwanzaa ("when our family gets together to celebrate what makes our community strong"). Given a patch at each house reflecting their particular holiday, Blue adds them all to the quilt, as Steve asks his young viewers, "What holiday traditions does your family have?"

In Nickelodeon's 2001 cartoon *As Told by Ginger*, the title character announces, "I've got latkes frying and gingerbread baking." Having just discovered she's one-quarter Jewish, the bubbly junior high student so enthusiastically reads up on "the traditions of my people" that she nearly turns her back on her friends' Christmas undertakings. "Mom," she finally realizes, "do you think we could actually celebrate Christmas *and* Hanukkah?" "We could celebrate the Fourth of July, for all I care," retorts Mom, expressing society's secular sentiment. Ginger arranges her party décor so "one quarter of the floor space goes to Christmas, one quarter goes to Hanukkah, and the remainder of the floor space is to be divided up equally among our visiting guests, no matter what their persuasion." After the decorations start a house fire, a teary Ginger comes to her senses. "I got totally wrapped up in being PC, obsessing about all the stupid superficial holiday things, and I forgot the most important thing of all—that the holidays are really about close friends and family. And right now, I don't care what holiday it is because I'm surrounded by both."

FESTIVUS, CHRISMUKKAH, AND MORE

So is Adam Brody's awkward teen Seth in Fox's sunny southern California soap *The O.C.* Father Peter Gallagher is Jewish and mom Kelly Rowan is "Waspy McWasp," so the Orange County rich kid introduces city-delinquent foster brother Benjamin McKenzie to his blended creation Chrismukkah. "I created the greatest superholiday known to mankind," Seth enthuses in 2003, "drawing on the best that Christianity and Judaism have to offer." He boasts that "highlights include eight days of presents followed by one day of many presents." The fictional brainstorm actually caught on with viewers flocking to the first-year soap's hip romances and family shenanigans. By its next holiday outing in 2004, production studio Warner Bros. was taking advantage of the grassroots enthusiasm by marketing Chrismukkah cards and wrapping paper. Not to mention a red velvet and white trim Yarmaclaus skull cap. Turning it commercial pretty much ruined Chrismukkah's coolness. But Seth's giddy gusto in the original episode still shines. When McKenzie's character is pulled over by cops after a drunken party, but then let go, Seth knows where the credit goes. "What we have here is a Chrismukkah miracle. You had Jesus working for you, right, and then you also had Moses, working together, the super team."

Not everybody is so inclined to mix and match their holidays. Especially those steeped in the American tradition of Christmas. The egalitarian political correctness of the 1990s had those folks blowing a gasket. Comic D.L. Hughley's volatile dad on ABC's *The Hughleys* goes ballistic in his 1998 episode, when in an effort to be fair to all holidays, his kids' suburban school decides to stage a winter solstice pageant. Hughley will have none of that. "All I wanna know is, why can't Jesus come to his own birthday party?" he insists. "We should have a pageant that reflects the traditions we grew up with," including "the baby and the manger, little elves, flying reindeer, something realistic." Other parents at a school meeting agree, seeking a show "where the kids still wear embarrassing costumes, *but* we know all the songs." One cautions that new rules prohibit "the promotion of any beliefs that are actually held by members of the community." "You can't celebrate nothing," argues Hughley. "You have got to celebrate something."

Which is precisely what happens. The kids of the neighborhood take over from their bickering parents, staging a show in the Hughley backyard that covers several somethings—explaining Hanukkah and lighting a menorah, enacting the Mary and Joseph story, even recounting the Dutch tale of Santa and Pete, the black sidekick who helps St. Nicholas deliver presents. (That story would be dramatized in CBS's 1999 TV movie *"Santa and Pete"* with Hume Cronyn and James Earl Jones.)

High schoolers do the omni-celebratory same in "A Very P.C. Holiday," UPN's 1997 *Clueless* episode. "In the spirit of our multicultural nation," the pageant staged by the movie spin-off's Beverly Hills brats proclaims "a lot of holidays from which to choose" in order to "wish all of you a happy whatever." The school's adults have given up completely. As one teacher drolly bemoans, "I knew it was over for me when the Trekkies declared themselves a religion and demanded to do a number in the pageant," now called upon to represent "Eastern religions, Western religions, New Age religions, old age religions, covens, cults and sects."

Yes, even "fringe" traditions have garnered tube time as cultural diversity has flourished. The 1991 *Northern Exposure* Christmas episode otherwise spotlighting Joel's Hanukkah dilemma comes to a climax with something else entirely—native Alaskans' raven pageant. The whole town has been drinking out of raven glasses at the local tavern ("hand-painted in Czechoslovakia—look at the details, you can see every feather") and adorning its trees with raven ornaments and raven lights. (A frustrated Joel asks the local store owner, "Do you have anything else besides Heckle and Jeckle?")

Finally, everyone attends the outdoor pageant at which a reenactment with drums and masks explains how "a long time ago, the raven looked down from the sky and saw that the people of the world were living in darkness," as Elaine Miles's native narrator–receptionist Marilyn tells it. The bird turns himself into a spruce needle and drops into water consumed by a woman, who then gives birth to a baby, actually the raven in disguise. The boy retrieves the ball of light that's been hidden by an evil chief, reverts to raven form, and carries the light into the sky: "From then on, we no longer lived in darkness." These echoes of the Christian nativity bringing its own kind of light to the world make a familiar story resonate in a fresh and inspirational new way.

On the other hand, there's Festivus, the comedic *Seinfeld* holiday invented and celebrated (so to speak) by Jerry Stiller as George's cantankerous father on NBC's sitcom in 1997. "When George was growing up, his father hated all the commercial and religious aspects of Christmas, so he made up his own holiday," Jerry Seinfeld explains, to the horror of Jason Alexander's George Costanza, who'd like to forget the whole thing. "Instead of a tree, didn't your father put up an aluminum pole? And weren't there feats of strength that always ended up with you crying?"

It all sounds great to Michael Richards as ever-jazzed neighbor Kramer, who seizes the idea and gets Stiller cranked up again about the dormant concept. "At the festival dinner," George's dad enthuses, "you gather your family around and tell them all the ways they have disappointed you over the past year!" Soon, the whole gang is gathered at the Costanza homestead. "Welcome, newcomers," declares Stiller. "The tradition of Festivus begins with the airing of grievances. I gotta lotta problems with you people!" And then for the feats of strength: "Until you pin me, George, Festivus is not over! Stop crying and fight your father!"

Irritating your family members is such a traditional part of the season. No matter which holiday it is.

Wild Collisions

Welcome to the 'chood, as the title star of *The Hebrew Hammer* likes to say. Comedy Central's deliriously wicked 2002 Hanukkah movie satire stars Adam Goldberg as a leather-clad, Shaft-styled Jewish avenger—"the baddest Hebe this side of Tel Aviv"—who makes it his business to defend his people. Of course, he does this while the movie good-naturedly indulges in lampooning every stereotype imaginable. (To pass the "Jew confirmation test" for the secret Jewish Justice League, Goldberg has to "demonstrate musical aptitude," max out the "whining scale," and show his, uh, circumcision.)

This wild satire's Christmas collision occurs when there's a new "anti-Semitic psycho Santa" at the North Pole: Andy Dick's deviously evil seed Damien. "The heir to the red suit" has reindeer kill his religiously tolerant father so he can destroy Hanukkah and let Christmas stand alone. With "this new meshuggener Santa Claus in power," Jewish Justice League leader Peter Coyote tells Goldberg, "the fate of Hanukkah rests squarely on your shoulders." The Hammer's crusade entails him "passing" as gentile at Kmart, enduring Shabbat dinner at his nagging mother's house, enlisting the aid of Mario Van Peebles's Kwanzaa Liberation Front, and finally resorting to the most dangerous, deadly weapon in the Jewish arsenal: passive-aggressively laying on the guilt ("What, I come all the way to the North Pole to fight you, you don't put out anything to nosh on?").

From his Star of David spurs to his pimped-out Caddy (fuzzy dreidels in place of dice), The Hebrew Hammer makes one hilariously "bad, bold, big-nosed Biblical brother" in this equal-opportunity-offender send-up.

CHAPTER 18

That Christmas Feeling:
How to Make a Holiday Show

If Christmas can be anything to any one of us—even Hanukkah or Kwanzaa—then writing a holiday-themed episode must open all kinds of possibilities for the Hollywood minds behind the TV shows we watch.

And it does. Ask series producers whether crafting that Christmas script is a burden or a delight. They'll say the latter.

"It just has a built-in emotional quotient that you always look for," says *Frasier* producer/writer Christopher Lloyd, who figures he's written a half-dozen Christmas scripts. "There's an emotional resonance to the holiday, and we always feel like that's going to make the storytelling easier."

Not just easier, says *Everybody Loves Raymond* creator Phil Rosenthal, but amplified. "We're a show that's based on a somewhat dysfunctional family, and you never see so much dysfunction as you do around the holidays." At Christmastime, he and his writers figure "we can really have fun with this, because if they're crazy during the regular year, think about during the holidays."

That enjoyment isn't purely professional, either. Though Rosenthal is Jewish, he gets as much of a personal kick out of all the holiday traditions as Christians who celebrate from a religious base. As a child of the 1960s, he grew up immersed in yuletide TV. "Listen, if you live in America, you don't have a choice. They're all over the place. Jewish, Hindu, Muslim, whatever—everybody watches the Christmas shows. I know 'Rudolph the Red-Nosed Reindeer' as well as any gentile. And I also know the deeper meaning behind it [the holiday], because I also know the 'Charlie Brown Christmas' special, which is the only one that gives you the *real* spirit of Christmas," he adds admiringly.

"What Jewish boy or girl doesn't feel a little jealous?" says Josh Schwartz, the twenty-something creator of *The O.C.*, Fox's trendy family saga. "Christmas has all the songs. It has the tree. It has the good characters, Rudolph and Frosty." For his show's first season, Schwartz merrily delivered a Christmas episode *and* a Hanukkah episode, rolled into one. His teen character Seth, son of a Christian father and a Jewish mother, dreamed up the somewhat tongue-in-cheek holiday of Chrismukkah—which became such a real-life cultural sensation that the following holiday season found marketers selling Chrismukkah cards.

Even a thoroughly unsentimental show like ABC's cheeky 1980s mystery/spoof *Moonlighting* can get into the act. Creator Glenn Gordon Caron playfully "broke the fourth wall," as he says, having characters talk to the audience, even acknowledging their own TV existence. "You know, life is unpredictable," Caron says. "Sometimes your life is a drama, sometimes your life is a comedy, sometimes your life is a musical." His first *Moonlighting* Christmas episode couldn't resist manger symbolism: A baby is left in a laundry basket by parents Joseph and Mary, who can't find a place to stay. Halfway through the episode, "they suddenly realize [and announce to viewers], 'Wow, we're in an allegory!'"

Caron unpredictably did something else for Christmas. "The dirtiest joke I ever told on network television was in that show, and it got completely by the censor." In going after the bad guys, sardonic detective Bruce Willis plays Santa, arriving literally through the chimney. "It takes some effort for him to actually get down and through the fireplace. And as he comes out, he says, 'That's the last time I try and jam myself into a tight hole with all my clothes on.' And the show just continues." The network didn't catch the double entendre until it aired.

But not all wicked impulses are followed. *Frasier* star Kelsey Grammer remembers plenty of Christmas story ideas that he and producers decided not to pursue. "We did have a time when I beat up Santa Claus. And also, I slipped on the radio show and said that Santa wasn't real. But we didn't do it. We just decided that we would hate for some little kid to watch *Frasier* that night and have us be the one to tell him. Who needs it?"

Other shows reflect their creators' estimation that we haven't been told enough. The prevailing picture of Christmas's historical connotations was challenged by *Nothing Sacred*, ABC's 1997 drama of an inner-city Catholic parish whose open-minded pastor was often embroiled in controversial issues. "Certainly for a Catholic priest, Christmas is a significant holiday and a significant ritual in the church," says producer David Manson, who cocreated the series with priest Bill Cain. "The hardest thing about doing a Christmas episode is there are so many clichés attendant to them. If we were going to do one, we wanted to do one a little subversive." Their hour reached beyond the ethereal focus viewers had come to expect of TV portrayals related to faith.

"The template we decided to apply to the episode was to look at it as a political story as opposed to a just religious story," explains Manson. About-to-be-arrested refugee activists from Central America take sanctuary in the pastor's church, in an echo of political and cultural clashes from the time Jesus was born (and also the time, as the script points out, when Jews won the liberation celebrated by Hanukkah). Manson says he and Cain wanted to "deliver the emotional punch that Christmas tends to have anyway, the sense of family and community. But instead of a little family huddled around the fireplace opening presents, it's about a community much larger and richer than we normally see in those episodes." That helped this provocative hour "cut through the sucrose quotient—those treacly, sweet elements that seem to be inherent to a Christmas episode—and gave it an edge."

A series based in a more intimate experience of faith and values took its own kinds of chances. In its first CBS season, *Touched by an Angel* celebrated Christmas with a literal, wings-and-all manifestation of the angel played by Roma Downey, who typically did her work in figurative person-to-person form. But, "knowing it was an angel show, people were expecting a big Christmas episode," producer Martha Williamson explains in the 1994 episode's DVD commentary, "and we wanted to give it to them." At the hour's climax, as a mentally handicapped boy proclaims the nativity to a packed church, Downey's character takes angelic flight—bathed in white light, levitating over the worshipers, and releasing a white dove.

What could have played heavy-handed seems to soar on wings of its own. Williamson notes that her original inspiration for the episode was not the elaborate exhibition, but the simple boy—"the meekest, the humblest, the most innocent of human beings delivering the good news of Jesus' birth." Yet she thought *Angel* fans expected "a beautiful, miraculous, explosive moment." And she believed this might be the only time she'd get to present Downey "in full regalia as an angel. We knew that we would probably never be able to do it again, but we always wanted to do it at least once." Indeed, Williamson says the network objected to the overt angelic portrayal, suggesting, essentially, "'Can you please take the Christmas out of the Christmas episode?' I said, no, the ship has sailed." So she got her white, weightless angel, "bathed in the glory of God," as Williamson describes it. "We said what we wanted to say with this episode."

It was an episode that she says "practically wrote itself." That same feeling is reported by the creator of a completely different experience—the twisted pop-culture cornucopia that is "Pee-wee's Playhouse Christmas Special." Comic Paul Reubens's goofy Pee-wee Herman character headed his own CBS holiday hour mostly because there'd been a 1988 Hollywood writers' strike. When it ended that fall, Reubens's Saturday morning series was in need of some immediate scripts to resume production. "We decided we could write a Christmas special quick," Reubens recalls on his commentary track for the program's DVD release.

"One of the things that made this special write itself, practically, and be written so fast, was the fact that there were just so many iconic kind of things to Christmas," says the soft-spoken performer behind the bluntly boisterous character. Reubens remembers simply sitting down and "making a list—fruitcakes, roaring fire, presents, Santa Claus, snow—all the things that we remember from all those Christmas specials." Each element got its own Pee-wee moment in the sun, alongside an amazingly eclectic parade of star cameos, among them Cher, Dinah Shore, Little Richard, Whoopi Goldberg, Magic Johnson, and Annette Funicello and Frankie Avalon. That, plus the kiddie show's popularity among adult viewers for its sly references and anarchic attitude, persuaded CBS to air the special in prime time. Reubens counts it "one of my favorite things I've ever done. I really loved working on it," he says, "and it did everything I hoped it would do."

Matt Groening savored his own chance to dabble in the Christmas TV special tradition with Fox's 1999 hour "Olive the Other Reindeer." Though the creator of *The Simpsons* had done holiday comedy on his weekly cartoon, he eagerly embraced producing this family perennial based on the popular children's book. "I'd always been fascinated with the idea of doing a big animated musical, and most animated Christmas specials are so lousy," he says. "I thought it would be really nice to give kids something they would really like."

Like many sitcom crafters, Groening came to the task as a child of TV and its holiday traditions. "Christmas is my favorite time of year," he enthuses, "and it's fun to take something that is so associated with sappiness and try to give it a little bite." Yes, "there's a sweet dog at the center" of the tale, he says, as Olive chases her dream to join Santa's sleigh team. But Groening tapped longtime David Letterman writer Steve Young to write the script. "So it's got this sardonic edge to it that makes you forget you're watching a cute little dog."

How did Christmas shows get so sweet, anyway? Groening puts the holiday in perspective with an astute observation. "One of the most biting stories of all time," he notes, "is Dickens's *Christmas Carol*."

In circling back to the holiday's nineteenth-century emergence as a profound social and cultural touchstone, we appreciate how all-encompassing Christmas can be. Its celebration reflects our lives as they change, and our human nature, which never does. TV's myriad reflections of the holiday, in all their variety and scope, have cumulatively assembled a fascinating sort of postmodern Pandora's box. Open up a TV Christmas, and you never know what you'll see. Except yourself.

CHAPTER 19

TV's Christmas Essentials: Choosing a Top 10

Everybody's got their own favorite Christmas show. Old, new. Silly, serious. Cartoon or live-action. Sentiment or satire.

After viewing hundreds of holiday episodes and specials spanning 55 years of television history, the following rank as my candidates for the most enduring Christmas TV of all time (DVD availability listed as of 2005):

The Jack Benny Program (1960, CBS)—Shopping has never been so surreal as in this clockwork black comedy perfected over two decades of radio and TV stagings. The venerable Benny takes his skinflint routine to the extreme, progressively aggravating clerk Mel Blanc in a comedy of errors that mushrooms insanely from the tiniest comic nugget. (Various DVD releases include those from Brentwood, Koch, Genius; VHS release from Universal remains a top-quality transfer.)

Married...with Children (1987, Fox)—Another pitch-perfect outing. The tacky Bundy family calmly eats Christmas pizza as the coroner removes a splattered Santa from their backyard. All the holiday outings of this subversive series are devilish fun. But this first-season farce grandly establishes its makers' ruthless sense of satire. (Fox Home Entertainment second-season DVD set)

Everybody Loves Raymond (1996–2003, CBS)—You can't choose just one. All of this Long Island family's Christmas gatherings are laugh-out-loud evocations of holiday hysteria. Husbands and wives, parents and siblings analyze each other's gifts, intentions, and festering resentments to inflame that delirious Christmas tension we recognize from our own "happy" holidays. (HBO Video season sets)

"Pee-wee's Playhouse Christmas Special" (1988, CBS)—Paul Reubens's haughty kid-nerd alter-ego lovingly sends up all the Christmas touchstones of both at-home and on-screen celebrations. Its gleeful litany of traditions wraps around a parade of quirky showbiz cameos to evoke everything beloved of the TV-era yule. (Image Entertainment DVD)

"The Judy Garland Christmas Show" (1963, CBS)—Here's the embodiment of what Pee-wee lampoons. The temperamental diva cozily hosts her kids, friends, singers, and dancers at "home," welcoming us to share their "spontaneous" festivity. Never was this conceit so seamless, so showy, and yet so casually convivial. (Pioneer Video DVD)

"A Charlie Brown Christmas" (1965, CBS)—The animated classic gently renders childhood traumas and triumphs. From its jazz ice-skating opening to its final sad-tree rebirth—with a heartwarming stop for Linus's unpretentious recital of the Bible's "real" Christmas meaning—this tartly sweet half-hour glows with the warmth we so seek from the celebration. (Paramount DVD)

Home Improvement (1991–98, ABC)—Christmas decorating goes over the top in Tim Allen's "more power" family sitcom, annually relishing American excess. But the series keenly eyed other holiday traditions, too, especially those involving children (the existence of Santa, church pageants, gift greed, and more). Its laughs were hard, while its heart was soft, and its reality relatable—a delicate blend Allen's vehicle managed to strike just right every time. (Buena Vista DVD season sets)

Northern Exposure (1991, CBS)—The meaning of the season is pondered by, and shared among, a variety of faiths and attitudes in one small Alaska town. Christian, Jews, and animists end up at the raven pageant, and family is redefined by the holiday arrival of an ex-serviceman's Korean kin he didn't know he had. (Universal Home Video second-season DVD set)

Nothing Sacred (1997, ABC)—Religion and politics collide in this provocative church drama as they did at the time of Jesus' birth. When Central American refugees take sanctuary in the series' urban parish at Christmastime, clergy and staff reconsider the holiday, in both history and modernity. Their personal reassessments of its holy meaning resonate more deeply than the insular certainty more common to "religious" depictions.

Little House on the Prairie (1974, NBC)—Michael Landon's nineteenth-century frontier dilemmas of gift-giving play out slowly to viewers living at a twenty-first-century pace. Yet this very plainness is what makes them so affecting. Holiday sentiment is stripped down to its purest expressions of family devotion and faith in this quietly sincere tearjerker. (Goldhil Video first-season DVD set)

OTHER TOP HOLIDAY EPISODE/SPECIALS:

Ozzie & Harriet
The Many Loves of Dobie Gillis
The Twilight Zone
Green Acres
M*A*S*H
Barney Miller
WKRP in Cincinnati
Night Court
thirtysomething
The Simpsons
Frasier
3rd Rock from the Sun
South Park
The Vicar of Dibley
Popular
Providence
Scrubs
Titus
The West Wing
Family Guy
"Mr. Magoo's Christmas Carol"
"Rudolph the Red-Nosed Reindeer"
MADtv (for animated parodies)
The Hebrew Hammer

And Your Favorite Christmas Show Is...?

Any best-of list provokes personal reflection, appreciation, and disagreement from all corners. So let's hear about your all-time top Christmas shows. You can vote online at TV Shows on DVD, since 2001 providing both the latest news on upcoming releases and comprehensive information on those already out: www.tvshowsondvd.com/christmas

The Worst Christmas Show Ever

"The Star Wars Holiday Special" stands head and shoulders above its rotten competition, like the towering Wookies that "star" in this misbegotten special-effects concoction. Designed by variety producers Gary Smith and Dwight Hemion to fill two hours of CBS airtime on November 17, 1978, it seems to last two days by the time Leah (played by Carrie Fisher) warbles a farewell "Star Wars"–theme carol.

Never encountered this novelty epic? No wonder. It never repeated, and word is "Star Wars" creator George Lucas tried to have every incriminating copy rounded up and trashed. (Blurry bootlegs can, however, be found at eBay and other unofficial acquisition points.)

The story, if it can be called that, revolves around Han Solo (played by Harrison Ford) flying his hairy Wookie pal Chewbacca home to celebrate "Life Day" while under attack from evil Imperial troopers. But most of this disjointed production's time is spent with Chewbacca's equally non-verbal wife, son, and father (named Malla, Lumpy, and Itchy!), as they wait at their high-tech tree house and moan and howl at each other for as long as 10 minutes at a clip. No subtitles. Just syrupy sentimental background music furthering the torture as they sluggishly call Luke Skywalker (played by Mark Hamill) on a video phone, watch TV cooking shows (comedian Harvey Korman in a sort of alien blackface drag), play a holographic Cirque du Soleil–style "doll" performance, and get hot under a virtual-reality hair-dryer helmet that delivers a cooing Diahann Carroll in what's essentially space-age phone sex.

Nonsensical? Wildly. This mind-numbing variety pastiche—let's not forget the Starship music video, Boba Fett cartoon and Beatrice Arthur cantina sketch/song—can only be ascribed to corporate spinoff greed, Lucas's apparent disinterest, and the controlled substances that were popular in the late 1970s. In their quick cameos, "Star Wars" stars Ford, Hamill, and Fisher look properly mortified (if not under the influence themselves). The videotape production values and visual effects are cheesy, the pace stultifying, the overall effect literally jaw-dropping. So bad it's good? No. Just dreadful.

Bibliography

The main research source for this book is the Christmas shows themselves. Over the past 20 years, I've taped more than 800 episodes, specials, movies, documentaries, commercials, and more—first on VHS, then on DVD. Many were captured in their original network airings, others on cable or in syndication, and a few in more out-of-the-way places: local cable access, even late-night filler reruns on public TV. Some were provided by friends. A few were acquired over the Internet.

Though studios have long marketed authorized video versions of Christmas movies such as *It's a Wonderful Life*, holiday TV shows were rarely available at retail in the relatively unwieldy VHS format (other than hard-to-find episode tapes from *St. Elsewhere*, for instance, or *The Jack Benny Program*). But with the recent popularity of TV-on-DVD, Hollywood's library keepers have finally unleashed a flood of season sets, themed collections, and one-offs that make accessible many long-sought tube yules—the Frank Sinatra–Bing Crosby variety pairing, Lassie's holiday tragedies and triumphs, and even *Have Gun Will Travel's* old-West Noel. That new bounty helped top off my own progressively acquired collection and made this book yet more comprehensive.

(Some good holiday DVD/video information sources: www.tvshowson-dvd.com/christmas; www.tvparty.com/dvdxmas.html; www.shokus.com/xmas.html; search.ebay.com/christmas-tv; www.amazon.com.)

OTHER KEY RESEARCH SOURCES

Books

Bianculli, David. *Dictionary of Teleliteracy*. New York: Continuum, 1996.
Brooks, Tim, and Earle Marsh. *The Complete Directory to Prime Time Network and Cable TV Shows*, 8th ed.. New York: Ballantine, 2003.
Eisner, Joel and David Krinsky. *Television Comedy Series*. Jefferson, NC: McFarland, 1984.
Encyclopedia Britannica. Chicago
Friedman, James, editor. *Hallmark Hall of Fame, The First 50 Years*. UCLA Film and Television Archive, privately published, 2001.
McNeil, Alex. *Total Television*, 4th ed. New York: Penguin, 1996.
Marill, Alvin H. *Movies Made for Television*. New York: Baseline, 1987.
Ritchie, Michael. *Please Stand By: A Prehistory of Television*. New York: Overlook, 1994.
Schulz, Charles and Lee Mendelson. *A Charlie Brown Christmas*. New York: HarperCollins, 2000.
Schwartz, David, Steve Ryan, and Fred Wostbrook. *The Encyclopedia of TV Game Shows*, 2nd ed. New York: Facts on File, 1995.
Zurawik, David. *The Jews of Prime Time*. Waltham, MA: Brandeis University Press, 2003.

Online

Essential Sources
TV Tome (detailed series episode guides): www.tv.com
Internet Movie Database (comprehensive movie/crew credits): www.us.imdb.com

Other Key Sites
Encyclopedia of Television, Museum of Broadcast Communications, Chicago (1,000 essays on history and trends): www.museum.tv/archives/etv
Nielsen Media Research (ratings/viewing information): www.nielsenmedia.com
TVparty! (loving repository of vintage video, TV memories): www.tvparty.com
Teevee (personal essays about television): www.teevee.org
Toon Tracker (cartoon history/info): www.toontracker.com
Wikipedia (wide-ranging user-edited encyclopedia): en.wikipedia.org

Additional Information
Newspaper/magazine articles: www.nexis.com
Christmas carols: www.hymnsandcarolsofchristmas.com
Christmas history/traditions: www.christmas-time.com, www.didyouknow.cd
Episode airings: www.tvguide.com

Audio Recordings

Radio's Greatest Christmas Shows. Radio Spirits CD set, 47122, 2003.
The 60 Greatest Old-Time Radio Christmas Shows. Radio Spirits cassette set, 44074, 2000.

Acknowledgments

My mom always let me watch TV to my heart's content, to an extent some would have considered crazy (on first thing in the morning to last thing at night). She even made a special stop every Tuesday morning so her obsessed little girl could grab the new issue of *TV Guide* the moment it hit the newsstand. Betty Werts gave me a huge head start on my eventual profession.

Another lucky leap came when I got an early chance to work in television through my high school years at the NBC affiliate WNDU in South Bend, Indiana. The station's 1970s TV-lampoon sketch comedy *Beyond Our Control* let a painfully shy nerd learn to write comedy, direct actors and technicians, edit videotape (back in the muscle-building days of hefty two-inch-tape reels), sell commercial time, and try almost anything else over the course of three years. *BOC's* guiding force, WNDU promotion manager Dave Williams, trusted 14-year-olds with the responsibility of producing a professional program from start to finish. His abiding respect for youthful smarts and energy (and skillful channeling of same) instilled those of us at the heart of the project with the resolve to live up to his high expectations, if not exceed them. The untold thousands of hours Dave shared with us, both professionally and personally, seven days a week, shaped dozens of accomplished careers like mine. His "kids" are now acclaimed Hollywood movie writers, directors, kids' show creators, novelists and journalists, as well as doctors, lawyers, and other "normal" careerists. More important, we're all better people for his loyal confidence in us, his understanding, encourage-ment, affection, wit, and all-around appreciation of teens as meaningful people. His was the kind of adult respect kids so desperately need and so seldom get as they strive to forge their future selves. Nearly 30 years later, Dave, we still miss you. Daily.

Other guiding spirits who know why I thank them: Joe Dundon from WNDU; David McHam from Southern Methodist University; Ed Bark of *The Dallas Morning News*; David Bianculli of the *New York Daily News*; Mark Dawidziak of the *Cleveland Plain Dealer*; and Gord Lacey of tvshowsondvd.com.

Christmas TV creators who graciously agreed to be interviewed, in per-son or by phone: Glenn Gordon Caron, Kelsey Grammer and Christopher Lloyd, Matt Groening, David Manson, Phil Rosenthal (and his *Everybody Loves Raymond* writers), and Josh Schwartz.

Also: Paul Ward and Larry Jones of TV Land; Lana Kim of Sci Fi Channel; John Solberg of FX; Janet Daily of CBS; Shari Rosenblum of Fox Home Entertainment; Craig Radow of Universal Home Video; Sasha Junk of Classic Media; Andy Edelstein and Ronnie Gill at *Newsday*; and Eric Levy and Daniel Harmon at Praeger/Greenwood Publishing.

Thanks most of all to Rich Bailey, my life's guiding spirit, who cheerfully puts up with watching Christmas shows in March and August, the same way he puts up with me year-round. Who'd have thought I could find such a generous soul—and he'd love TV as much as I do?

Index

About the Author

DIANE WERTS initially worked in television as a writer/director/editor for "Beyond Our Control," the award-winning Midwest sketch satire of the 1970s and 1980s. Her writing has appeared in *TV Guide*, *The Los Angeles Times*, and other publications. She served two terms as president of the Television Critics Association, as well as on juries for the American Film Institute and the Banff International Television Festival. She now works as television writer for New York's daily newspaper *Newsday*.